CIVIC EDUCATION

By Donald W. Robinson

In collaboration with
Harold E. Oyer
Elmer F. Pflieger
Daniel Roselle

National Council for the Social Studies
A DEPARTMENT OF THE NATIONAL EDUCATIONAL ASSOCIATION
1201 Sixteenth Street, N.W.   Washington, D.C. 20036
Price $4.00 paperbound; $5.00 clothbound

NATIONAL COUNCIL FOR THE SOCIAL STUDIES

Civic Education Project Team

Chairman:

Donald W. Robinson
Associate Editor, *Phi Delta Kappan*

Harold E. Oyer
Superintendent of Public Schools
Elkhart, Indiana

Elmer F. Pflieger
Director, Department of Social Studies
Detroit, Michigan, Public Schools

Daniel Roselle
Professor of History
State University College
Fredonia, New York

Advisory Committee to the Civic Education Project

Stanley E. Dimond, *Chairman*
University of Michigan

Adeline Brengle
Elkhart, Indiana, Public Schools

Rose Brennan
Torrington, Connecticut, Public Schools

Richard E. Gross
Stanford University

William H. Hartley
Towson State College (Maryland)

Merrill F. Hartshorn
National Council for the Social Studies

Franklin Patterson
Hampshire College (Massachusetts)

Natalie J. Ward
Los Angeles, California, Public Schools

To
Howard E. Wilson
1901–1966

This book is dedicated to Howard E. Wilson, a pioneer in civic education, Past Secretary, Past President, and loyal supporter of the National Council for the Social Studies. Dr. Wilson first attracted national attention by his investigation of the status of citizenship education in the State of New York, a study which resulted in the publication in 1938 of the book *Education for Citizenship*. He was one of the team members who wrote in 1940 the volume *Learning the Ways of Democracy*. In his last year of active service before his untimely death, he continued his support of civic education projects at the University of California at Los Angeles, where he served as Dean of the School of Education, and he strongly supported the project that culminated in this report. In a long and varied career as teacher, author, international educator, and dean, he always gave major interest to the social studies and civic education.

NATIONAL COUNCIL FOR THE SOCIAL STUDIES

Officers for 1967

The National Council for the Social Studies is the Department of Social Studies of the National Education Association of the United States. It is the professional organization of teachers of social studies. It holds a series of meetings each year and publishes materials of significance to those interested in this field. Membership in the National Council carries with it a subscription to the Council's official journal, *Social Education*, the monthly magazine for social studies teachers, and the Yearbook. In addition, the Council publishes bulletins, pamphlets, and other materials of practical use for teachers of the social studies. Membership dues are $9 a year. Applications for membership and orders for the purchase of publications should be made to the Executive Secretary, 1201 Sixteenth Street, N.W., Washington, D.C. 20036.

Promising Practices in
Civic Education

PROMISING
PRACTICES
IN

PREFACE

Here is essentially a most helpful NCSS handbook for civic learning and action. The many socio-civic qualities and competencies identified in this volume are organized for reference under 11 citizenship goals. These goals or overall categories were established by our visiting team of observers as they followed citizenship activities in visits to 83 schools in 27 states. Although the focus is frequently on the social studies class, the heart of citizenship education, promising practices were often identified in many other elements of the school program as well. The socio-civic goals of society, those of the school, of citizenship education, and of the social studies are so intermingled that it was not possible to delineate a single, all-encompassing definition of citizenship education. These difficulties proved a virtue, however, for as a result, we are provided with a wide variety of examples that have application in numerous and different situations.

The Vietnam war, integration marches, youth in revolt, the "hippy" epidemics, narcotics arrests, draft card and even flag burning have all brought adults a mounting degree of irritation and worry. The pendulum of public concern now, once again, swings toward the challenges of citizenship education. This volume appears at a propitious time, with its valuable guidelines which should enable instructors to help channel youthful energy and concern into positive citizenship practices.

Herein we are introduced again and again to the means that teachers and schools are employing to meet the dilemma of citizenship education: How are we to promote healthy value orientations at the same time that we develop objective young social analysts? We are indebted to our team of observers—Harold Oyer, Elmer Pflieger, Donald Robinson, and Daniel Roselle—for the insights they have provided toward answering the foregoing dilemma. To the pupils, teachers, and officials of the many schools contacted, who so graciously received our representatives, the National Council for the Social Studies is very thankful. We appreciate the efforts of NCSS leaders and committees, especially the guidance of the Advisory Committee chaired by Stanley E. Dimond, who helped shape the study and eventually this report. On behalf of the writing team we express our appreciation to Aleta Clayton for her editorial assistance and for seeing the manuscript through the printing process. We also extend our gratitude to the Danforth Foundation for its support in financing this study.

Richard E. Gross

INTRODUCTION

ORIGINS AND PURPOSES OF THE STUDY

In the fall of 1963, negotiations were begun by the Committee for Educational Policies (now the Council on Civic Education) for support of an integrated study of civic education. The Danforth Foundation of St. Louis granted $500,000 for the study, which included four separate projects. One of these, conducted by the Survey Research Center at the University of Michigan, was a nationwide survey of political socialization of high school seniors. Another, centered at the University of California at Los Angeles, concentrated on the construction of a 5th-grade teaching unit on due process of law. A third, located at the Lincoln Filene Center at Tufts University, was concerned with content analysis of social studies textbooks, as well as a study of political socialization. Finally, the fourth project, under the sponsorship of the National Council for the Social Studies, was a survey of promising practices in civic education. That survey is reported in this volume.

The Council on Civic Education was eager to have a survey of promising practices because it believes that such a study can:

1. Show how civic education projects and enterprises are developed within the total framework of the school and its encompassing community.
2. Stimulate, encourage, and aid good projects now being developed.
3. Identify qualified personnel in the field who can be drawn into other activities that develop in this area.
4. Provide teachers with specific information and ideas that will enable them to improve their regular programs and practices.
5. Provide teachers and schools with criteria that will assist them in evaluation of their own programs.
6. Help identify needs and gaps in existing programs.
7. Provide data and information that can be utilized by other projects supported by the consortium.

From time to time useful reports have been published about citizenship education. They include, notably, the 1940 report by the Educational Policies Commission titled *Learning the Ways of Democracy;* the 1954 Yearbook of the American Association of School Administrators, *Education for Citizenship;* and the 1960 Yearbook of the National Council for the Social Studies, *Citizenship and a Free Society.* Only the first of these, written over a quarter of a century ago, was based directly on extensive classroom observations. Although the present survey may be considered by some a restudy of the area covered in *Learning the Ways of Democracy,* no such replication was planned and no comparison with the earlier study is included in the present report.

PROCEDURES

In the spring of 1965, the Advisory Committee of the National Council for the Social Studies to this project appointed a four-man team to conduct the survey of promising practices in civic education. Its specific assignment was "to prepare and publish a report on outstanding civic education programs at the junior and senior high school level (grades 7–12) in the schools of the United States. The survey should include both public and private schools. The survey should include an evaluation and selection of promising new projects and practices as well as those programs that have been carried out for a period of time. Consideration should be given to surveying and including programs designed for students of varying abilities (who will possess the same privileges of citizenship). Programs for the non-academic student as well as those who are talented need to be examined and reported."

During July 1965, letters were sent to state superintendents of education, state and local social studies supervisors, and officers and former officers of the National Council for the Social Studies, inviting nominations of schools reputed to have promising practices in civic education. The project team met in Washington in mid-August and began its work by examining information submitted with the names of the 300 schools nominated for visitation. Seventy-five schools were selected, representing all geographical areas and including junior high schools, senior high schools, and combination junior-senior high schools. They were of a wide variety—public, parochial, and independent schools, inner-city, suburban, and rural consolidated—located in communities ranging in population from under 2,000 to more than a million. A few of the 75 schools selected declined to participate on the grounds that they did not consider their offerings worthy of inspection and national reporting or because they felt the program for which they were nominated was an innovation too new for public examination.

The project team spent approximately one month in Washington corresponding with the schools selected for visitation and establishing guidelines for the visits. From Labor Day until Christmas 1965, the project team visited 83 schools in 27 states. Frequently a visit to one school led to an invitation and visit at another school in the same city. In each case, one, two, or three members of the project team observed a school for one, two, or three days. An exception was Detroit, where three members of the project team stayed a full week to obtain a more nearly comprehensive picture of the ways a large metropolitan school district organizes its resources for civic education.[1]

---

[1] The fourth member of the project team, Elmer Pflieger, is associated with the Detroit school system. His knowledge of the Detroit schools gave the team a unique opportunity to study in depth this metropolitan school system. To reduce the possibility of bias, he chose not to join in the team's visits to Detroit schools and did not assist in writing those portions of this report that deal with the Detroit school system.

In each school visited, attention was first given to the program or practice for which the school was nominated. Conversations with the principal, department chairmen, teachers, and students usually suggested other activities worth observing. Visits were not formally structured, and project team members moved freely throughout the schools without prearranged schedules, going wherever they sensed the possible existence of an interesting activity. They visited libraries, cafeterias, classrooms, and offices. They talked to administrators, teachers, and students. They did not spend excessive time examining published courses of study or educational objectives; instead, they sought to observe what was actually being done. In every school the project team was cordially and hospitably received and encouraged to probe wherever it wished. None of the schools visited was reluctant to let the public know what it was doing in the area of civic education.

Some aspects of training in citizenship may have been slighted in this report simply because they were not brought to the attention of the project team. The absence of any reference to promising practices in map-reading in the junior high schools, for example, does not mean that map-reading is being neglected. It means only that the schools visited apparently did not consider their techniques outstanding enough to bring them to the team's attention.

Most of the activities reported in this volume were observed at first-hand by one or more members of the project team. Exceptions usually concerned activities that had already taken place or were planned for the future; these were described to project team members by persons directly involved. A few reports included herein are from schools which were on the original itinerary but which team members were unable to visit because of time limitations or scheduling difficulties.

Only two schools had pilot projects of major research programs. One was in a school where teachers and students were experimenting with an inquiry approach; the other was an experimental social studies curriculum related to the Carnegie Tech project.

ORGANIZATION OF THE REPORT

The team members agreed on the basic organization of the report and each member arranged his own notes in line with this organization. The chairman of the team then prepared a rough draft based on the material that appeared to lend itself to effective reporting. A few school practices that were favorably reported had to be omitted because there was insufficient information for persuasive reporting. The most significant change in the agreed-upon outline necessitated in the writing was the elimination of a chapter on teaching about the necessity for world peace. This omission was dictated by the paucity of material.

The rough draft was circulated among the team members, and several revisions were prepared in the light of the suggestions received. At a three-day conference in July, 1966, divergent views were reconciled and the script approved for editing. Team members continued to offer suggestions during several additional edited revisions, so that this published report represents as complete a consensus of team thinking as could be secured within a reasonable time span. This report is strengthened by all of the virtues of committee reporting and hampered by its faults. No one of the team members writing alone would have produced exactly this report, but all are in essential agreement with most of the content as published.

The first three chapters of this report identify the project team's beliefs concerning contemporary educational challenges, goals for civic education, and methods for approaching these goals. In Chapters 4, 5 and 6, a large number of school practices are described, arbitrarily grouped according to the citizenship goals they most strongly exemplify and without any implication that other goals are not present. Behind a promising practice is usually found a person, a program, or a set of conditions that permits the practice to flourish. Consequently, the project team attempted to identify and report on some of the background conditions, and on outstanding teachers encountered during the survey. Chapters 7 through 11 discuss administrative arrangements and other factors that facilitate civic education. Finally, Chapter 12 presents a restatement of civic education ideals in the light of the practices observed in the schools, along with an affirmation that these ideals can be more widely and more effectively applied. The aphorisms scattered throughout this book were copied from classroom walls and bulletin boards; they express ideals to which students were daily exposed.

One other aspect of the report should be stressed. In school visits, team members observed Orientals, Mexicans, Negroes, and Caucasians working together, oblivious of racial differences. In this report, the religious or racial composition of a school is sometimes mentioned, but only to clarify a description.

PURPOSE, SCOPE, AND LIMITATIONS OF THIS REPORT

The situations cited in this report are not presented as typical of all American secondary schools. Instead, they illustrate what can be done and is being done in meaningful civic education in selected schools. The task is largely one of encouraging and helping more schools to lift their instruction to the level of the most effective techniques and tools already at their disposal.

Although individual schools are identified and are commended for their promising practices, inclusion in this report in no way implies that such a school is a "best" school. On the other hand, large numbers of schools with equally promising practices in civic education have gone unreported. We salute these schools and express our regrets that it was not possible to give every deserving school the attention to which it is entitled.

The reader should not expect to find many dramatic innovations reported here. Some practices reported—group discussion, for example—are simply excellent uses of techniques as old as education and well-known to most teachers. Others, if not completely unique, have a freshness or originality of approach that tempts one to think of them as innovations.

Because this is a report of promising practices, the reader might justifiably expect to find examples of good instruction in every area related to civic education. However, with a limited number of schools to observe and a wide variety of practices to consider, a comprehensive survey of any single practice was out of the question. Although the infusion of sociology and anthropology into the curriculum is recognized as potentially promising, for example, the team was unable to make a systematic study of this trend. The report includes only isolated references to the study of anthropology, as at Verde Valley, rather than a methodical treatment. The same point is true of other topics. The report refers to teaching about communism, but it does not presume to offer all the effective approaches to this important topic. It simply describes the several ways of teaching about communism that came to the attention of the team, with comments about the promising aspects of these approaches. Similarly, the report mentions favorably the heterogeneous grouping plan at Yorktown High School. This should not leave the reader with the impression that the team unreservedly favors heterogeneous grouping. The team did not make a systematic study of grouping practices—or of simulation or team teaching—but it did report those arrangements that were brought to its attention that seemed worthy of mention.

The role of the team during a school visitation was essentially that of a reporter. There has been no attempt to editorialize by eliminating mention of what might be considered undesirable. If a total situation were deemed worthy of reporting, it was reported as it was observed, not as the observer might have idealized it. Project members would not attempt to defend every detail of the class scenes reported, although they would contend that every situation reported was useful in the school where it was observed.

The project team has made no attempt to be categorical about what constitutes a promising practice. The report presents observations of practices that appeared praiseworthy in the light of the goals stated in Chapter 2, and the project team hopes that reporting these practices will in fact contribute to the attainment of these goals. Many practices were regarded as useful even when specific values could not be documented. Teachers and principals agree that conferences with their counterparts from other schools, for example, are among their most rewarding experiences. Even though specific benefits cannot be substantiated, such experiences are of value if the participant knows they have helped him.

The conclusions reported in Chapter 12 of this report are based on the observations made in the course of visiting 83 schools and on the professional judgments of the observers. Although these conclusions—like most conclusions in the social sciences—are not empirically provable, the project team believes them to be valid. This does not mean, however, that these conclusions will remain valid as changes occur in society. Further, an unusually rapid adoption of radically new practices is likely to take place in the years immediately ahead, as a result of increased Federal support for education. New procedures were initiated xvi / PROMISING PRACTICES

under the auspices of Title IV of the Elementary and Secondary Act of 1965, and there have been massive infusions of funds and attention into the social studies curriculum by both government and private foundations.

If the reader finds encouragement in the practices reported in this volume, he will be further encouraged by the realization that civic education is likely to take substantial strides forward in the coming years. The advances of the next 10 years should far surpass those of the present or any preceding decade.

CONTENTS

PROMISING PRACTICES IN CIVIC EDUCATION

The thing I wanted most of all
in the world was to know what was
going on in the world, to find something
to say to whatever happened—
to sass it back.

Carl Sandburg

CHAPTER **1**

Citizenship in an Age of Change

In one sense, desirable citizenship traits in a democratic society remain the same today, in the midst of rapid cultural change, as they were hundreds of years ago. Effective participation by the individual in public affairs continues to require the same four essentials: knowledge, thought, commitment, and action. In application, however, each generation redefines good citizenship to fit the demands of its times. Effective participation in American society during the remaining decades of the 20th century clearly calls for many different traits and competencies than were appropriate in 16th-century England or colonial America.

It is therefore relevant to consider civic education in the United States within the context of the dominant challenges of 20th-century life. The promising practices seen by the project team in 83 schools throughout the nation grew out of national conditions, and neither the schools nor the project team can claim that the specific practices that served civic education in 1965 will remain appropriate as the coming years bring other changes in the nation and the world.

Preparation for citizenship in an increasingly urban environment presents new challenges for schools.

THE THEME OF CHANGE TODAY

The most important factor contributing to the evolution of the meaning of good citizenship in the United States has been the nation's expanding concept of democracy, from colonial times and the Jeffersonian and Jacksonian eras through the civil rights movement of the 1960's. This concept of democracy embraces the right of the individual to his own unique combination of traits and interests and the right and responsibility of citizens to participate fully in public affairs. It is a concept of human worth that has been alternately advanced and jeopardized by the accelerated tempo of change in the 20th century.

Science and Technology as Agents of Change

Many changes in 20th century life have resulted from scientific and technological developments. One profile of the scope and speed of change can be found in March's *Thesaurus*, which lists and defines 1,800 words and phrases that came into use during this century. Under the letter "A," for example, the entries include A-bomb, accelerator, aircraft, allergy, amino acids, anti-acids, anti-freeze, antihistamine, and automation.

Other yardsticks can be used to measure the pace of contemporary change. Today's large industries—automobiles, aviation, radio, television, computers, plastics, and dozens more—did not exist 65 years ago. At least half of today's occupations have come into existence within the past 40 years.

As other technological advances have done in the past, development of atomic energy and automation of industrial processes will inevitably bring unemployment and empty leisure to some categories of workers while it stimulates the aspirations and creativity of others. Another inevitable byproduct of technological transformations, population mobility, is already a prominent feature of American life.

Gradually, society adapts to reconcile the social structure to the technological innovation, but in today's world, this adaptation also entails centralization of power and leadership, particularly in creating new

Computer components small enough to fit in the eye of a needle are among the wonders of modern technology.

roles for government. In response to the problems that arise as the small town gives way to megalopolis, the Federal government established the Department of Housing and Urban Development. As automation spreads, the Federal and state governments have instituted retraining projects. Because the inadequacies of one area are often carried to another by mobile pupils and teachers, complicating the problems of teaching and learning, the Federal government has extended more programs of financial assistance to schools. The program of the Great Society is largely an effort to deal with the dislocations and inequities resulting from technological change. In responding to problems arising from technology, however, government draws attention to another concern: Can centralization of power and leadership be reconciled with autonomy for the individual?

Equally important questions are raised by the influence of technological change on international relations. Some nations, thrust into pivotal positions in the balance of power between East and West, pursue intense nationalism and divisive internal struggle while proliferation of nuclear weapons continues. Technology has transformed some agricultural economies within a single generation, while in others, the problems of famine, disease, and poverty are not likely to be solved within the foreseeable future. Underlying these concerns are the Cold War, Vietnam, and the ever-present hazard of nuclear warfare.

The Nation in 1965

The year 1965 was one of dramatic advances. An astronaut walked in space, as his earthbound colleagues pushed ahead with plans for a rendezvous of four astronauts travelling at 17,000 miles per hour. Man's arrival on the moon was scheduled to occur in less than five years. The economy surged, as employment reached an all-time high. The automobile industry set another record; color television gained widespread use; and stock market averages reached a new peak. Continuing efforts to bring civil equality for Negroes took a step forward with the Civil Rights Act of 1965. Congress passed legislation on voting rights, poverty, medicare, and education.

The year 1965 was also one of trouble. Violence erupted in Selma, Montgomery, and Watts. In other parts of the world—Laos, the Dominican Republic, the Congo, and on the India-Pakistan border—brutal fighting occurred. The war in Vietnam escalated to a full-scale military involvement, with no end in sight. While the national economy boomed, with a gross national product of more than $650 billion, 35 million Americans continued to live in poverty. While the ecumenical movement in religion made gains, the idea that God is "dead" provided a popular source of controversy. In almost every city in the nation, urban planners faced increasingly complex problems in meeting man's spiritual and practical needs. Throughout the world, the population explosion and depletion of natural resources caused increased concern.

The School's Response to a Changing World

High school students in 1965 lived in a world of unprecedented contrast and paradox. Their task of understanding the world around them, always a formidable challenge for adolescents, had never been more difficult. Fortunately, many schools are deeply concerned with the need to prepare students for effective citizenship.

In 1965, as the war in Vietnam became a major center of controversy, Sunset High School near Portland, Oregon, was one of many that incorporated the Vietnam debate into its school program. Civil rights was another issue for debate in schools throughout the nation, and in some cases, the school's response extended to other activities as well. In cities as widely separated as Detroit and Selma, for example, high school students marched in demonstrations with the approval and supervision of their school authorities. In Meridian, Mississippi, encouraging signs were seen as students sought ways to improve the image of their state and to implement school integration.

Efforts of schools in 1965 to meet rising problems of juvenile delinquency took many forms. In Los Angeles, for example, respect for law and order was made an emphasis throughout the school system. In Portland, Oregon, schools received the cooperation of the Oregon Bar Association in preparing appropriate study units. In numerous schools, student government shared responsibility for fostering respect for law and order.

The schools have been assisted in their response to poverty by new programs of Federal assistance, such as the Vocational Education Act, the Manpower Regional Development Act, and the 1965 Elementary and Secondary Education Act. Many schools have benefited from Federal leadership and funds.

Technological aids such as computerized record-keeping and teaching machines are being used widely, and some schools have inaugurated flexible scheduling, team teaching, independent study plans, and the elimination of grade levels. The curriculum has been revitalized, especially in mathematics and science, where new programs have been introduced on something approaching a nation-wide scale. Curriculum revision in the social studies is directing more attention to the Non-West and to international affairs. New material from the behavioral sciences, stressing intellectual processes rather than accumulation of information, is being infused in social studies courses.

Equally important, educational writing indicates that schoolmen have become conscious of change and its implications and are seeking to know what demands tomorrow will make on today's education. They may not agree in their predictions of the educational needs of the next decade, but their concern is likely to improve the quality of the student's preparation for adult life.

Having reviewed some of the changes in 20th-century society, in the nation during 1965, and in current approaches to education, we are in a position to examine the implications of change on civic education.

REDEFINING CIVIC EDUCATION FOR TODAY'S WORLD

The problems confronting citizens today give urgency to the search for effective civic education. Our responses to the challenges are shaped by the nature of our democratic society. Unlike a closed society, in which an officially authorized ideology can be imposed on the young without deviation, our democratic society relies on continual reexamination of beliefs, so that outworn convictions may be discarded without sacrifice of the essentials of our democratic heritage. Thomas Jefferson said it well:

I am not an advocate for frequent changes in laws and constitutions. But laws and institutions must go hand in hand with progress of the human mind as that becomes more developed, more enlightened, as new discoveries are made, new truths discovered, and manners of opinions change with the change of circumstances. Institutions must advance also to keep pace with the times. We might as well require a man to wear, still, the coat which fitted him when a boy, as civilized society to remain ever under the regimen of their barbarous ancestors.

Also unlike a closed society, in which citizens have well defined roles, our democratic society encourages individuality and diversity. In a nation as diverse as ours, it is neither desirable nor realistic to insist on a single definition of good citizenship and a single set of traits and competencies for all to share in full measure. Can we say, for example, that the foreign affairs expert is a poor citizen if he fails to take an interest in each local election? Can an active, sensitive citizen be condemned because he resists knowledge of economics, art, or science?

The open-ended responsibility democracy places on its citizens makes it difficult to define civic education in precise terms. Citizenship in our society does not depend on the individual's acceptance of an externally imposed role; instead it depends on his participation in the processes of society. Civic education in a democratic society does not require fixed adherence to a static ideology; instead, it calls for flexible responses to changing conditions.

Possible Approaches   Although this report offers no precise definition of civic education and no checklist of requirements that must be shared by all good citizens, the project team does assert that a variety of traits and competencies can be associated with good citizenship and a variety of means can be used to foster civic education.

In a sense, good civic education gains much from a good liberal education, differing mainly in immediate objectives and priorities. Willingness to participate in decision-making in matters of public policy is of high priority to society and is less important in terms of personal goals; well developed aesthetic values may be crucial for a fully realized life for an individual but of less consequence to society. Yet, both serve society. In our democracy, experiences that cause the individual to be well informed, analytic, committed to democratic values, and more effective in his participation in society also serve the interests of society. Fred T. Wilhelms, in his definition of a liberal education, comes close to the project team's idea of civic education:

A liberal education—and I take it that is what we are all about—is something more than a calculated dosage of technical instruction in a series of disciplines that have come to be called the liberal arts. The disciplines are essential, but a liberal education lies in their use for human purposes. They are powerful engines; but they stand useless if they are not hitched to the train of human affairs.[1]

Civic education, as the project team sees it, embraces most human affairs and is nurtured in many ways. The Council on Civic Education has suggested:

Civic education is a process comprising all the positive influences which are intended to shape a citizen's view of his role in society. . . . Civic education is, therefore, far more than a course of study. It comes partly from formal schooling, partly from parental influence, and partly from learning outside the classroom and the home. Through civic education our youth are helped to gain an understanding of our national ideals, the common good, and the processes of self-government. Similarly, our youth are helped to comprehend the meaning—both within the United States and throughout the world—of freedom for themselves and all men, for the individual and for the group, in creed and commerce, in ballot and daily behavior. They are helped to understand the various civil liberties guaranteed in our Constitution and Bill of Rights and the accompanying civic responsibilities by which alone they can be achieved.[2]

Assumptions

In preparing this report, the project team assumes that civic educaton practices can be learned and taught; that the school's role in civic education is not confined to the social studies or any other classroom; and that the school is not the sole agent of civic education.

---

[1] National Association of Secondary School Principals, *Spotlight.* Number 67: March–April 1965.
[2] Council on Civic Education, unpublished statement.

The first assumption underlying this report, that civic education can be taught, runs counter to the ideas of many scholars. Jacques Barzun, for example, says, in his classic *Teacher in America:*

You know by instinct that it is impossible to "teach" democracy, or citizenship, or a happy married life. I do not say that these virtues and benefits are not somehow connected with good teaching. They are, but they occur as byproducts. They come, not from a course, but from a teacher; not from a curriculum, but from a human soul.[3]

Barzun is correct in saying that the benefits of education come largely from the character of the teacher and that more is learned in school than is formally taught. This position, however, does not lead inevitably to the conclusion that attention to civic education is futile.

Implicit in Barzun's position is a conviction the project team fully supports. Civic education is a process rather than a narrow competency, a focus or concern rather than a prescribed set of actions, and it takes place whenever a conscientious effort is made to prepare students for any form of effective participation in society.

The second assumption made in this report is that the role of the school extends beyond the classroom. Although social studies departments remain a major influence, citizenship values can be and often are communicated through courses in literature, science, and art, among others, and through student activities outside the classroom. When a school has a comprehensive commitment to civic education, reflected in every activity within or outside the classroom, it builds a bridge between the academic and the practical life.

In making its third assumption, that the school is not the sole agent for civic education, the project team affirms that the community as a whole shares in the responsibility of preparing students for citizenship. The fact that the community shares responsibility for civic education raises several questions for schools. In some programs, activities of the school and community may best be done cooperatively; in other programs, one or the other of these agents of civic education is better equipped to meet the needs. Some local school authorities give only

---

[3] Jacques Barzun, *Teacher in America.* Atlantic Little, and Brown, 1945. p. 9.

slight attention to the efficient division of responsibilities between school and community. Yet, without such attention, duplicated effort, critical omissions, misplaced responsibility, and overall deficiencies in civic education are all but inevitable.

CONCLUSION

More than ever before, civic education today seeks to create citizens who are informed, analytic, committed to democratic values, and actively involved in society. Because civic education is a living process rather than a set of immutable beliefs to be transmitted to youth, it accomplishes its objectives by responding creatively to changing conditions.

The tempo of change in the contemporary world, which is in large measure a result of technological and scientific developments, presents unique challenges to students as future citizens and to schools as agents of civic education. A narrow definition of civic education, which would limit the school's role to what might take place in a social studies department, is not likely to prepare students for the full range of citizenship challenges they will face. When, instead, a school is committed to preparing students for any and all aspects of effective participation in society, it will find opportunities for civic education virtually everywhere —in an industrial arts or music appreciation class as well as in the civics class; in a biology club or political discussion group as well as in the classroom; and in cooperation with the community and other schools as well as within its own program.

> We believe that no society
> can survive and advance unless its citizens
> understand its underlying purposes
> and values; unless they know
> where we are going and why.
>
> Paul R. Hanna

CHAPTER **2**

Goals for Civic Education Today

The objectives of a knowledgeable, analytic and committed citizenry, effectively participating in society, have been shared throughout history by democratic societies, however varied have been the interpretations of these terms.

In the context of the world today, the need for knowledge was described by Secretary of State Dean Rusk, in an address before the American Association of School Administrators, in 1964:

I, for one, am just a little skeptical that in the elementary or perhaps even in the high school classes there is a good opportunity to solve the Kashmir question. And I don't think our young people get much benefit from problem-solving where the problems are taxing the capacity of the mind of man himself. But if they have begun to achieve the foundations of geography and history and a rudimentary knowledge of other peoples, I would suppose that they could learn a great deal about the basic elements which enter into these situations. The specific problems will change many times over before they get very far; they change

13

week by week. But there are enduring elements of information and understanding which could well preoccupy their time and their purposes and their activities . . .[1]

In contrast to Secretary Rusk's emphasis on the importance of specific knowledge, an American history teacher stressed analytic judgments reached through specific knowledge:

A good citizen must learn the ways of finding out facts, ideas, and values. He must develop the ability to know: where to find information, how to evaluate it, and how to communicate his findings to others. But good citizenship is not just frothing at the mouth; rather, it involves making precise, analytic judgments.

Despite the difference in emphasis, these two statements are not in conflict. Information is insufficient without analysis, and the validity of analytic thinking depends on firm grounding in fact. The interrelation of these two aspects of the educational process is the key to effective education for a truly discerning citizenry—one made of citizens who possess sound standards of judgment and who subject all new ideas and situations to rigorous appraisal before reaching a decision.

But knowledge and the ability to analyze it are not sufficient without the citizen's expression of his ideas and conviction in meaningful action. One need not go to the extreme of Thomas Huxley, who said "The great end of life is not knowledge but action," in order to believe in the necessity for a committed and involved citizenry. Richard W. Poston took a more moderate position when he said:

Can the principle of a democratic society with its tradition of freedom succeed in the modern world? . . . The answer to that question will depend upon the action of people within their communities, for without thought, action, and participation by the people in their own community life, no democratic society can long exist.[2]

---

[1] Quoted in Mortimer Smith, A Citizen's Manual for Public Schools. Little, Brown and Company, 1965. p. 8.

[2] Richard W. Poston, Democracy Is You. Harper and Brothers, 1954. p. 11.

There are many paths to good citizenship and many goals for the schools to foster.

Within the context of knowledge, analysis, commitment and effective action, this chapter will identify 11 goals for civic education. Six methodological approaches by which the schools can serve these goals will be discussed in Chapter 3. In Chapters 4, 5, and 6, practices found in the schools that serve goals of civic education will be described, and in successive chapters attention will be directed to administrative arrangements which reflect the six methodological approaches and which help to implement civic education goals.

Thoreau criticized education that made a "straight-cut ditch out of a free, meandering brook." A similar protest may be raised against any attempt to mandate a single path for good citizenship. The categorization of goals and approaches in this report should not be interpreted as an attempt to define attributes required of all good citizens.

The 11 goals listed in this chapter collectively represent aspirations for citizenship in our society; individually they may be found in good citizens in varying measures and with differing emphases. The school can serve its role in civic education, however, by exposing students to the full spectrum of goals for citizenship and trusting that these students will, as citizens, incorporate some—if not all—into their own lives.

Classification of civic education goals into 11 areas is no less arbitrary than classification into three or six or eight goals. It is simply an organizational device, one of many that could have been used in this report. The project team would go further, and say that the reader may add to the list of 11 goals given here or may feel that practices described in this report as most closely related to one civic education goal instead have a stronger relation to another. Objections such as these are welcomed, because they contribute to awareness and discussion of the goals of civic education and actions to promote these goals.

Two final words of warning are needed. The project team considers all these goals equally important; neither the order in which they are presented nor the space given to their discussion reflects any attempt to assign priorities. Finally, the project team offers its listing of goals with the realization that reexamination and revision will be needed as changes occur in our schools, our nation, and society.

THE GOALS

1. Knowledge and skills to assist in solving the problems of our times.

2. Awareness of the effects of science on civilization and its use to improve the quality of life.

3. Readiness for effective economic life.

4. Ability to make value judgments for effective life in a changing world.

5. Recognition that we live in an open-ended world which requires receptivity to new facts, new ideas, and new ways of life.

6. Participation in the process of decision-making through expression of views to representatives, experts, and specialists.

7. Belief in both liberty for the individual and equality for all, as guaranteed by the Constitution of the United States.

8. Pride in the achievements of the United States, appreciation of the contributions of other peoples, and support for international peace and cooperation.

9. Use of the creative arts to sensitize oneself to universal human experience and to the uniqueness of the individual.

10. Compassion and sensitivity for the needs, feelings, and aspirations of other human beings.

11. Development of democratic principles and application to daily life.

Goal 1: Knowledge and Skills for Solving Problems From the membership roll of the United Nations to the names of the states of the Union, from the interpretations of the Constitution of the United States to the essential data about international travel, conditions have changed significantly since the end of World War II. Because change is so characteristic of our age, future citizens need information that is reasonably current and is presented in such a way that they will recognize its impermanency.

Reference points, as well as ephemeral facts, are subject to change. Not long ago, civic education in the school was based on the lessons of history, and the models of Greece and Rome were commonly used. Today, civic virtues are more likely to be derived from current analogies and are almost as likely to be drawn from sociological or anthropological sources as from historical sources.

Critical thinking skills are among the most important for the American citizen to develop. As these have been described in *Education for Democratic Citizenship*, the citizen

(a) locates and evaluates evidence relevant to the issues at hand;

(b) analyzes the elements of a controversial issue and weighs the motives of interested parties;

(c) understands the methods and devices of the propagandist;

(d) reserves his reasoned decision until considerable evidence has been

Education for space-age students involves learning knowledge and skills for as yet unknown challenges.

weighed, and then takes a working hypothesis which he acts upon if action is necessary;

(e) subjects this working hypothesis to future modification if new evidence warrants it.[3]

Related skills invaluable to the American citizen in decision-making are "those of *gathering information* through reading and listening; of *interpreting information* by organizing logically and evaluating accurately; and of *communicating information* through speaking effectively and writing lucidly."[4]

---

[3] *Education for Democratic Citizenship.* 22nd Yearbook of the National Council for the Social Studies, 1951. p. 157.

[4] "Skills for Democratic Citizenship in the 1960's," by Helen McCracken Carpenter in *Skill Development in Social Studies*. 33rd Yearbook of the National Council for the Social Studies, 1963. p. 15.

A third group of skills involves the effective use of techniques of group participation through awareness of decision-making as a process. The importance of these skills has been stressed by Vice President Humphrey:

. . . *Luckily, in the last few years, a number of fine books have been written by people with experience in government at many levels. The great improvement, in my mind, has been that they deal with government as a process rather than merely as a structure. Students now are able to get a much more realistic view of government and an appreciation of its dynamic, human component. Specifically, some of the concepts that are now put across are the tremendous role of group action in politics [emphasis added], without the connotation that somehow such activity is evil.*[5]

Goal 2: Awareness of the Contemporary Role of Science

Technical and scientific advances, at the same time that they contribute to man's well-being, threaten daily the stability of our social and cultural traditions if not our very existence. Recent reports suggest that the day is not far off when intelligence can be chemically increased, when humans will visit the moon, and when the average life span may exceed 100 years. In the early 1960's molecular biologists reported that they were on the verge of discovering the specific relationship between the geometric shape of the molecules present in cell chromosomes and the specific genetic characteristics of a living organism. Scientist Oscar E. Lanford described some implications when he said, "This discovery, which in the scientific circles is known as 'breaking the genetic code,' will mean that man is close to the point at which he can by laboratory procedures vary, in a predetermined way, the hereditary characteristics of his offspring."[6]

---

[5] Letter from then Senator Hubert H. Humphrey to Daniel Roselle, dated May 23, 1958.

[6] Extract from address by Dr. O. E. Lanford, delivered at his installation as president of the State University of New York College at Fredonia, N.Y. May 1963.

A good citizen recognizes that these and other achievements and imminent advances in technology and science have far-reaching implications for individual man and society. Whether they improve or reduce the quality of life, whether they bring new freedom to man or new destructiveness depends on society.

Goal 3: Readiness for Effective Economic Life

Recent technical advances in industry present the American citizen with economic problems of great complexity. Vice President Humphrey has reported, "Between 1960 and 1970, estimates are that 22 million jobs will be eliminated [in the United States] by automation and more efficient production techniques." He added, "At the same time an additional 12.5 million new persons will have moved out of classrooms and into the labor force for the first time. We shall have to provide close to 300,000 jobs per month just to keep up with the current effects of automation and new labor force alone."[7]

In 1964, President Johnson summed up the situation when he said, "In this political democracy, what you have and what you own and what you hope to acquire is not secure when there are men that are idle in their homes and there are young people adrift in the streets, and when there are thousands that are out of school and millions that are out of work, and the aged lying embittered in their beds."[8] Economic security and economic opportunity—like political and social democracy —are vital factors in the health of our country, and employability and education are inextricably intertwined.

Goal 4: Value Judgments for a Changing World

Values, as Robin M. Williams, Jr. says, "are not the concrete goals of action, but rather the criteria by which goals are chosen."[9] The rapidity of change in the United States today presents a dilemma for citizens in choosing values. At a time when astronaut

---

[7] Hubert H. Humphrey, War on Poverty. McGraw-Hill, 1964. p. 152.

[8] Cited in Ibid., p. 31.

[9] Robin M. Williams, Jr., American Society, a Sociological Interpretation, Alfred A. Knopf, 1960. p. 400.

John Glenn's space capsule is already considered dated enough to be placed in the Smithsonian Institution, possession of current facts—the facts of the moment—does not guarantee of an "informed citizenry" with "sound values." Thus, an American statesman declares:

Although the individual citizen today is caught up in a vast web of associations—legal, commercial, social and personal—he too often finds no general community of values which he can share. He seeks a consensus with which he can achieve harmony and direction and purpose in his contact with public affairs.

Participation in political life first requires this identification with and sharing of some community of values. But it is this very relationship which is being eroded and chipped away by the growing complexity and specialization of modern life.[10]

An American educator adds:

Change in our own time has had a profound effect on the social character of people. This effect has been widely noted and studied, but its implications for responsible citizenship in a free society have not been appraised adequately or taken into sufficient account in making policy for our schools. Change, among other effects, has made it increasingly difficult for the individual to gain an adequate inner sense of self. Some of the most evident social facts of our time are impermanence, diversity, and movement. In consequence, stable values and a sense that one's life is coherent and meaningful are harder to come by than they were even a generation ago.

The search for self is a central task of adolescence. The questions of adolescence are those of identity: "Who am I? Where am I heading? What do I believe in?" To the degree that firm personal values and agreement between one's values and actions are not achieved, the search for self fails. The result is a modern phenomenon: The adult adolescent —the chronically uncertain, restless, and often irresponsible adult.[11]

---

[10] Senator Jennings Randolph, "The Citizen and His Public Responsibilities," in *Vital Speeches of the Day*, Oct. 15, 1963. p. 10.

[11] Franklin Patterson, *High Schools for a Free Society*. The Free Press, 1960. p. 66.

The special dilemma facing adult and adolescent citizens today springs largely from the accelerated tempo of change in the postwar world. Change brings conflict between the persisting values of the past and the emerging values of the future. The adolescent is in a most difficult position. He is often asked to reconcile seemingly conflicting loyalties. His values quite properly reflect in part the judgment of his parents, from which he may not be ready to dissent, and in part his independent judgment, on which he may not yet place full reliance.

Many of the dilemmas persist into adult life. Even well integrated teachers may have difficulty, from time to time, when change introduces conflict between their allegiance to state or nation and family or religion. Conflict and disagreement are not to be treated as a failure of human intelligence. In many instances, conflict is the beginning of a painful but necessary adjustment to new realities.

Goal 5: Receptivity to New Ideas, Facts, and Ways of Life

It is difficult for some men to forego what Crane Brinton has called "the delights of certitude." Yet, we must be willing to abandon some of these delights for a world in which yesterday's facts are today's old wives' tales. Our objective must become to develop the student's ability to conceptualize and evaluate, to function in the midst of world change.

Man has spent centuries developing social controls—religious rites, patriotic rituals, social taboos—to permit the operation of an orderly society by restraining individual impulses. Today, many of these external controls, seen as contrary to contemporary concepts of democracy and individualism, are being discarded in favor of understanding, insight, self-discipline, and voluntary cooperation. A vital society maintains equilibrium between controls operating for continuity and forces working for change.

The contemporary citizen may believe with Lin Yutang that "nothing is very new that is not at the same time very old," without permitting the past to blind him to the present. "Democracy is not an abstract concept of the kind that can be set forth mathematically in terms of pure ratiocination," writes Pierre Teilhard de Chardin. "Like so many of the notions on which modern ideologies are based . . . it was originally, and to a great extent still is, no more than the approximate expression of a profound but confused aspiration striving to take shape."[12]

As soon as we enter the town meetings and classrooms where specific issues are discussed, it is apparent that new ideas are often troublesome. The inescapable conflict between the old and the new that constitutes the core of social and political struggle seems unavoidable. It can be made less divisive and less destructive if schools successfully involve students in the process of dealing with new ideas. By learning the techniques of group action, as well as of individual study, students can better disagree without being disagreeable.

The goal of receptivity to new ideas obviously does not mean instant acceptance of new doctrines, which is as inappropriate as fixed resistance to innovation. The ideal condition is an open-minded willingness to hear and test all proposals, old and new, without prejudice, and to select those most consistent with one's own principles and most efficacious in the immediate situation. Acceptance of this goal presumes a willingness to admit controversial issues into the classroom.

Many persons are concerned about the need for greater exposure to new ideas in high school. In a sense, however, all of education should be a continuous presentation of new ideas, ideas that are certainly new to the student, sometimes new to the teacher, and occasionally new to the entire community. Obviously, it is necessary to use good judgment in the pursuit of ideals such as receptivity to new ideas. Because of the diversity of backgrounds in our vast country, some ideas may appear normal and wholesome in one community and dangerously revolutionary in another. The use of good judgment and caution, however, does not denote persistent reluctance to face the facts of a changing world.

A committee of Harvard professors wrestled with this problem 20 years ago in writing *General Education in a Free Society*. Their discussion of the topic concludes with this paragraph:

How far should we go in the direction of the open mind? Especially after the first World War, liberals were sometimes too distrustful of enthusiasm and were inclined to abstain from committing themselves as though there were something foolish, even shameful, in belief. Yet

---

[12] Pierre Teilhard de Chardin, *The Future of Man*. Harper and Row, 1964. p. 238.

especially with youth, which is ardent and enthusiastic, openminded-ness without belief is apt to lead to the opposite extreme of fanaticism. We can all perhaps recall young people of our acquaintance who from a position of extreme skepticism, and indeed because of that position, fell an easy prey to fanatical gospels. It seems that nature abhors an intellectual vacuum. A measure of belief is necessary in order to pre-serve the quality of the open mind. If toleration is not to become nihilism, if conviction is not to become dogmatism, if criticism is not to become cynicism, each must have something of the other.[13]

Goal 6: Participation in Decision-Making

No American citizen is expected to know the facts and figures on each matter handled by society. As Evron and Jeane Kirkpatrick point out, "For-tunately, democracy does not require that all men be equally expert in their knowledge of politics or public policy. Fortunately—because if democracy required every citizen, or every voting citizen, or even most voting citizens to understand and judge the myriad of complex issues which confront the nation in this age of technical specialization, international involvement, and inter-dependence, democracy would be impossible."[14]

Further, they say, "It is important to recognize our dependence on experts and to disabuse ourselves and our students of the notion that "good citizenship requires omniscience concerning public policy and the institutions by which it is made."[15]

When alternative plans of action are proposed about major issues of public policy, however, citizens can participate in the process of in-quiry, discussions, and debate leading to a decision. E. E. Schatt-schneider, who believes that the power of the people in a democracy depends on the importance of the decisions rather than on the number of decisions made by the electorate, defines democracy as "a competitive political system in which competing leaders and organizations define the alternatives of public policy in such a way that the public can par-

[13] *General Education in a Free Society.* Harvard University Press, 1945. p. 78.
[14] Evron M. Kirkpatrick and Jeane J. Kirkpatrick, "Political Science," in *High School Social Studies Perspectives.* Houghton Mifflin, 1962. p. 101.
[15] *Ibid.,* p. 102.

ticipate in the decision-making process."[16] Such participation is a basic responsibility of a good American citizen.

Contributing to the formation of sound public opinion is such an important function of the citizen in a democracy that the nature and quality of citizen participation deserves more attention than it has received. The characteristics of the citizen able to contribute effectively are listed by John Payne as follows:

1. *He arrives at his decisions on public issues by a process of reflective or critical thinking and acts individually or in a group to implement his decisions.*

2. *He is loyal to the basic ideals of democracy.*

3. *He upholds conventions and institutions which preserve the democratic heritage, while maintaining a readiness to make changes to meet new conditions and new times.*

4. *He appraises the services of public servants for competence, honesty, and interest in the general welfare.*

5. *He thinks and acts on the assumption that an informed public opinion is not in itself necessarily good. He believes that good public opinion conforms to the ideals of democracy and humanitarianism and insists upon the use of critical thinking as a method.*

6. *He continually supports policies and practices which encourage the free flow of information at home and works for agreements which will extend these policies and practices to the international scene.*

7. *He considers factors involving personal adjustment in reaching personal and group decisions.*[17]

Goal 7: Belief in Equality and Liberty

It may have seemed logical for John Randolph of Roanoke to say in his day, "I love liberty, and I hate equality." Today, this schism in the democratic ideal is archaic. In the new social mathematics of our times, the simple division between liberty and equality has been replaced by the equation: "Democracy = Liberty ×

---

[16] E. E. Schattschneider, *The Semisovereign People.* Holt, Rinehart, and Winston, 1961. p. 141.

[17] John Payne, "The Teaching of Contemporary Affairs." 21st Yearbook of the National Council for the Social Studies, 1950. pp. 3–11.

Equality."[18] Max Lerner describes the situation in these words:

There are two major meanings—or better, a double aspect of meaning—of the idea of democracy. In one aspect it is free or constitutional government, a going system for assuring the safeguards within which the will of the people can express itself. In this phase—set off the more sharply because of the rise of the new totalitarianisms—the emphasis is on the natural rights of the individual and the limited powers of government, on the separation of powers, on civil liberties, on the rule of law, and the protection of freedom and property against the arbitrary encroachments of the state.

In the second aspect the democratic idea is egalitarian. In this phase it emphasizes the rule of the majority. It presents the spectacle of a demos unbound, a whole people striving however imperfectly to make social equality a premise of government . . .

The recent American experiences in the context of world events have made it clear that in neither of these phases can democracy stand by itself, whether as constitutional government or popular government, "property rights" or "human rights," antistatism or welfare state. These are not different and self-sufficient "brands" of democracy, to be purchased from the shopwindows of history according to the taste, tradition, or means of a people; nor, to take the other extreme, are they merely semantic quibblings—verbal variations of the same democratic reality. They are polar ideas within the same field; or to vary the figure, they are currents in the same stream of historic tendency. They are complementary aspects of how political communities in our time have tried to answer the central problems of power, welfare, freedom, and creativeness. They are parts of each other, each of them either barren or dangerous unless set in the context of the other.[19]

Goal 8: National Pride and International Cooperation

A citizen need not idolize every aspect of the American past, while he remains proud that he is unalterably linked to it. He can find identification and purpose in this part of the inaugural address of John F. Kennedy: ". . . the torch has been passed to a new

---

[18] Leslie Lipson, The Democratic Civilization. Oxford U. Press, 1964. p. 543.
[19] Max Lerner, America As a Civilization. Simon and Schuster, 1957. pp. 362–363.

generation of Americans—born in this century, tempered by war, disciplined by a hard and bitter peace, proud of our ancient heritage—and unwilling to witness or permit the slow undoing of those human rights to which the nation has always been committed. . . ." A citizen demonstrates his pride in his American heritage by willingly meeting his responsibilities; he votes, obeys the laws, educates his children to understand his country's traditions, and, in time of peril, defends his nation.

At the same time, a good citizen makes a conscientious effort to understand how other human beings in other lands view the world and its development. He does not demand that all people fit a single mold; he recognizes and appreciates the contributions to civilization made by other peoples. As early as 1916, the famous *Report* of the Committee on the Social Studies urged "cultivation of a sympathetic understanding of (other) nations and their peoples, of an intelligent appreciation of their contributions to civilization, and of a just attitude toward them . . ."[20]

It has never been more important for American citizens to understand other cultures than it is today, when 121 nations are joined in the United Nations, when all of the capitals of the world are within a few hours of travel time from each other, when global dissemination of news is virtually instantaneous, and when the world faces the threat of nuclear war.

Recognizing that human existence depends upon peaceful relations among men, the concerned citizen strives to reduce national hatreds and to strengthen international cooperation and order. He works with his fellow men to build a world of law and order.

In a society of changing values, ideological conflict is inescapable. Some individuals cling to traditional patterns, while others embrace newer codes. Some are highly impatient with the pace of international cooperation, while others resolutely hold to nationalistic postures. The result has been a clash in public opinion over every move in our foreign relations. The teacher who deals with current problems in social studies classes cannot easily ignore controversial issues, nor can he with impunity indulge in indoctrination.

---

[20] Cited in Henry Johnson, *Teaching of History.* Macmillan, rev. ed., 1940. pp. 113–114.

The twin ideal of loyalty to our nation and its achievements along with devotion to international cooperation and peace is difficult to attain. Yet, it is no more difficult to realize than was reconciliation between science and religion, once thought impossible. Further, if pride in the accomplishments of one's nation is coupled with an urge to help it contribute to the peace of the world, the ideal promises heightened pride. This is a worthy as well as a formidable goal.

Goal 9: The Creative Arts and Humanistic Awareness

In the search for self-discovery, citizens look increasingly to the creative arts, to music, painting, sculpture, literature, and related fields. The arts help man to realize the uniqueness of his personality by sensitizing him to a variety of human experiences. Harold Taylor describes the importance of this function in these words:

Until the individual becomes sensitive to experience and to ideas, until they mean something to him personally, or, to put it differently, until he becomes conscious of the world around him and wishes to understand it, he is not able to think creatively either about himself or about his world. His sensibility, his values, his attitudes are the key to his intellect. It is for this reason that the arts, since they have most directly to do with the development of sensibility, are an essential component of all learning, including scientific learning.[21]

The citizen who strives to enlarge his vision views mankind in the mirror of the arts, and in the process he discovers the unique features of his own image.

As is true in so many areas, the strengthening of the individual citizen by artistic growth also enriches the community and the nation. As Vaughan Williams said in a letter to the students of an English school which had decided to name one of its buildings for him:

I am very much pleased to think that one of your houses is to bear my name. I am myself a musician, and I believe that all the arts, and

---

[21] Harold Taylor, Art and the Intellect—Moral Values and the Experience of Art. Museum of Modern Art, 1960. p. 13.

These girls at Monmouth Regional High School are enjoying an exhibit of student art.

especially music, are necessary to a full life. The practical side of living, of course, is important, and this, I feel sure, is well taught in your school; such things teach you how to make your living. But music will enable you to see past facts to the very essence of things in a way which science cannot do. The arts are the means by which we can look through the magic casement and see what lies beyond.[22]

Today, the importance of the arts as an integral part of our life is being recognized increasingly in our schools and by our national leaders. As President John F. Kennedy said, "Both Roosevelt and Lincoln understood that the life of the arts, far from being an interruption, a distraction, in the life of a nation, is very close to the center of a nation's purpose—and is a test of the quality of a nation's civilization. That is

[22] Schools and the Fine Arts: What Should Be Taught in Art, Music, and Literature, Occasional Paper 9. Council for Basic Education, 1966. p. 16.

why we should be glad today that the interest of the American people in the arts seems at a new high."

This heightened interest is evident in the schools. The proposals approved under the Elementary and Secondary Education Act include several for introducing or improving art programs. Among them are these, as reported by *Education Summary:*

One project will bring music, art, and drama to children in schools in seven rural Kansas counties. Touring groups will give demonstrations and performances, bring along exhibits. A professional composer will be hired to visit schools and to write music for children to perform. A professional artist will also be hired to demonstrate and lecture. (Madison, Kansas.)

Another school district is planning a center for the performing arts. Possibilities under consideration include a state-supported symphony orchestra, a repertory theatre, an art exhibit, a children's ensemble, performance by national groups and artists on tour, weekly films, a collection of books and audio-visual materials. (Monett, Missouri.)

Goal 10: A Compassionate Citizenry

As the philosopher Martin Buber points out, each person has a responsibility to treat every other person as a "Thou," not as an "It"—that is, as a fellow human being and not as an object of political, economic, or social exploitation. In an age of increasing "depersonalization," compassion for others and sensitivity to their feelings and needs are essential.

In Asia the average life expectancy is only 45 years; the great majority of Africans cannot read or write; in the Middle East, thousands of children waste away from brutal diseases; and in the United States more than 35 million people live in poverty. A compassionate citizen realizes that sensitivity to the conditions of others is a necessary first step to intelligent civic behavior.

The concept of civic education embraces intellectual experiences and a great deal more, including the kind of education which may be advanced through the wisdom of the heart. Frederick Mayer identified it as the road of Buddha and Jesus and said, "Such wisdom goes to the center of things; it establishes harmony and a sense of contentment. It creates balance and perspective. . . . Education thus becomes a way of living rather than an empty theory."[23]

Goal 11: Development and Application of Democratic Principles

Citizens establish principles as intelligent guides to democratic behavior, rather than as inflexible censors of conduct. In the words of Francis Biddle, the citizen-philosopher has a responsibility "not so much to formulate a rationalized and comprehensive system as to develop what Jacques Maritain calls 'an adequate ideological formulation,' expressing the American view of civilization in new symbols and fresh language."[24]

It is of prime importance, however, that the citizen translate his principles into action. "What Americans have done," writes historian Henry Steele Commager, ". . . is to realize, to institutionalize, to actualize, the principles and doctrines and values inherited from older civilizations, to translate them, that is, out of the realm of theory and doctrine and into the realm of practice, *to transform them from bodies of cherished opinion to bodies of felt activity and practice.*"[25] The citizen must continue to test his principles on the basic issues of his own times, and to apply these principles as effectively as possible in an ever-changing world.

CONCLUSION

Concepts of citizenship are intertwined with socio-historical developments, and what is true of the study of history is equally true of the study of citizenship. However much we may wish for a Lydian touchstone by which to measure the civic behavior of men, there is no single answer to the question: "What makes a good citizen?"

---

[23] Frederick Mayer, *A History of Educational Thought.* Charles Merrill, 1960. pp. 126–127.

[24] Francis Biddle, "Freedom and the Preservation of Human Values," in *Preserving Human Values in an Age of Technology,* The Franklin Memorial Lectures, Volume IX, edited by Edgar G. Johnston, Wayne State University Press, 1961. p. 68.

[25] Henry Steele Commager, "Human Values in the American Tradition," *Ibid.,* pp. 29–30.

Equally important is the fact that the 11 goals described above are man-made guidelines and not absolute rules of nature. The comment of Oliver Wendell Holmes—"I prefer champagne to ditch-water but I see no reason to suppose the cosmos does"—has particular relevancy for anyone bold enough to draw up standards for human conduct. What is more, the goals are all interwoven into highly complex patterns, and none can be understood fully except in relation to the others.

Underlying these 11 goals are three major tasks for good civic education in the United States today. We need to: (1) Create an informed citizenry; (2) Develop an analytical citizenry; and (3) Promote a committed and involved citizenry.

Most of the students interviewed by the project team expressed similar views concerning the need for informed citizens, Linda Ellis at Henniker High School in Henniker, New Hampshire, said, "A good citizen is one who finds out information before making a decision." Donald Schueman of West Leyden High School in Northlake, Illinois, said, "A good citizen is someone who knows his country and understands the laws—not only obeys them but understands them." Information is not a permanent collection of "facts" pinned down for all time. Nevertheless, it is a prime necessity for the citizen to keep himself as well informed as possible about the facts of the past and the present.

An analytical citizenry is also essential, and students indicated their agreement in many ways. A boy at Darien High School in Darien, Connecticut, pointed out: "Lots of times things come up where the crowd is against your position, and I think you face discrimination against yourself. At that point it is necessary for a good citizen to think and analyze for himself and to do what he thinks is right—notwithstanding the feelings of the crowd." Annie Price of Dubose Junior High School in Alice, Texas, said, "A good citizen is one who can listen intelligently, be impartial—that is, objective—and analyze. And one who has the courage to stand up for what he believes in." A boy at Oakland Technical High School in Oakland, California, stated, "A good citizen thinks and questions until he understands the laws of the land. And if, as a result of his questioning, he finds bad laws, he sees it as his duty to change them [by regular, legal means]." An analytical citizen runs the risk of reaching some unsound conclusions. Aristotle, for example, once concluded that women have fewer teeth than men, and the learned Pythagoras taught that it was dangerous to let swallows rest on the roof of a house. Yet, analysis remains a key tool to assist the citizen in solving the problems of the contemporary world.

Other students drew attention to the need for a committed and involved citizenry. Marla Overby of Labette County Community High School in Altamont, Kansas, said, "The most important things are to vote, and to serve on juries, and perform duties such as that—and also to help other people willingly." John Hausner at Phoenix West High School in Phoenix, Arizona, noted, "A good citizen is one who looks out for the other fellow as well as for himself. He participates in elections, community projects, and other things." Moira Stacey at Rim-of-the-World Junior-Senior High School in Lake Arrowhead, California, said, "A good citizen is a person who is responsible—to himself, to people, to the country, and to all of society." Glenn Keife of De La Salle High School in New Orleans, said, "A good citizen is one who knows what his duties are and practices them, and gets others to do so, too." And Mary Chris Roman, a student at St. Scholastica High School in Chicago, said, "It should start right on the community level. If a good citizen thinks something should be changed, he contacts others; thus he plays an active role—he participates."

It must be reaffirmed that the making of good citizens is not just the responsibility of the school, but of the community as a whole. This key point—so often stated and so often forgotten—was brought home again and again to members of the civic education project team. It is reflected most sharply in this comment taken from the team's observation notebook:

This morning we walked about the slum area that surrounds the school we visited yesterday. It was a different world from the shiny make-believe, coffee-break, excuse-me-sir, Utopia of the Central Administration Building. There were ugly houses and filthy streets, beer cans rusting in the sun and people rusting with them. There was dirt that could not be swept away by memos or television programs or speeches. It was horrible. What are we doing talking about citizenship education? How can the schools turn out good citizens when slum communities are negating the academic niceties? Education is not enough—is not a universal panacea—is not the solution. The attack has to be many-

sided: better education; better housing; better clothing; better jobs; better everything.

All the sweet talk about citizenship seems to go out the window when you see a child sitting in the gutter playing with a rat's tail—and when you know that probably the child's only sin was being born in the wrong neighborhood. How long will it be before all communities develop a conscience and act?

*If it's good enough for today,
it's not good enough for tomorrow.*

Harvey Handel, Principal
Oneida Junior High School
Schenectady, New York

CHAPTER **3**

Approaches for the Schools

How well a school succeeds in serving the goals of citizenship depends on its convictions about civic education and its sensitivity to the needs of its students. The following six assumptions about the school's approaches are offered here as guidelines.

1. The school can develop the rational abilities its students bring to decision-making.

2. The school can provide students with opportunities for realistic examination of the issues of our time.

3. The school can make realistic contact with the total environment of its students, adjusting its expectations, curriculum, and instruction accordingly.

4. The entire school—its goals, personnel, organization, curriculum, and climate for learning—can mirror a commitment to democratic values.

5. The school can offer a variety of experiences through which students can learn and practice behavior appropriate to multiple goals.

6. The school can help develop both academic excellence and effective citizenship.

ASSUMPTION 1: DEVELOPING RATIONAL ABILITIES

In their approaches to the decision-making process, the various disciplines stress different factors. To the theologian, certain values derived from religious experience, such as faith, hope, and love, are likely to appear most crucial to the process of decision-making. To the economist, other values derived from society, such as economic security and success, are likely to appear most important. The biochemist may emphasize the importance of chemical balance in the body; the psychoanalyst may consider paramount selected experiences from early childhood. Each of these factors may enter into decision-making, but the most basic factor is rational thinking.

Although the schools have assumed varying degrees of responsibility for helping students to acquire skills, the cultivation of competence in rational thinking remains the central task. It is the task that probably cannot be accomplished on a broad scale by any other institution, and it calls for factual evidence to apply in correcting erroneous beliefs.

ASSUMPTION 2: REALISTIC EXAMINATION OF ISSUES

Society and its schools often tend to protect the young from reality, especially from those aspects that are "unpleasant." Situations that conflict with the values they are attempting to implant in the young are often neglected, and unenviable traits such as conspicuous self-seeking, corruption, or faithlessness are commonly ignored. Violence, torture, and inhumanity may be screened out, on the basis that "children will have to grow up soon enough." Embarrassment or guilt may result in concealment of other aspects of reality.

In some schools, students receive a highly edited view of social and political phenomena. The study of government, for example, may be reduced to charts which purport to show how a bill becomes law. The students who memorize the charts and recite the steps through which a piece of legislation travels will learn little about how political choices are usually made and what factors influence political decisions. Other administrators and teachers—apparently, a growing number—are pursuing a different policy. They have conscientiously attempted to provide realistic exposure to the major issues of our time.

Realistic discussion on an abstract level is found at Yorktown High School in Arlington, Virginia. Alex Anderson and Mack Smith introduce their students to a study of government by having them examine what happens in a group which has no government. Students of Julie Stindt, sociology teacher in Detroit's Denby High School, are given realistic exposure to social issues at an action level, by attending and participating in meetings of at least two community groups during a semester. Many in this predominantly white school work with families in Detroit's worst slums; others have established a library and a nursery play area for children in a culturally deprived Negro area.

A school-wide concern with realistic treatment of contemporary issues is found at Fairmont Heights High School, in Prince George's County, Maryland. Principal Gholson and his staff have initiated a program they call "Operation Awareness," to "help students to explore and become involved in significant aspects of American life beyond the walls of the school." Activities include experiences in social, governmental, scientific, technical, and recreational aspects of metropolitan Washington, D. C., and in a creatively structured co-curricular program in the school. The staff is now moving toward involvement of parents in the program. Seminar groups have been organized to insure a continuing dialogue on significant issues between school and community and among parents, teachers, and students.

Public high schools in the United States are in an exposed position,

Vice President Humphrey greets students seeing Congress in action.

vulnerable to criticism, and subject to attack from several directions at once when they become involved with "real" issues. It is much safer to screen material to be learned and avoid the risk of offending any part of the school's public. But commitment to a viable democratic society demands that loyal, useful citizens learn to assess and improve the existing order of things. This assessment is not likely to be made intelligently unless the schools provide opportunities to examine the real issues.

The significant issues of contemporary society should be examined honestly. Every care should be taken to avoid superficial, biased, careless, or unscholarly treatment.

ASSUMPTION 3: ADJUSTING THE SCHOOL TO THE STUDENT'S ENVIRONMENT

If we accept as a basic premise that civic education is designed to affect the student's perception of society and his role in it, the school must make contact with the environment in which the student lives. Unless the content, methodology, and school climate are attuned to the conditions the student sees in his daily life, talk about civic education becomes a meaningless exercise and is likely to be a vehicle for self-deception. Making contact with the real world of the student poses different problems in different types of communities, such as the transitional neighborhood, the big city school, or the school preoccupied with college entrance.

Many teachers have had personal experience with only one world, usually the middle-class, upwardly mobile, highly verbal world from which so many teachers are recruited. The difficulty arises from the rapidly changing population in many communities. Teachers who have learned to understand the real world of the student in their school may suddenly find new students in their classrooms, students with very different values and standards. This change in school populations results from the rapid shifting of racial, ethnic, or socio-economic groups. The population shift is accompanied by a shift from traditional middle-class values, which have dominated public education for many years. The schools are often not ready with a new curriculum, goals, organization, and, most important, appropriate intellectual and emotional postures by teachers and administrators. One can sympathize when a counselor complains that "I cannot understand these kids. They're different." But one cannot overlook the absence of the follow-up statement, "But I'll try to learn enough about them so that I can."

Central High School in Kansas City is one of thousands of schools that have experienced a rapid shift in school population. As in most cities, the change has been in the direction of lower achievement, less motivation, more problems of adjusting to the school. Jim Boyd, Central's principal, has worked with his staff to get the best possible performance from each individual. "Forget about group norms," he says. "Work for individual improvement." It is a simple statement, but it is one that is rarely heard. It reveals a commitment to the basic democratic value of the primary importance of the individual.

Some systems sponsor excellent in-service courses and workshops to prepare teachers for changing populations. And some principals are like Guy Varner of Cleveland's Lincoln High School, who says, "Our students are not as high-powered scholastically as they used to be, but they have a much better attitude; they are more cooperative and certainly much more appreciative."

Students in large urban areas are likely to become cynical about government, especially local government. Many of them are told from childhood, "You can't fight city hall." "It doesn't make any difference who wins." "They'll all gouge you sooner or later." Sometimes teachers are caught in the same hopeless cynicism. Some teachers, however, are doing something about this cynicism. Bob Donaldson's class at Denby High School in Detroit proved that "You can fight city hall, and, furthermore, you can win." His students studied conditions in Detroit's Receiving Hospital. When they found facilities inadequate and budget requests insufficient to bring improvement, they organized 1,000 students to campaign for more funds. As a direct result, the city council appropriated an additional $500,000.

Sometimes the big city school serves a slum neighborhood, where education is not looked upon as a road to a better way of life but as an obstacle to be crossed or circumvented, where authority does not represent security but an enemy to be fought and outwitted. If the slum area happens to be a Negro neighborhood, the attitude toward school and authority may reflect hopelessness generated through years of discrimination. A refreshing exception to this all-too-common attitude is found in the *esprit de corps* at Fairmont Heights High School in Prince George's County, Maryland. Here, students have developed a strong sense of loyalty to the school and pride in its accomplishments and in their individual contributions to the school. If anyone cuts across the well-kept, student-planted lawns and flower beds, a student is likely to say, "Hey man, get off my lawn."

In another school, preoccupied with preparing its students for college entrance, a department chairman stated, "We would like to experiment with newer and more promising methods of teaching, but we cannot risk change until the Regents exams are completed in grade 11." Yet, some of the best academic high schools in the country—schools that send many graduates to top colleges—are as much concerned with developing citizenship qualities as with training students to succeed in college. Mount Hermon School in Massachusetts is a good example. There, the Director of Research says:

> If we want students to value intelligence . . . morality . . . social concern and an appreciation for the arts . . . rather than good looks, cars, and personality and a gay social life, we should arrange the school program so that it is through stressing those values that students obtain recognition from the institution and, more importantly, their peers.

Frederick Bauer, social studies chairman at Mount Hermon, states it this way. "We are trying to make these kids see that they are part of the human race."

ASSUMPTION 4: MIRRORING DEMOCRATIC VALUES

If a school is really serious in its commitment to democratic values, it will find that the process of translating ideals into action requires a high degree of resourcefulness, intelligence, effort, and cooperation. The Rockefeller Report asserts that "To care about democracy is to care about human beings, not *en masse*, but one by one." This value is incompatible with the statement made by some teachers in transitional neighborhoods, "You should have visited our school when we had a better class of kids, before 'they' moved in." Neither is it consistent with a concern for human beings "one by one" to neglect the problems of slow learners or to isolate the culturally deprived in programs that accentuate their alienation. Finally, in a school which has a totalitarian climate, talk about our nation's democratic values becomes a mockery.

Seldom do such schools have sheer disregard for democratic values. Usually, they can be charged with lack of resourcefulness, effort, and cooperation, with a failure to think through the implications of democracy and then give adequate attention to translating ideals into reality.

The social studies department at Yorktown High School, Arlington, Virginia, is one which has thought through this problem. The teachers there say:

It seems imperative to bring faith and actuality together by dispensing with the idea of one level of instruction for an entire class to begin thinking in terms of a level of instruction according to ability levels of the individual students. This has the immediate value of allowing the truly gifted student to pursue areas of independent study, while bringing him into touch with reality by making him communicate the results of his study with those who are less capable.

Social Studies Chairman David Turner and his department have devised numerous, creative ways to teach significant material to students of all ability levels.

ASSUMPTION 5: SERVING MULTIPLE BEHAVIORAL GOALS

One facet of the democratic heritage in the United States is acceptance of pluralism. This commitment upholds the rights of others to interpret, behave, and dream differently within the framework of the democratic process, without being viewed with suspicion or treated as second-class citizens. It must include recognition of the need for many kinds of learning experience and acceptance of many different student reactions to the same experience.

The different aspects of citizenship are not learned all at a time, or from a single experience. Each aspect requires specific kinds of learning although there may be some overlapping. Ralph Tyler suggests:

To develop attitudes, it is necessary (a) to provide an environment which stimulates an assimilation of desired attitudes, (b) to provide experiences which evoke feelings of certain types, or (c) to give opportunities to make the kinds of intellectual analyses which reveal the consequences of the events, ideas, or possibilities sufficiently to cultivate either a favorable or unfavorable disposition. Interest can be cultivated primarily by seeing to it that the areas in which interests are to be developed are satisfying.

To extend sensitivity, students need an opportunity to react to feelings and to identify with feelings of other people, whether in the reality of actual experience or as described in fiction.[1]

A panel discussion may be a poor way to present many types of information, but it can cause students to react to different points of view and with empathy to other people. Research, involving many sources of information, may be a poor source for developing democratic attitudes, but it can develop skill in handling, analyzing, and judging the validity of evidence. Student council committees may discourage divergent thinking, but they can provide an excellent means for developing skill in reaching a consensus. Patriotic ceremonies may not always promote awareness of the Constitution as a dynamic, living document, but they can be extremely useful in developing pride in and identification with our cultural heritage. Participation in a political campaign may not lend itself to careful analysis of issues and may strengthen preconceived biases, but it can supply an abundance of information, promote understanding of the work of politicians, and foster an inclination to become more active in community affairs.

ASSUMPTION 6: ACADEMIC EXCELLENCE AND CITIZENSHIP

The frenzied post-Sputnik effort to "up-grade" high school education, the "knowledge explosion" which multiplies the amount of information to be learned, the return of university scholars to curriculum-making—

---

[1] Quoted in Hilda Taba, Curriculum Development: Theory and Practice. Harcourt, Brace and World, 1962.

Attentive learning in a debate class at Trinity High School, Bloomington, Illinois.

all these combine to add substance to the high school curriculum. Usually, the emphasis is on content formerly delayed until college years.

Many changes resulting from this recent activity were urgently needed. Citizenship education, for example, was sometimes associated with soft pedagogy. The theoretical was often completely sacrificed to what was thought to be practical. On the other hand, excellence in recent times has too often been equated with quantity rather than with quality. "Excellence," according to Paul Woodring, "is not achieved by piling on more work . . . Excellence is achieved only when the student is led to think more deeply and about more important things."

A persistent fallacy is the belief that rigorous academic standards are incompatible with development of the individual student's capacities for citizenship. Rigorous study of judiciously selected data is instead essential for civic education. At the same time that rigorous academic standards are applauded, however, the student's sensitivity to civic issues should not be neglected. The hazards of school emphasis on intellectual perfectionism are noted by William S. White:

> Of course, the function of the high prep school is to teach the young and to prepare them for the future. Nevertheless, it does not follow that they ought to be put through a prolonged intellectual torture chamber in which appalling exertion is rewarded only by ceaseless warnings that unless they do better they will surely never get into College X or the University of Y.
>
> But this is what is happening in many school and prep school classrooms. And some of these agonized little characters are turning to academic cheating, lest they let down Mom and Dad.
>
> The country seems seized with a doctrine of high-school perfectionism so extreme as to call into question the rationality of the whole business. Is it really necessary for high school seniors—not just the dullards but also those who could pass exams their college-trained parents never could—to be prodded and chivvied in this way?[2]

CONCLUSION

To summarize, Chapter 2 identified 11 goals of civic education:

1. Knowledge and skills to assist in solving the problems of our times.

2. Awareness of the effects of science on civilization and its use to improve the quality of life.

3. Readiness for effective economic life.

4. Ability to make value judgments for effective life in a changing world.

5. Recognition that we live in an open-ended world which requires receptivity to new facts, new ideas, and new ways of life.

6. Participation in the process of decision-making through expression of views to representatives, experts, and specialists.

7. Belief in both liberty for the individual and equality for all, as guaranteed by the Constitution of the United States.

8. Pride in the achievements of the United States, appreciation of the

---

[2] William S. White, "High School Pupils Pressured to Perfectionism," in *The Phoenix Gazette*, December 1, 1965. p. 7.

contributions of other peoples, and support for international peace and cooperation.

9. Use of the creative arts to sensitize oneself to universal human experience and to the uniqueness of the individual.

10. Compassion and sensitivity for the needs, feelings, and aspirations of other human beings.

11. Possession of principles consistent with our democratic heritage and application of these principles in daily life.

To implement these goals, Chapter 3 offers six guidelines for the schools in their approach to civic education.

1. The school can develop the rational abilities its students bring to decision-making.

2. The school can provide students with opportunities for realistic examination of the issues of our time.

3. The school can make realistic contact with the total environment of its students, adjusting its expectations, curriculum, and instruction accordingly.

4. The entire school—its goals, personnel, organization, curriculum, and climate for learning—can mirror a commitment to democratic values.

5. The school can offer a variety of experiences through which students can learn and practice behavior appropriate to multiple goals.

6. The school can help develop both academic excellence and effective citizenship.

The following chapters will report on practices that serve these goals and exemplify these approaches to the tasks of civic education.

Eric W. Johnson, Vice Principal of Germantown Friends School and teacher of 7th-grade English, talks with enthusiastic students.

CHAPTER **4**

Creating an Informed Citizenry

GOAL 1: KNOWLEDGE AND SKILLS FOR SOLVING PROBLEMS

"Cleveland, comme bien des cités Américaines, suit la marche du temps par son béton, son verre, ses vues, at ses sons, que l'homme appelle civilisation."

"Cleveland, like most American cities," begins Peggy, the pretty 8th-grade girl, "follows the march of times . . ."

Peggy and her classmates at Cleveland's Wilbur Wright Junior High School are learning French and learning about their own city at the same time. An important part of their study material consists of booklets such as *Qu'il Faut Savoir Sur Cleveland Et Les Services Publics*, prepared by the city's Chamber of Commerce for the benefit of French-speaking newcomers to the city.

Mrs. Barbara Ball, the able and enthusiastic teacher, says, "Instead of just studying French, we also aim to make this course a positive help to students in learning about their community and how to live together with peoples throughout the world."

Studying social and political affairs and a foreign language at the same time is by no means unique. It reflects a growing recognition that the knowledge and skills that contribute to effective citizenship come from

47

many sources. The knowledge explosion has extended the boundaries of scholarship in the social sciences as well as in the natural sciences and has added new realms of understanding to be mastered. Studies once reserved for college, such as sociology and anthropology, are being introduced into the high school curriculum. Geographical areas, especially Africa and Asia, which were once given only nominal attention have now become fields of intensive study. An awareness of motivations that make men think, feel, and act as they do is another aspect of the knowledge explosion in secondary schools. Further, the knowledge and skills associated with citizenship are usually found in unfamiliar arrangements today. Combinations of social science disciplines to create new social studies courses or, in collaboration with other departments, new humanities courses, are increasingly common. Still another change is the gradual relaxation of the view that certain material must be learned by the 10th grade, others by the 11th or 12th, and that other learning should be reserved for college. Students now are being encouraged to read, study, and learn in wider fields.

Evidence of these changes in current social studies practices will appear in the episodes reported throughout this chapter. It will appear, as well, in later chapters whose titles may direct attention to other facets of civic education but whose content will also be concerned with knowledge and skills.

Drawing Relationships Between Facts

At West Leyden High School in Northlake, Illinois, a contemporary problems course has, as one of its goals, the development in students of "a critical attitude toward generalizations about human behavior." Joachim Schneider, social studies department chairman at West Leyden, explains the goal in these words:

A critical attitude toward generalizations about human behavior is a highly important and controversial aspect of the course. Man's thinking is frequently based on many generalizations about people that will not stand up to fact or the findings of social science research. When generalizations are challenged, frequently you feel threatened and react emotionally and aggressively. However, we do not want an alternative which is as bad. We don't want our students to accept all the claims of the pseudo-scientist. We hope that our students will begin to realize the difficulty of establishing the truth of a proposition, yet concurrently to recognize the possibility of developing generalizations that will give them the increased ability to predict and understand what people do.

This attention to somewhat abstract aspects of learning is in no sense an evasion of the responsibility to handle solid, factual material. Rather, it is a way to help students relate the facts and ideas they will meet in this course to the larger problems of humanity and to the smaller problems of the self—a function that is essential if a full use is to be made of knowledge. The reading list suggests that the students are exposed to a variety of ideas. It includes the following among its 17 titles: *Patterns of Culture, The Status Seekers, Darkness At Noon, What We Must Know About Communism, Mirror of Man,* and *The Nature of the Non-Western World.* In addition to reading, students are often exposed to experiences which provide direct information on each problem. For example, Schneider's description of a unit in this course called "Minority Life and Prejudice in the United States" suggests a wide variety of sources of information:

In this unit we have a small group discussion over selected questions concerned with prejudice. The group reports after two or three days of talk. The individual members of the group then evaluate their experiences. We take a trip to Chicago's South Side to visit Dunbar High School, Public Housing, slum districts, and some social agencies. . . . We read extensively in the area of human relations and hear speakers on these topics. We have talks with representatives of the National Conference of Christians and Jews, the Urban League, Johnson Publishing Company, the Chicago Housing Authority, Dunbar High School, and others who work in the field of human relations. This unit is quite controversial. I believe it is interesting and challenging, because it involves an examination of deep personal values.

Special problem areas of concern to American citizens are sometimes brought into the U. S. history course. At Passaic Valley High School in Little Falls, New Jersey, U. S. history is required of all students during their junior and senior years. In this school, the last of the four semesters of American history includes these six units:

 I. *U. S. Becomes a World Power*
 II. *United Nations*
 III. *Economics and the World Around You*
 IV. *Public Opinion and Propaganda*
 V. *Politics and Government in America*
 VI. *American Democracy and Communism*

Although these topics depart from the subject matter of the strictly historical and chronological history course, they are areas of significance that link American history with current problems.

In Rino Pettiross' ancient history class at Glastonbury High School in Connecticut, at the time of the project team's visit, students who had been reading Plato were engaged in a discussion of the Greek philosopher's ideas, a discussion frequently punctuated by references to *The Republic* and by reading paragraphs to reinforce a point.

STUDENT: Socrates says that the laws of the state should be obeyed, even if a person does not agree with all of them. He said that the state married his parents.

TEACHER: What does "The state married his parents" mean? What is he trying to say?

STUDENT: That he gained what he has—knowledge and other things—from the state.

TEACHER: Now, for what is Socrates trying to gain respect?

STUDENT: Laws.

TEACHER: Yes, he's trying to show respect for laws. Now, what has put him in jail?

STUDENT: The laws of the state.

TEACHER: The same type of law that "married his parents" put him in prison, didn't it?

STUDENT: Socrates could have left the city, but he didn't. He agreed to abide by the laws.

(He reads a key section from Plato that makes this point.)

TEACHER: Have you tried to place yourself in Socrates' position? Try it. What is Socrates thinking?

STUDENT: *He is worried about his children.*
TEACHER: *What else?*
STUDENT: *What people are going to say?*
TEACHER: *What else is bothering him?*
STUDENT: *His conscience.*
TEACHER: *Yes, this is the thing that bothers him greatly.*

At the close of the period, the visitor asked a number of students, "Why is it important to study ancient history at all? After all, these events occurred many centuries ago and these people are long dead. Why should we not just study contemporary affairs and issues?"

These are some of the answers. "Some of our greatest literature comes from this period. It has influenced our lives." "One reason for studying ancient history is to know about the people who came before you." "We can learn from the past by observing their mistakes and not making similar ones." "Ancient people built the foundations of our culture."

The answers are not always assured or even completely accurate. Letter-perfect responses, however, come only from limited—and generally unimaginative—instruction and learning based on drill. They are seldom possible when students are asked to interpret the facts they have learned, to examine them in different arrangements and different contexts, thereby transmuting them from information to knowledge.

Students acquire a wide range of information in the increasingly popular but not yet common anthropology courses. The anthropology course offered at Germantown Friends School in Philadelphia includes these eight units:

    I. *Origin of Man and Natural Selection*
   II. *Paleolithic Man (Java, Peking, Heidelberg, Neanderthal, Upper Paleolithic)*
  III. *Neolithic Man*
  IV. *The Races of Europe and the Culture of a Nomadic Group— The Arabs*
   V. *Polynesia*
  VI. *Polar People*

VII. *The New World*
VIII. *Sumer and Ancient Babylonia*

The reading list for the course reflects the comprehensive world view promoted by the teacher, Howard Platt. The 25 volumes on this list were selected to help the students become informed about the ways in which man has adapted to his world and shaped the world to his needs. Among the titles are Montagu's *Man—His First One Million Years;* Eiseley's *The Immense Journey;* Lawrence's *Seven Pillars of Wisdom;* Mead's *Coming of Age in Samoa;* Nordhoff and Hall's *Pitcairn's Island;* Freuchen's *I Sailed With Rasmussen;* Chiera's *They Wrote on Clay;* and Kramer's *History Begins at Sumer.*

In the same school, the second semester of the 8th-grade social studies course includes a study of China and a study of Africa. At the time of the visit, Africa was the subject and the 13- and 14 year-old students were already remarkably knowledgeable. Their teacher, John Emerson, led them into an exploration of the geography of Africa, as well as the relation between 19th-century and 20th-century views of Africa held by European nations and America, and an examination of traditional colonialism and present-day variants. These 8th-graders were eager to handle ideas, followed the direction of their teacher in grasping relationships, and were reading at what a few years ago would have been considered senior high school level.

This class, like many the project team visited, was conducted primarily as a teacher-led discussion, with the students responding to the teacher's questions and only occasionally injecting a query of their own. Almost never, however, was this exchange in the nature of a catechism. Seldom could the teacher know in advance exactly what response his questions would elicit. The sequences of questions were designed to probe understanding, present new conjunctions of facts, and provoke new ideas in the minds of students.

TEACHER: *What do we mean by colonialism?*
STUDENT: *One government taking over an area it has not previously had and calling it a colony. Or taking over people of another culture.*
TEACHER: *How have a few people been able to take over larger areas as colonies?*

STUDENT: *Because they have metal weapons; they have modern technology. Sometimes they use persuasion.*

TEACHER: *Why did not primitive peoples develop their own resources?*

STUDENT: *They don't have the tools or the knowledge or the need for more resources.*

With each exchange the concept of colonialism as control of one people by another was developed more fully. Then Emerson asked, "Is control good or bad? What controls exist over you?" Students responded with reports of assorted restrictions at home and at school, and again the teacher asked if controls are good or bad, desirable or undesirable.

The answer appeared to be obvious to everyone at the same time: controls can be either good or bad. From here it was a short jump to the idea that colonialism can be either exploitation of underdeveloped people or development of the resources and bringing an advanced culture to areas that can profit from such cultures, or both.

From this point, the teacher led the discussion into today's concerns. Why do African people want to change, and what is progress? What is the difference between classic colonialism and something like the Peace Corps? The Peace Corps, said a student, is trying to teach people how to use their own resources; it is not trying to exploit their resources.

The students in this 8th-grade class learned, at the same time, about African history and geography, various concepts of colonialism, and current issues such as emerging nationalism and the effect of the Peace Corps on U.S. foreign policy—all in a context of critical thinking.

Making Imaginative Use of Resources

Centennial Junior High School at Decatur, Illinois, seeks to provide 7th- and 8th-graders with knowledge about themselves, their immediate community, and the larger world scene through a three-pronged resource program meeting every Friday. The three parts of this course are the student resource phase, the community resource phase, and the world resource phase. The student resource phase requires participation in a club of the student's own choosing. The community resource phase consists of visits to occupational and cultural centers in the immediate area. The world resource phase is brought to the student through films depicting world activities.

The places visited in the community phase of this program include a tractor plant, the local television station, a food processing plant, the Post Office, the County Building, a hospital, and a local florist. The value of this kind of learning experience depends on the care with which a site to be visited is selected and equally on preparation by students and teachers for the trip.

The team was frequently impressed with the importance of planning as an essential ingredient in effective learning. Spontaneous insights arising from an unplanned or improvised classroom situation are valuable and the effective teacher is quick to sense these sparks and exploit them to build a continuing fire of interest. Spontaneous excitement and insight occur most frequently, however, when the teacher has carefully planted thought-provoking information in the student's path.

The need for careful preparation for a visit to a local factory is as necessary as it is for a debate on American foreign policy .In some ways the former takes even more time, because preparation is required for logistic problems as well as for an understanding of the factory's processes and function. Preparation might include the examination of detailed industrial facts and concepts, which become far more meaningful to the students as a result of the trip. Frequently in civic education, there is no adequate substitute for the field trip—the face-to-face exposure to the live situation of adults at work in industry, in business, in executive offices, in the courts, and in the legislatures.

At the Hopkinton High School in New Hampshire, where the 9th-grade social studies course has been given the traditional title of civics, the process for gathering substantive information for the course is unique.

In 1964, the freshman civics class at Hopkinton made a town survey. As the study proceeded, it became evident that many points were vague and sources of exact information uncertain. The students decided that the thorough research needed to secure reliable answers to some of their questions could more easily be justified if the answers were made available to the entire community. A class committee constructed a questionnaire on the town government, and then solicited questions that the townspeople also might wish to have answered.

Groups of students participated in conducting the survey based on student questions and in tabulating the results. To find answers to their own and citizens' questions, the students consulted town reports and interviewed town officials, studied the state-revised statutes and volumes such as *Selected Duties of New Hampshire Selectmen* and *Town Meeting in New England,* and interviewed the state tax commissioner. The students then published the results of their study in a pamphlet circulated throughout the town.

There seems little question that the experience of polling the citizens and compiling an informative booklet assured a far wider range of investigation and subsequent information. Even more important, it stimulated the interest of the students in local government.

Knowledge is likely to seem more worthwhile to students when it comes from experiences that have stimulated their interest, provoked their curiosity, and called their initiative into play. These experiences are not only satisfying, but they also encourage the student to seek further similar experiences which, in turn, lead to acquisition of additional knowledge.

Many current issues can be better understood and more intelligently discussed in the classroom with the aid of data found in significant documents, magazine articles, or news columns. Searching out copies of the current federal budget, the text of a presidential address, or a pertinent editorial in the *Saturday Review* is not always a productive use of students' time. An increasing number of schools, accordingly, have turned to the quick, easy, and relatively inexpensive process of reproducing the printed word through various copying machines. Alert teachers are developing teaching strategies based largely on their ability to make available to each student in their classes a copy of data not found in texts, library books, or the almanac. Despite their added chore in securing reprint permission from an author or publisher, teachers find this method an effective and rewarding way to expand the sources of information available to students.

In a government course at the Horton Watkins High School at Ladue, Missouri, students are presented with a series of neatly mimeographed readings which outline key issues in the lesson and present information not available in the text. Some of these readings are reprinted from other sources and some are written by the instructor.

An example is Reading 38, "Legislative Decision-Making: The Human Element," which presents several cogent paragraphs summarizing the increased complexity of a Congressman's duties, followed by a reprint called "A Day in the Life of Senator Dirksen." This is accompanied by three salient questions for the student to bear in mind as he reads:

1. Which of the activities described in the reading relate to Dirksen's role as a legislative decision-maker?

2. Which of the activities are merely favors for constituents?

3. Which of the activities seem to you to be of major importance? Minor importance?

In a history course at West Leyden High School, H. J. Paske encourages students to enlarge their knowledge and skills by using the resources of college history departments. His students once noted a discrepancy among published sources in regard to the location of General Howe during the Battle of Trenton. The students then addressed this letter to 25 historians:

A historical matter has come to the attention of our West Leyden High School American history classes. A controversy has arisen over the precise location of British General Howe during the Battle of Trenton, various sources giving conflicting information as to his personal whereabouts. We feel this question is important, not for the sake of clarity alone, but primarily because it seems inconceivable that nearly two hundred years could have passed with conflicting reports persisting. We would appreciate any information concerning this question that you might have. Thank you for your cooperation.

Responses ranged from a terse "If it is important for you to know this detail, I'm afraid it will be necessary for you to undertake the research" to a two-page letter describing in detail how they might proceed to locate information and verify it. One history professor confessed that he was personally unable to throw light on the matter but offered the names of four specialists in the military history of the Revolution to whom they should write. Another took time to comment:

> With regard to your second point, I have to say that it is not surprising about an affair that occurred 200 years ago. This is not an uncommon circumstance in history at all. There are thousands of incidents on which the evidence is conflicting. The minutiae of history are extremely difficult to uncover. Then, too, sometimes participants in events undertake to cloud the record in order to preserve their own reputations.

An occasional exercise like this is most useful to afford students an appreciation of the kinds of problems with which historians contend.

Although the development of skills and techniques is seldom described on paper or included in a course outline, this consideration is usually prominent in a teacher's planning. Certain assignments with their accompanying instructions are designed to develop the skills of constructing or interpreting charts and graphs or evaluating sources of information. Other assignments provide practice in organizing material, arriving at generalizations, test-taking, or presenting effective oral arguments.

Miss Joyce Fulton, who teaches American government at Woodside High School in California, plans for the acquisition of knowledge and the development of skills to assist in solving political, economic, social, and cultural problems by a particularly perceptive selection of material related to crucial issues. With the aid of ditto and mimeograph machines, she then makes copies of the material available to each student. It is important to note that Miss Fulton obtains from the publisher specific permission before duplicating copyrighted material.

Equally important, she presents the facts and ideas so that students may learn the essential skills of analysis and decision-making. To this end, she provides pages of explanation and check-sheets prepared to fit each assignment. These have included checklists for evaluating news reports; advice on radio news-listening; guides for panel chairmen; instructions on preparing a critical analysis of a magazine article; practice outlines; procedures for oral reports; checklists for reactions to the Congressional record; and "What a Free Society Expects of You—The Citizen," and several other statements on how to interpret the news and detect slanted news in mass communications.

In another example of skills-development, American history students at McCluer High School in Florissant, Missouri, are given a three-page lesson sheet explaining how a research paper should be prepared. The lesson sheet includes advice on reference sources, outlining, choosing a subject, attribution, bibliographies, and final form.

Similar helpful materials are often provided on the subjects of how to study, outline, and take a test. The usefulness of these materials depends on whether they reach students at the right time, accompanied with the right follow-up by the teacher. Although a few "natural" scholars quickly pick up the study skills needed in high school, most students must be taught specific skills. Conscientious teachers usually take the time to do this.

Acquiring Knowledge and Skills Through Student Clubs

The acquisition of knowledge and skills is of course not limited to the classroom. Student clubs play an important part in preparing students for knowledgeable citizenship. A case in point is the Current Events Club of Redford High School, Detroit, which drew a record attendance of 150 students and a dozen faculty members to a meeting addressed by a graduate of the school, now a district coordinator for the John Birch Society. Students took full advantage of their opportunity to obtain first-hand information about this organization. With no show of animosity, they listened patiently, questioned sagely, and emerged with authentic, first-hand facts about the John Birch Society which will help them to arrive at more nearly valid attitudes toward it.

Political clubs thrive at some schools and provide knowledge of practical politics to supplement the more theoretical learnings of the classroom. The students at Yorktown High School in Arlington, Virginia, for example, support both a Republican and a Democratic Club, and apparently with nearly equal enthusiasm.

In 1964, members of the Young Republicans Club, for example, helped to organize a mock election in the school. They also went to the airport to greet the Republican candidate for President. They assisted at various Republican headquarters by typing envelopes during the campaign, organized and operated a baby sitting committee for voters during the election, and were ushers for an Arlington County Republican Convention. At first hand, they learned about politics.

At John Marshall High School in Richmond, Virginia, young partisans of both persuasions join forces in the Young Americans Club. In the words of the sponsor, this club was organized several years ago by a group of "alert, politically conscious, predominantly conservative but open-minded students." In 1965 there were 38 members. They frequently sponsor speakers representing several sides of an issue. In 1964, for example, they brought in speakers to explain the Democratic and Republican platforms. On another occasion some of the members brought in the film "Operation Abolition." This sparked an explosive discussion which the sponsor believes was a good experience for all. The group also attended a John Birch Society meeting. Another club activity was a mock election for which club members planned the details, put up campaign posters, manned the ballot boxes, and performed other routine duties that accompany an election.

At the time of the project team's visit, the Young Americans Club was interested in the juvenile jury system. The members had read about its operation in Terre Haute, Indiana, and in Jacksonville, Florida. They had corresponded with officials in these two cities and were making plans to work with one of the Richmond municipal courts on this project. Miss Horne, their sponsor, said that the group has been largely self-propelled from its origin, with responsibility for lining up programs and projects and following through on its own. "They are sincerely interested," according to Miss Horne, "in relating themselves to the community and to the nation." Miss Horne seems to be an ideal choice to sponsor this group, because of her ability to keep channels of communications open, so that both sides of political issues can be heard.

A bipartisan club of this sort is especially useful in a school or community where either liberal or conservative sentiment is overwhelmingly dominant, a setting in which the minority view, accordingly, would be less likely to receive impartial airing in classroom discussion. In a club, the pressure to agree with the teacher is not as likely to be present.

At Southwest High School in Kansas City, students organized a Law Club, open to sophomore and junior boys with satisfactory grades and an interest in law. Applicants for membership must submit a summary or analysis of a legal case. Although membership is limited to boys, girls may attend the bi-monthly meetings devoted to mock trials, talks by prominent lawyers, and discussion of legal problems.

At Hollenbeck Junior High School in Los Angeles, the History-Makers Club meets weekly, after school. Programs feature sound and picture recordings of dramatic and historical episodes of the 20th century; illustrated talks on topics such as World War II aircraft, history in fiction, and the 1948 Presidential election; reports by students; and records of speeches by political leaders of this century.

The knowledge and skills acquired by students cannot be neatly and accurately listed in a course outline or an administrative report. It is obvious, however, that they result from after-school club programs as well as from scheduled classes and that the gains thus achieved can be highly important to citizenship training.

Teaching About Communism

A Florida school states that its first objective in the teaching of communism is to "develop a greater appreciation of the American heritage, democratic processes, freedom of opportunity, enterprise under law, and the will to preserve that freedom." Above and beyond this generally accepted objective of strengthening appreciations of democratic processes through knowledge of other systems than our own, the study of communism can have additional benefits for the future citizen. Some of these are suggested in the objectives of the elective Russian seminar offered for seniors at Euclid High School in Euclid, Ohio:

1. To develop a better understanding of the Soviet Union and the Russian people.
2. To see the continuity between Russia before the 1917 revolution and the modern communist state.
3. To understand the nation's political, social, and economic developments.
4. To appreciate the nation's cultural contributions.
5. To compare and contrast the Soviet Union with the West.

6. To encourage continued study of the Soviet Union.

7. To further develop pupil skills in history and other social studies disciplines, as well as in other "humanities" subdivisions.

8. To promote American values of democracy as contrasted to communism and totalitarianism.

Approaches to the organization of course or units designed to provide knowledge of communism vary considerably, as is evident in the following listings of major headings taken from a number of course outlines. A unit in the 12th-grade government course at Central High School in San Angelo, Texas, covers eight areas:

  I. Background
  II. Karl Marx and Friedrich Engels
  III. Central Concepts of Marxism
  IV. Lenin's Changes of Marxism
  V. Stalin's Contributions
  VI. Khrushchev's Contributions
  VII. Progress of Communism
  VIII. Difficulties Faced by the Soviet Union

The public schools of Richmond, Virginia, offered a tentative unit outline for use in the 12th-grade government course:

  I. Phases of American Culture
  II. Philosophers and Theories of Society Preceding Marxism
  III. History and Origin of Communism
  IV. Events leading to the Russian Revolution of 1917
  V. Russian Revolution of 1917 and Subsequent Events
  VI. World War II
  VII. Post World War II Period
  VIII. Khrushchev—Revival of "Peaceful Coexistence"
  IX. International Communism
  X. The Communist Party in the United States
  XI. International Communist Party
  XII. Some Methods used by the United States to Combat the Russian Offensive
  XIII. Some Methods Proposed to Obtain the Offensive

Dade County, Florida, has a 12-week unit in the 12th-grade government course:

I. *Introduction*
II. *The Communist Ideology*
III. *The Communist Party*
IV. *The Soviet System*
V. *Khrushchev in Power*
VI. *Social, Political, and Economic Concepts for Evaluation and Summary*

Published materials and films on the subject of communism have recently been prepared in abundance and most course outlines include lengthy bibliographies.

How effectively such instruction equips the student to contend with dilemmas—such as that between the need to uphold the democratic rights and freedoms of all citizens and the necessity to protect those rights and freedoms from those who would subvert them—cannot be known with any certainty. The effectiveness must vary with a number of factors, including the knowledgeability and competence of the instructor in the course.

What kinds of knowledge do the students acquire in units on communism? These sample test questions may provide an indication:

Circle the correct answer to each of the following questions.

1. Which of the following trends in the United States have been most contrary to the predictions of Karl Marx?
    (a) *growth in size of corporations*
    (b) *division and specialization of labor*
    (c) *the development of foreign trade*
    (d) *the development of a "salariat class"*

2. The "Communist Manifesto:
    (a) *was critical of the Utopian Socialists of the 19th century.*
    (b) *attempted to justify the Communist Revolution which had taken place in Russia in 1917.*
    (c) *was a document issued by Marx and Fourier.*
    (d) *was a brief revolutionary statement issued in 1848.*

3. Karl Marx stressed the division of men into classes based on:
    (a) their station in the social life of a society.
    (b) the economic system employed.
    (c) their relationship to productive property.
    (d) their acceptance or rejection of the materialistic concept.

4. Karl Marx believed that capitalist nations would destroy each other in wars for:
    (a) world domination.
    (b) national prestige.
    (c) foreign markets and sources of materials.
    (d) spread of religious ideals.

5. All of the following are views held by Karl Marx except:
    (a) history is mainly determined by economic forces.
    (b) under conditions of capitalism there is a constant class struggle between capitalists and workers.
    (c) communist society should be ruled by an elite class.
    (d) capitalism is inevitably doomed to give way to communism.

6. Karl Marx believed that the condition of the proletariat could be improved fundamentally only through:
    (a) trade-unionism.
    (b) the elimination of private property.
    (c) capitalistic reforms.
    (d) proletariat control of one of the leading political parties.

These six questions and 45 similar items are used in the test on communism taken by seniors at Miami Beach High School following their study of the state-required unit on Americanism versus Communism.

An essay test during the same course asks students to answer four of these five questions:

1. State and explain thoroughly any three of Marx's theories. Give at least one criticism of each theory.

2. Name three leaders from any period of Russian history and describe two contributions attributed to them.

3. State and explain at least two basic philosophical differences between Marx and Lenin.

4. Explain clearly and thoroughly Hegel's theory of dialectics and Feuerbach's theory of materialism and give an example of each.

5. Explain at least five major causes for the undermining, weakening, and fall of the Czarist regime in 1917.

If a school agrees that one goal of civic education is the acquisition of knowledge and skills to assist in the solution of political, economic, and social problems of our times, it would seem important to include knowledge about the major competing ideology we face today and the countries that have embraced it. The thorough and comprehensive effort that has gone into the preparation and presentation of such units in some schools deserves the term "scholarly."

GOAL 2: AWARENESS OF THE CONTEMPORARY ROLE OF SCIENCE

A quality of a well-informed citizen in today's society is awareness of the role of science and technology. Today, scientific advances with inescapable social implications include wonder drugs, lunar probes, atomic energy, and almost unbelievable precision of measurement in a dozen fields. In certain schools throughout the nation, the study of science is contributing to civic education.

Learning Science by Doing

In 1964, when an inquiry-centered laboratory course in physical science was introduced into the Glastonbury High School in Connecticut, 40 students enrolled. In 1965, after the student body had had an opportunity to hear these 40 students speak about the excitement of learning science by doing, the enrollment climbed to 160.

A teacher said, "This course is giving students basic preparation in the scientific attitude. They will need this as citizens, as voters, and as employees in business and industry." The course is based on the philosophy that science must be taught as a process, not merely as an organized body of facts.

The philosophy of the program may be summarized as: (1) science is a process, a state of mind, an approach to a problem; (2) science is best learned by applying the process to the problem in the proper state of mind; (3) science courses should provide carefully selected problems which will receive scientific treatment; and (4) science teachers must provide materials, equipment, atmosphere, questions, and direction in the assault on the problem.

A thousand miles west of Glastonbury, a dozen 7th- and 8th-graders talked about their hobbies as they waited for the start of the meeting of their after-school Science Club at Edison Junior High in Wheaton, Illinois.

The visitor chatted with a 7th-grader whose hobby for the past six years was tropical fish. He was one of a group of six students interested in this hobby and he was considering a project on fish breeding. In his tank he had a single piranha. When he was asked if he planned to breed the piranha, he said, "Oh no, breeding would require a 500-gallon tank which would cost about $500." When he was asked if there is any danger of piranha eating each other, the boy said, "Yes, if there is too much difference in the sizes. The big ones will eat the small ones, but if you keep them all about the same size there is no danger." Another club member had seven fish tanks containing 35 species and still another member had 28 fish. The club's enthusiastic sponsor, Mr. Phelps, is confident that a valuable learning experience is afforded these boys by giving them the opportunity, freedom, encouragement, and facilities to pursue their chosen interest area.

Many adults who were denied the experience of studying science as a process and who were not encouraged to develop their own spontaneous interest in scientific areas feel totally inadequate in this age of accelerating technological development. For effective life in society, students will need a reasonable understanding of scientific method, scientific processes, and scientific discoveries.

The recently improved courses of study in the physical and biological sciences are designed not only for the capable and the advanced student but also for the slow learner and the poor reader. The *Biological Sciences Curriculum Study* (BSCS), first released for general distribution in 1963, indicated that although most students did well, some students had difficulty with the reading materials. Because most of these students were able to benefit from the emphasis on laboratory experience and because many showed unsuspected ability to think through biological problems while dealing with them in the laboratory, it appeared that a

Students learn science by doing laboratory work.

presentation which placed even more stress on laboratory activity could make BSCS biology appropriate for all students. As a result, a special edition of high school biology was prepared for students who were slow readers.

In the Pershing High School in Detroit, students whose reading level is at the 5th grade or lower are enrolled in a special biology course based on this BSCS material, with stress on experiment, programming, and inquiry. The course work centers in the laboratory, where students can see, make, and handle things. Mrs. Sylvia Gonek, a biology teacher at Pershing High School, says, "The students are particularly interested, of course, because of the stress on lab work." The course is within the abilities of the student and is designed to bring out biological concepts.

Mrs. Gonek obviously appreciates the place of science in preparing effective citizens. She says:

First, the students must learn to work together in the laboratory. Second, in discussion, they must learn to appreciate that no one knows everything about a subject. Third, this course introduces them to scientific concepts of which every thoughtful citizen should be aware.

Fourth, we give the student a chance to talk and to express his ideas rather than having the teacher do all the talking.

The sophistication of science instruction is frequently startling. In an 8th-grade general science class at Kearns, Utah, the lesson material on radiation, sunlight, and rays is equivalent to what was recently considered very solid senior high school material. These 8th-grade students study infra-red rays, ultra-violet rays, cosmic rays, x-rays, and radio waves.

In a number of other schools, the project team found science teachers aware of the importance of science in developing basic civic virtues. At Fairmont Heights High School in Maryland, for example, Mr. Bonds emphasizes careful observation and the importance of planning ahead. He reports that one of the most effective lessons learned by students each year comes when their first experiment fails because they do not make provision for maintaining laboratory conditions over the weekend.

Special Programs in Science

In Ladue, Missouri, student assemblies, planned by a joint committee of four faculty members and four students, emphasize the dramatic NASA program and others, on the assumption that all students should be aware of the scientific and technological implications of the space age. With models of space missiles, dramatic experiments with liquid fuels, and nontechnical descriptions, all students absorb some further understanding of the space program.

At nearby Webster Groves High School, the students enjoy a variation in their science program when they spend a full day at the school camp. Here, a biology class or general science class can exploit a natural outdoor setting for a lesson in biology or photography.

Using Scientific Inquiry for Critical Thinking

Perhaps more significant than any single course, either in social sciences or the natural sciences, is the increasing evidence of the scientific attitude on the part of teachers who are attempting to use empirical evidence to evaluate the effectiveness of any course content or method.

Typical of the best of this scientific inquiry is the following memo from science teachers directed to the curriculum director of the school system of Ladue, Missouri: "Would you please criticize the enclosed instructional objectives that we have written for the first few topics of our course? I have also enclosed a test that was given over the first three topics of the enclosed objectives."

As the materials illustrated, these teachers were using an analytic approach toward the preparation of their course. An initial experiment in observing a burning candle, for example, was developed so that the student would learn to differentiate between quantitative and qualitative observation and would become aware of the role of his senses in making these observations. The objective was for the student to recognize the limitations of his senses and the necessity for utilizing instruments to measure qualities not directly observable by the senses. Throughout this extended science course, all instructional objectives are phrased in terms of what the student should be able to do. Students construct, calculate, recognize, determine, and define, and they carry on a dozen other activities supplementary to reading, learning, or memorizing.

Individualized and Multidisciplinary Science Instruction

The Monmouth High School at New Shrewsbury, New Jersey, offers an advanced science course for seniors of high interest and ability. Selected students take the three regular science courses (biology, physics, and chemistry) one year ahead of the normal time. In their senior year they are free to enroll in a science seminar which provides opportunity for individual research projects and instruction in advanced and multidisciplinary science topics.

When the project team visited this informal class, the two instructors were talking with individual students while other students talked with one another and scanned books and journals seeking clues or suggestions for a topic which they would pursue for their major project. The students were expected to explore possible topics for perhaps eight weeks before finally adopting a topic.

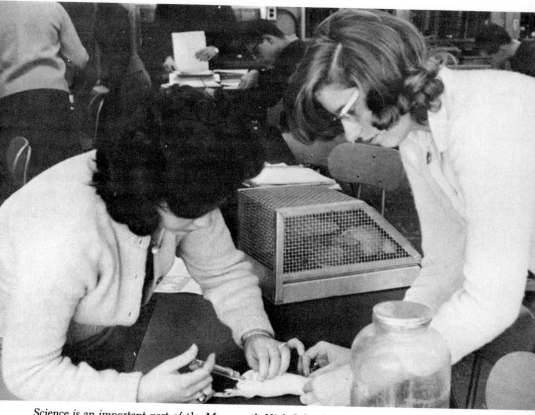

Science is an important part of the Monmouth High School curriculum.

This course is planned to fill the gaps in their knowledge of areas such as astronomy and the earth sciences, which tend to be neglected in the three regular courses. In addition, the instructor cooperates with the social studies department and includes a specific unit entitled "Science and Society," dealing with the social implications of science and technology.

The school also participates in the Junior Science Colloquium, conducted at the Fort Monmouth Research and Development Center, where students present papers during a two-day symposium. This school also takes part in the State Science Day conducted by the New Jersey Science Teachers Association, by entering the competition for prizes based on scores in written tests in biology, physics, and chemistry.

In addition, the science department deliberately approaches urgent current problems such as population control, birth control, and space science. The department chairman emphasizes the importance of providing a serious and scientific knowledge of sex to high school students. He admits that forthright scientific presentation of knowledge in areas such as sex is likely to arouse anxieties and complaints from some parents. This he accepts as one of the hazards of the profession, and he insists that teachers and school administration must accept such complaints as a normal problem.

In a climate of unfettered scientific inquiry, students can become knowledgeable, inquiring citizens, likely to remain aware of the tremendous effects of scientific discoveries.

GOAL 3: READINESS FOR EFFECTIVE ECONOMIC LIFE

Twelve students in an elective course in a California high school, their desks arranged in a seminar circle, leaned forward eagerly to participate in the discussion.

"Why are people content to stay in areas like Appalachia even when there appear to be more opportunities for a good life in other places? Why don't people move?" asked Roger Boedecker, the teacher. A lively discussion followed.

"People are not as well educated in Appalachia, so they can not see the possible advantage of a move," one student said.

"It's the risk of failure. Even though a farmer barely ekes out an existence in an underdeveloped area, he doesn't want to take a risk, because it might turn out worse," said another.

"I don't understand really why they should move. After all, they are eating, maybe not as much, but they are living. They are not dying. They are making it in a way."

The course is not all discussion. Readings include substantial offerings such as The Great Ascent, The Nature of the Non-Western World, The Rich and the Poor, The Worldly Philosophers, and several books dealing specifically with problems of Latin America, Asia, and Africa.

The unit headings are:

I. United States Foreign Policy: Guide for the Free World
II. National Power: Instrument of Foreign Policy
III. Economics: Key to Modern National Power, Independence, and Peace
IV. The Underdeveloped Nations: A Problem of Universal Concern
V. Latin America: The Non-West
VI. The United States and the Underdeveloped Nations: A Problem in the Role of Free World Leadership
VII. Asia: Problem in Power, Population, and Politics
VIII. Africa: Problem in Cultural Superimposition (Moslem, European, and Tribal) and Nationalism

The proposed theme topics, 65 in all, include questions such as:

Why might it be said that the Marshall Plan satisfied both U. S. national ideals and interests? How does foreign aid satisfy both ideals and interests?

What examples may be offered to demonstrate how a nation's power may be affected by the shifting importance of natural resources it possesses or controls?

What predictions may be made for the future of Latin America if the production of goods and services continues to lag behind the population growth of the area?

The difference between this course and the classical economics taught in some high schools is apparent. Here, the study of principles is made meaningful by relating it to concrete and urgent problems. Or, to state it another way, the teaching about current problems is related to learning principles.

This course was not planned only for students headed for college. Roger Boedecker, teacher at Rim-of-the-World Junior-Senior High School, made clear that it was designed to broaden the experience of all students. "The course," he said, "is not for the purpose of establishing a direction in economic thought, but to stimulate the thinking of the student and deepen his understanding."

In addition, this school provides a substantial unit on "Corporate Enterprise: A Unit in American Economic History" as an introduction to the second semester of the 11th-grade course in American history. Teachers of American history recognize that the history of our nation, especially in the period following the Civil War, cannot be understood without some grasp of the problems arising from the relations between the government, the consumer, and corporate industry. To help students attain this grasp of economic relationships, an appropriate background of learning about corporate organization has been included.

A very different, but equally substantial, economics course is offered at the Mount Hermon School in Massachusetts, as a discussion and seminar program. The primary books include: *The Making of Economic Society* and *The Worldly Philosophers* by Heilbroner; *The Great Crash* by Galbraith; *Stages of Economic Growth* by Rostow; *Economic Reasoning* by Robinson, Morton, and Calderwood; and Orwell's *Animal Farm*. The supplementary texts are: Warner and Fuchs' *Concepts and Cases in Economic Analysis*; Samuelson, Bishop, and Coleman's *Readings in Economics*; Mark and Slate's *Economics in Action*; and materials from the Federal Reserve System. The course regularly uses the most recent material from the Sunday edition of *The New York Times*.

This full-year elective for seniors at Mount Hermon School is much closer to the traditional economic theory course than is the international economics course at Rim-of-the-World. At Mount Hermon School, the topics to be covered during the first term include: Objectives of an Economy; Economic History; Gross National Product; American Capitalism; Classical Theory; Utopian Systems; Supply Theory; Communist Theory; Changing Economic Ideas; the Idea of Equilibrium; Elasticity in Theory; Marginal Analysis; Keynesianism; Aggregate Analysis; and the Great Depression.

The schedule is punctuated with occasional reading days, when the student goes to the library rather than class to do some of the reading required in the course. This also affords the fine instructor, Frederick Bauer, additional time for reading and administrative tasks.

The bi-monthly current news lessons are based on assignments in *The New York Times*. The economic theory is tied to concrete problems not only by the bi-monthly current events lessons but also by individual assignments.

Vocational Emphasis

Midway geographically between Rim-of-the-World and Mount Hermon School is the Labette County Community High School of Altamont, Kansas, where an entirely different contribution to economic training is made. Here, in a town with a population of 700 and a four-year high school for 860 students from the surrounding agricultural community, a major function of education is to prepare students for useful social and economic lives. Seventy percent of the students will not go to college. The majority enroll in practical vocational programs as well as academic courses.

Often, college preparatory students also take vocational subjects, one or more of the music courses, or individual music lessons. It is not at all infrequent for the valedictorian of the class to have majored in machine shop, electronics, or vocational home economics. A typical schedule for an 11th-grade girl might include one period daily in orchestra and one period in practice or instruction in piano. Two periods might be spent as a paid secretary within the school. Her other classes might include chemistry, American literature, advanced algebra, and typing.

Boys may major in one of a number of different trades in the trade school. The choices are auto mechanics, machine shop, welding, metal

Machine shop at Labette County Community High School.

processing, drafting or agriculture. If a student maintains a "B" average in all subjects, he may be eligible for a trade school diploma. This is a high honor and jobs are apparently easily available to these graduates, because the reputation of the trade school at Altamont is well known throughout Kansas.

A follow-up report on Altamont indicates that practically all of the boys who are trained in shop find jobs in machine shops or related areas after graduation. Trade school teachers maintain an informal placement agency and the department chairman receives more requests for promising graduates than he is able to fill.

Many people in the community bring their automobiles and machine tools to the school shop for repair or processing. The facilities include an elaborate body and fender repair shop. When asked whether the shops in the community objected to the competition of the school shop, which charges only for the cost of materials, the teacher replied that at one time there were strenuous objections. These have stopped, for the body shops are happy to get the trained workers prepared in the school shops.

The school also maintains a 20-acre farm, where the boys carry on agricultural projects, dividing their time among three major areas: animal husbandry, crops, and the farm shop. Of the 110 boys enrolled in agriculture in 1965, over 50 percent planned to go on to college. All have gained deeper understandings of economic security and economic opportunity and greater readiness to assume economic responsibility as a result of their experience at Labette.

Practical Applications of Economics

Instruction in economics at the New Albany High School in Indiana is divided between a class and a club. Donald Moore teaches the economics class and sponsors the Investors Club, which started in 1962 and which had, three years later, 55 members. Half of these members were in the economics class. Current or past enrollment in economics is a requirement for membership in the Investors Club. This club follows a planned program of background learning in the field of investment, beginning with learning about a charter. Speakers have included a local lawyer, a bank president, a stock broker, a representative of the Federal Reserve Bank, a realtor, the manager of a clothing factory, and the personnel director of Colgate-Palmolive Company.

The members assess themselves a small weekly fee and invest money in common stock. New business for each club meeting includes presentation of analyses of companies by students and recommendations for the purchase or sale of stock.

Moore, the sponsor, feels that there is definite value in this club in making students aware of the business world. He told the project team that he considered the buying and selling of stock as simply a motivating guideline for learning economics. It also gives students a sense of responsibility. The club planned to send a representative to the annual meeting of stock holders of the Sperry Rand Corporation, in which they hold stock. At the invitation of their brokerage firm, 12 members attended a symposium on financial problems. At a recent meeting, the students viewed a film of the annual conference of IBM stockholders.

The senior boy who was the treasurer of the Investors Club said:

The buying power of young people today is growing. Here is our outlet to apply what we learn in economics class. We have almost 100 percent attendance at the Monday evening meetings at school. We now own three shares of Sperry Rand Corporation, coissued to the sponsor and the club. We went to our first meeting uncommitted, but voted to have Merrill, Lynch as our broker. There was no solicitation from them. The formation of the club and the decision to buy common stock was based largely on the model of one boy in the school—a very industrious boy who has earned, saved, and invested, and has accumulated an unusual amount of money for a high school student. So we bought common stock. We are speculating and we know it. At this point, each of the 55 or 60 members, about 35 boys and 25 girls, has contributed so little to the club that the hope for excessive profits could not very well be the motivation for the large membership and high attendance level. The students are here more to learn than to earn.

All of the members, he told the project team, are busy, serious students, who will give up a Monday evening for this meeting because it seems like a worthwhile learning experience for them. They have a genuine interest in applying in practice what they are learning in economics

Typewriting classes provide many students with economic mobility.

about our economic system. They are also interested in the Investors Club as an adult experience which gives them an added opportunity to identify with adults.

In his regular economics class, Moore uses six weeks for a study of competing economic systems. He feels the average student can do well in economics and wants to extend the economics course and have it replace the senior problems course.

The organization of this economics course is different from the offerings at either Rim-of-the-World or the Mount Hermon school and is based on these eight units:

I. Our Expanding Free Economy: Meaning, Characteristics, Purposes

II. Nature and Problems of Business Enterprises: What to Produce and How to Produce It

III. Money and Banks

IV. Government and the Allocation of Resources

V. *Economic Growth and Stability*
VI. *International Trade*
VII. *Labor, Wages, and Labor Unions*
VIII. *The Farm Problem*

About a third of Mr. Neuman's class in modern problems in Oregon's Lebanon High School is given to economics, running the gamut from family budgets to federal financing. On the day of the project team's visit, the students were given a typed sheet describing a hypothetical family budget problem. They divided into groups of three or four to formulate an acceptable family budget. During the next meeting of this class, the small-group work continued, and eventually one student from each group was asked to present his budget proposal to the entire class—and to defend it.

The value of this sort of problem-solving approach, when accompanied by appropriate presentation of significant principles, seems to be substantial.

The following statements from students are typical of their ideas of the value of this budget lesson:

1. *Learned to compromise . . . found out how important it is to work together as husband and wife to make up a suitable budget even though problems arise.*

2. *Learned the procedure in preparing a budget . . . managing money, saving, and regulating expenditures.*

3. *Learned what are the real necessities . . . that they vary in different families but are important things to think about when paying bills. Must know how to arrange budget in order to pay bills.*

4. *Learned the terms that have been heard a number of times from various sources but never applied to an actual experience.*

5. *Learned of the problems that could easily arise in the early years of marriage and be a major factor in "breaking up" a good marriage relationship.*

Attention to how-to-do-it problems such as filing an income tax return or constructing a family budget can become gimmicky. But if such exercises are introduced in moderation to illustrate the applicability of principles learned, they link learning and living and provide motivation and meaning for the less obviously practical aspects of a course.

The most promising approaches to economic education avoid the extremes of exclusive attention to theory or total involvement with practical problems. Theoretical problems are best understood when they are accompanied by appropriate applications. Applied procedures are most easily mastered when the user understands the principles behind the practice.

The American high schools described here provide a wide variety of approaches to economic education, and they are by no means unique. In Illinois' Maine Township High School, West, for example, the economics course places heavy emphasis on the problems of the underdeveloped nations. In the high schools of Kansas City, Missouri, an attempt is made to blend abstractions such as the law of supply and demand with the practical problems of credit buying and the dangers of patronizing loan sharks.

In-Service and Work-Study Programs

In a very few schools, including those of Richmond, Virginia, a sequential program of economic education for the entire school system is being developed.

In Richmond schools, under the guidance of Ray Hines, teachers at all grade levels attend in-service programs and contribute to the writing of the syllabus. One hundred teachers and principals are enrolled in a television course to prepare them for the introduction of the new economics courses. The aim of this system-wide program is to "help the children of Richmond to be conversant with the terms and familiar with the concepts that will make them more literate and effective citizens."

Some schools expose their students to a kind of economic education through work-study or distributive education programs. Sometimes programs of this type offer no more instruction than does the after-school or Saturday job that a student finds for himself. At their best, however, they offer substantial guidance and instruction correlated with the realities of holding down a job.

Some cooperative, work-study programs are far more sophisticated than others. In one Midwest high school, a full-time director handles this department, which includes four divisions. The office-occupations students divide their school day between secretarial and other office work and class attendance. The diversified-occupations students include boys who work part-time in various skills and trades. The third division, called extended education, is for students of lesser ability, who may be placed in non-skilled jobs. The fourth, called cooperative careers, is largely for girls in home economics, usually placing them in food service jobs in restaurants and hospitals.

Vocational Guidance   A very special approach to the problems of education in economic security and economic opportunity can be found in Wood County, West Virginia, in Appalachia. The work of people like Superintendent Grant Venn (now Associate Commissioner in the U.S. Office of Education) becomes of prime importance in raising the level of effective citizenship. Venn told the project team:

> If the student is locked out of society, locked out of a job, he sees no value in education or in the traditional values of God, mother, or country. Our education must be concerned with all factors which lock people out of society. In a community which sends most of its young people to college, or in which industry trains its own workers, vocational training may not be relevant. But in a community where many are "locked out" of the economy, it is relevant.

What can the public high school do to educate its students for economic participation in a system that has little place for individuals with limited background? Grant Venn initiated a three-pronged program of intensive vocational counseling with students and parents, a broad expansion of vocational course offerings, and an aggressive placement service designed to make the school the major agency providing the first or entry job for every graduate. In addition, the placement service plans to keep an active record of the employment history of all graduates until the age of 21. Although this program differs greatly from the academic economics courses at the core of economic education at Mount Hermon School, for example, it is highly relevant to the needs of students in Wood County, West Virginia.

Now that the school has begun to place emphasis on getting students entry jobs, students have begun to take school work more seriously. The percentage of high school graduates may increase markedly. English, history, and other academic subjects are no longer merely hurdles to graduation, but prerequisites for the job that may really materialize with graduation. New courses have also been adopted to prepare students to be diesel mechanics, bookkeepers, waitresses, computer programmers, office machine service repairmen, apprentice salesmen, nurses' aides, and television repairmen.

Grant Venn believes that schoolmen must make substantial adjustments in their notions of the school's function. Among the principles he lists are these:

1. *Establish a new basis for awarding credit in educational institutions so that an individual can move back and forth between formalized learning and the world of work.*

2. *Concentrate on developing basic skills in reading, writing, and computing; job opportunities are few for those who lack basic intellectual skills—fewer now than has been true throughout our history.*

3. *Strive to understand the future occupational patterns and the role of the school in preparing young people for working in an automated society.*

4. *Devise new approaches in teacher preparation for the occupational areas, particularly bringing aides into the educational system to become assistants.*

5. *Develop pre-technical programs for high schools along lines unlike traditional vocational education.*

6. *Have the universities recognize the importance of education for occupations and give it status; otherwise we will develop a duo-system and a "schizophrenic situation."*

7. *Develop better preparation for guidance workers in occupational information so that they can give young people a broad understanding of their role in the world of work.*

8. *Assist every student who enrolls in the schools to make the transition to a next step, be it work or education, because everyone will ultimately benefit.*

Venn feels there is a need for a differentiation between entry skills and more permanent job skills. This is necessary for analysis purposes because of the need to retrain many workers (probably four times in a single lifetime of work) to compensate for the rapid obsolescence of skills, particularly in the productive and distributive occupations. Preparation for entry skills is a joint function of educational institutions and industry itself, with the bulk of the responsibility probably resting with industry, says Venn. Beginning with the premise that an unemployed citizen cannot be a fully effective citizen, his ideas and his program can be viewed as a comprehensive and an urgently-needed approach to one aspect of civic education.

CLASSROOM DIALOGUES

The teachers and classes mentioned above were not unique in encouraging informed thinking. Similarly, the classroom dialogues offered below are not intended as ideal models but as good examples of the variety of effective classes observed.

Teaching Democratic Concepts in a Reading Skills Class

The classroom of Mrs. Martha Denz, reading teacher at High Point High School in Maryland, was equipped with shelves of books for general and specific reading assignments, four table-desks for individual study, a bulletin board featuring a "Peanuts" cartoon strip, a variety of magazines and newspapers, a file where students could place clippings they found, and a number of copies of *Reader's Digest*.

It was a "working classroom," and Mrs. Denz herself seemed to blend into it. She wore a simple, dark dress, soft leather shoes, and a black headband that circled her hair like a tilted halo. She needed no makeup—and she used none—to accentuate a refreshingly wholesome face. When she spoke, she did so calmly but with assurance.

Seven students were in the class. Mrs. Denz smiled at them and said, "Please write on your paper the Pledge of Allegiance." She gave them considerable time to do this, but it was soon apparent that some students could not finish the assignment.

"Steve, how would you like to read what you have on your paper?"

"I haven't finished yet."

"That's all right," she said. "Read what you have so far."

" 'I pledge allegiance to the flag of the United States . . .' "

As this student paused, Mrs. Denz asked each of the others, "How do you spell 'allegiance'?"

Several of the seven students had misspelled the word, and Mrs. Denz made the necessary corrections. Then, leaning forward against her desk, she asked, "Bill, what did you think 'allegiance' means?"

"Loyalty."

" 'Loyalty.' What does 'loyalty' mean?"

"It's a feeling you have—something that you feel toward someone or something. A feeling that makes you want to be true to someone or something."

"An 'allegiance' is 'loyalty' or this 'feeling'?"

"Yes, that's it," the student said.

" 'Loyalty'—that word is going to be useful to us." Turning to another student, she asked, "Diane, can you use the word 'allegiance' in a sentence?"

The girl could not do this immediately, and Mrs. Denz asked several leading questions to help her. The girl began to show new interest in the problem.

"Diane, our discussion just now shows that 'allegiance' probably means something a little different to you than it does to Bill. That's perfectly all right. Each person has a right to his own ideas. Now, can you give us an example of the use of the word?"

The girl, encouraged by her teacher, said, " 'The man owes allegiance to his government.' "

"I see. You stress that we are pledging allegiance or loyalty to our government, or, on a broader basis, to our country," Mrs. Denz said. Then, addressing herself to the class, she asked, "But what do we say in the first part of the Pledge of Allegiance?"

A student volunteered, " 'I pledge allegiance to the flag of the United States . . .' "

"To the flag? That's interesting. But what does that mean? How could we explain to the foreign students in our school what we mean by allegiance to the flag?"

Another student quickly answered, "Our flag stands for something—just as their flags stand for something."

"Yes," she agreed, "and do we have a word meaning 'stands for something'?"

There was no immediate response, and Mrs. Denz remained silent to give students time to think. Then the first student, who earlier had defined allegiance as loyalty, said, "I think I know—'symbol.' 'Symbol' means 'stands for something.'"

"Another word: 'symbol,'" she said. "Very good. So the flag is a symbol for our country, and the word 'symbol' means 'stands for something.' Let's be sure we all understand this. 'Symbol' means 'stands for something.' Now perhaps we are ready to explain to the foreign students at our school what we mean by 'allegiance to the flag.' What could we say?"

"Well, we could explain that we are saying that we have loyalty to all the things our country stands for."

"That would certainly help them to understand, Bill. Of course, the word 'loyalty' still might give someone a little trouble."

"That's what I was thinking, Mrs. Denz," another student interjected. "That's the whole trouble with words like 'allegiance.' They're too general. You can't touch them or picture them or anything. They're just . . . just . . . ."

"Just what, Linda?"

"Oh, I don't know. Just something we have in our minds. Just an idea."

"An idea? Of course, an idea. Another fine word, and the exact one you have been searching for," Mrs. Denz said. Then she asked her final question for the unit, "All right now. What are we really saying when we declare, 'I pledge allegiance to the flag of the United States . . .?'"

A student, smiling, replied, "I 'believe in the idea of loyalty to the *symbol* of what my country stands for.'"

"Excellent!" she said. "Our class has worked out the problem well, and we now have a better understanding of the meaning of 'allegiance.' And, as a bonus, we know more about the meaning of three other words—'loyalty,' 'symbol,' and 'idea.'"

In this unit Mrs. Denz had thus strengthened the language development of her students. At the same time, she helped them to understand important concepts of democracy.

Then Mrs. Denz began another exercise, designed to increase the students' knowledge of the meaning of words while developing good citizenship by helping them to understand themselves better. Earlier, she had written on the blackboard:

I AM	YOU ARE	HE IS
1. cautious	discrete	timid
2. bookish	studious	well-read
3. brilliant	intelligent	knowledgeable
4. prominent	conspicuous	noticeable
5. economical	miserly	frugal
6. stubborn	firm	obstinate
7. tipsy	drunk	inebriated

To begin this exercise, Mrs. Denz asked each student to think about himself and others, and—using the three words in each of the seven groups—to fill in the lines, "I am . . ." "You are . . ." and "He is . . ."

When the class finished, Mrs. Denz had the students discuss the meaning of each of the words until they understood them. This was the "language development" aspect of the activity. Then she turned to a consideration of the values expressed by the students' choices. This was the "citizenship" aspect of the activity.

Her first question was addressed to a student who had said little during the pledge of allegiance exercise.

"Bob, will you read what you put down for number 6?"

" 'I am firm.' 'You are obstinate.' 'He is stubborn.' "

Speaking to the entire class, Mrs. Denz asked, "Did anyone else in the class have the same response?" Several indicated they did. She returned her attention to the first student, asking, "Now, why did you describe yourself as 'firm' and others as being 'obstinate' or 'stubborn'?"

"Being 'firm' made me seem better than being 'obstinate' or 'stubborn' so I put it down that way."

"What do you mean by saying 'better'?"

"A better person. You know, someone you could like more."

"I see," she noted. Then, looking at another student who seemed eager to continue the thought, she said, "Steve?"

"And if you were talking directly to a person, you wouldn't want to make him feel too bad so you'd call him 'obstinate' rather than 'stubborn.' "

"Clift," she asked another, "what about the statement, 'He is stubborn'?"

He answered with a smile, "Well, when we say 'he' it shows that he—the other person, that is—probably isn't there. So we can be as rough as we want and call him 'stubborn.' "

"That's clear," she agreed. "But why do we do this? Is it always true that each of us is—as Bob puts it—a 'better' person than others?"

"No. Sometimes it isn't true at all."

"Then why do we do it?"

There was no immediate response. Finally, a student said, "I guess it's only natural for a person to think more of himself than of others—I mean to have a better picture of himself than of strangers."

Mrs. Denz interrupted, "If we wanted to use another word for 'picture' we could say 'image.' "

"All right," the boy continued. "That's a good word—'image.' Well, we want to have a better image of ourselves than of others."

"Is that a good idea? Is it wise to see yourself as better than others?"

"Not always. It could be bad."

"In what way could it be bad?"

"Well, if you twist things around like that and always make yourself seem better than other people, it's not fair to them and they'll know it."

A girl then commented, "And then they could get very angry at you and cause trouble or have nothing to do with you."

Another student responded, "That's so. Trouble is, you don't always know you're doing this." He laughed. "Maybe everyone in the world should take this course and learn about pictures."

"Pictures?" Mrs. Denz asked.

The boy, smiling, corrected himself. "Images, that is—images. Maybe it would be better if everyone knew about them."

The bell rang. As the class left, the students jokingly scolded each other by repeating, "I am economical. You are frugal. He is miserly." "Not me," someone said. "I'm economical."

Through this exercise, Mrs. Denz had helped her students to learn more about themselves, their values and relations with others.

When asked to describe her objectives in this course, Mrs. Denz answered, "I am trying to help the individual student to know himself better—not just to improve his reading score. To help him to know where he fits in as a citizen—and that he does fit in." She could well have added that by urging her students to examine critically words such as "allegiance," "loyalty," and "image," and by dramatizing the obstacles to objective insight into oneself, she was providing her students with self-perpetuating tools for citizenship.

A Systems-Analysis Presentation in a Social Problems Class

Thirty-five 12th-grade girls sat in the classroom at St. Scholastica High School in Chicago. Each was different; yet, in their white blouses, charcoal gray blazers, gray skirts, and black or gray knee-length stockings, they also looked very much alike. When Sister Mercedes entered, they rose with a single rhythmic movement and bowed their heads, and she led them in a brief prayer.

Sister Mercedes leaned gently against the podium in front of the class and looked around the room. It was neat and uncluttered, but it contained familiar classroom objects such as an American flag, a broad-faced clock, a bulletin board with newspaper clippings, and—because it was October—two ears of colored corn. A figure of Christ on a brown cross hung on the east wall.

Sister Mercedes, the white and black of her habit accentuating the roundness of her face, spoke slowly and quietly.

"Today we are going to consider the domestic features of our society."

She drew on the board:

"On your way to school today, what did you come in contact with that was done by the government?"

"The white line in the center of the street!" a student replied. "That was done by the government."

"What value was allocated here?"

"Safety, and justice—for every car must obey the line."

"Can any of you give other examples of contact with the government?" Sister Mercedes asked.

Several students did so. Then, she added an inner rectangle to the diagram on the board:

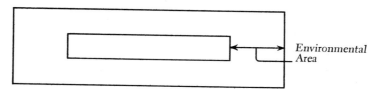

"Now on our diagram, note that the lines are not separating people, but activities. The outside area"—she indicated the area between the two rectangles—"represents what might be called our 'environmental area.' What might we place in it?"

"I believe that education belongs in the environmental area," a student said, and another added, "Yes, and economics should be placed there." A third student said, "Certainly, religion." A fourth contributed, "And family."

"Keep thinking," Sister Mercedes said. "What else might we place in this area?"

"Does recreation belong there?" a student asked and then affirmed.

"Also resources," another student added. "Resources are extremely important."

Sister Mercedes kept adding to the diagram as the students responded:

Education	Economics	Climate
Resources		Religion
Recreation	Ethnic	Family

"Now, can you think of any of these environmental factors that people are not satisfied with? Anything in our locality, for example?"

"Some people did not like it when they cut down trees to make way for a road. I remember hearing a number of complaints about that. Would that be an example?"

"What do you think?" she prodded, "Do you think it is a good illustration?"

"Yes, I think it applies here."

"All right. Any other examples?"

"Some people are not satisfied with federal aid to education."

"Can you explain further?"

"I mean that they are not satisfied with the amount given by the Federal government to education."

"I see. All right, anything else?"

"What about economics?" a student asked, "We might use the recent sugar quota bill as a bill that a number of people were not satisfied with. At least the newspapers indicated that this was the case."

Sister Mercedes, using a piece of chalk as a pointer, said, "So we have out here"—she indicated the environmental area on the diagram—"a number of tensions. For example, there may be problems under Family. We even have a Family Court to help work them out. You noted that there may be things going on that cannot be settled immediately. These 'rumbles' are there because people don't all agree on how these problems are to be settled. We call these differences of opinions *wants*. A *want* may result in a *demand*."

At this point she added to the diagram:

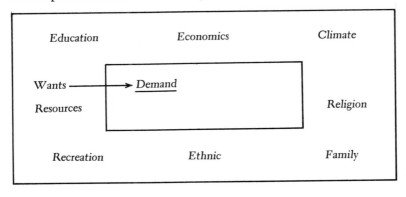

"Eventually who is going to make a decision on demands?"

"Authorities."

Sister Mercedes adds the word "authorities" to the diagram:

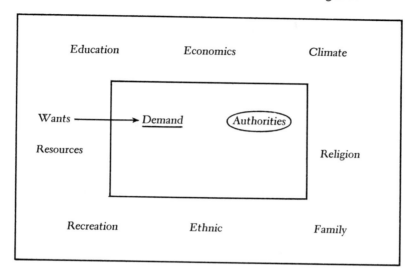

"'Authorities' is such a broad term," Sister Mercedes commented, "We had better probe more deeply into its meaning. How do people get picked to be authorities?"

"In the United States they are generally elected."

"Is there a set way of going about the election? If so, where does it come from?"

"From rules."

"How do these rules originate?"

"The rules are in basic documents, such as the Constitution."

"What underlies the Constitution?" she pursued. "Did the persons who drew up the Constitution have to agree on certain things?"

There was no immediate response from the class, so Sister Mercedes said, "Let me ask you again. What underlies the Constitution? Does it show any consensus on the part of the authors?"

"Yes, it does," answered a student. "For example, it shows general agreement that civil liberties should be protected."

"Does anyone want to add to this?"

"The Constitution shows consensus on civil liberties and on many other points, too. The Constitution really expresses values in general. That's it, *values!*"

"Values! I see. It is because you have certain values that you react. Let's look at the situation again." Sister Mercedes pointed to the diagram. "We said that there are *wants*—that wants lead to *demands*—and that *authorities* decide on the basis of *values*. Up here we're going to place the word *regime*—that represents values, norms, and structure, or how we have set up our government."

The blackboard diagram became more complex:

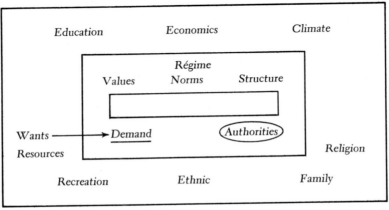

"This harried political system of ours is bombarded with demands— this is especially the situation in a democracy, where everyone has the right to express what he wants. What can be done in a democratic society to lessen the bombardment? Do we have ways of regulating the demands? Is there any method by which our demands reach the authorities? Does our organization—diagrammed on the blackboard— make it possible?"

"There are different people in charge of various organizations. They are like 'gate keepers,' and we contact them to express our demands," pointed out a student.

"Yes," another student added, "there are people we see who take our case to the authorities."

"We might call this the principle of subsidiarity," Sister Mercedes said as she wrote "Principle of Subsidiarity" on the board. "As you indicate, there are certain known channels or ways through which we can reach authorities. On the local level, there are people such as the aldermen; on the state level, there are state representatives; and on the national level, Congressmen. When you channel a series of similar demands you make a *national* issue—and then the authorities often step back and let the public debate and discuss it until a consensus develops. Is there anything that your newspaper does to help formulate an issue?"

"One newspaper I examined pointed to an issue by describing conditions in a local jail," said a student. "It did the same thing when it reported charges of voting fraud at an election."

"Why does a newspaper do that? What is the newspaper saying?"

"It is saying, 'You ought to do something about the situation.' "

"I see. The newspapers were almost creating a demand. Now are there any wants that people might not demand of government? Is there anything in the back of our minds that determines what we should and should not ask government?"

"Our *values*. Our values determine it."

"All right, what about values? Do they remain the same? Can you think of something that 20 years ago we might not have gone to the government about, and yet today many accept as a government responsibility?"

"Care of the poor."

"Anything else?"

"Medicare."

"What was Medicare called when discussion about it first began?"

"A form of socialism."

"So, if such matters are accepted for serious discussion and consideration today, it indicates that there have been changes in attitude. Changes in attitude do occur. I wonder—*is this one of the most important conclusions we have worked out today?*"

The bell rang sharply as Sister Mercedes said, "Think about that question, and we shall continue our discussion tomorrow." Then she threw her arms wide open, smiled warmly, and said, "See you on Thursday!"

A member of the civic education project team met with several of Sister Mercedes' students after class. They commented:

"I like this class. We can express our ideas freely. Also, it's not all book facts; it's related to life—we apply it to our own life, and we see how world events are related to us."

"I like the class so much that I put it down as my favorite course on my application for college. I'm crazy about it. Sister Mercedes gives us several sides of each issue; she involves the students; she helps us to apply ideas to our own day; and she encourages us to think. Sister Mercedes is fabulous!"

Had she heard, Sister Mercedes—an intelligent, sincere, and compassionate woman—might have been embarrassed by the word "fabulous," or perhaps she has become accustomed to the situation. After all, in a recent yearbook of St. Scholastica, the *Scholastican*, the student editors printed above her photograph, "Freedom is *Tremendous!*"

Three features of the class were outstanding. First, Sister Mercedes stressed important concepts and values rather than unrelated facts, and she used diagramming effectively to clarify complicated relationships. She based much of her work on David Easton's *A Systems Analysis of Political Life* and *A Framework of Political Analysis*. She said, "I want to show relationships between political, economic, religious, educational, familial, and other aspects of society." Secondly, she stimulated the thinking of the students. Sister Mercedes stressed this point when she said:

I want to give my students an understanding of what society is, and what the functions—and responsibilities—of the individual are in regard to maintaining and changing society. This is done so that they can use this to understand other societies—that is, to open up "international communication." Therefore, it is essential that they understand the thinking behind their attitudes and decisions.

Finally, she related the study to the contemporary world of the students and contributed to their development as good citizens. In response to the question, "How does the work you are doing in this course in social problems help your students to become good citizens?" Sister Mercedes answered:

The students become aware of the complexity of problems; they *realize that problems must be handled at the level of institutions—that is, through institutional change or modification or adjustment; they learn to see relationships between man's activities; they develop an understanding of how they can modify society; and—I hope—by these and other ways, they see their responsibilities as citizens.*

A Teacher Sets the Stage for Thinking

"Have humans the right to control the lives of humans in order to save humanity?" With this question William Witbeck sent his 7th graders on to their next class. He told them, "We'll begin with this question when we next meet in our small discussion groups. Think about it, especially in the light of today's demonstration." During the preceding hour Mr. Witbeck had held the rapt attention of both class and visitors as he demonstrated an idea and provoked thought.

The class, at Oneida Junior High School in Schenectady, New York, met in a room large enough to accommodate the 60 7th-graders who are members of this special humanities class. Ordinarily, Witbeck meets members of this class in discussion groups of 15 to 20 each, but occasionally, as on the day of the project team's visit, he meets the total group for a demonstration or a presentation.

It was a peculiar setting for an academic presentation. One student walked in to class with an electric extension cord, while another carried in an electric plate. The teacher brought in an aluminum container of popcorn kernels. The sight of these items created interest on the part of students. The equipment was set up, and Witbeck began the lesson. "The problems that people meet are largely the problems of people. For our lesson today I want to use these materials to have you think about people and their problems. Let's see whether they can help us. What do we have here?"

Answers from students led to the following list:

Popcorn popper
Popcorn kernels
Stove for heat (energy)
Oil
Salt and butter

Witbeck then related the demonstration to people, their relations, and their problems, as the kernels of corn cooking over the burner began to pop. Through discussion he developed with students the analogy of kernels in the popper to people on earth. The list on the blackboard now looked like this:

Popcorn popper—Earth
Popcorn kernels—People
Stove for heat—Human energy (life force)
Oil—Food
Salt and butter—Culture

"What relationship do you see between the kernels and the popper and the people and earth?"

Several suggestions were made. Finally, Witbeck heard the suggestion he wanted.

"Just as the kernels are exploding and are expanding the aluminum foil and filling the popper, people are exploding and filling the earth—it's the population explosion."

Witbeck went further. He helped students to see that "man with man creates problems for man," and also that "man with man can solve man's problems."

"We will talk more about this in our small groups later. Our popcorn is ready. Let's take a look," he said, opening the foil covering the cooked popcorn, "and you tell me what it means to you in terms of our listing on the board."

As they looked, students noted that some kernels had come to the top. On the bottom were other smaller kernels, many of which had not even popped. From the students came these ideas, which were written on the blackboard.

The kernels at the top exemplify the survival of the fit.

Each man's situation is determined by his position in the world in relationship to other men.

The rich get richer, and the poor get poorer.

Then, without advance notice to the pupils, Witbeck took a piece of cardboard and pushed the popcorn toward the first few rows of pupils.

Everyone grabbed for it, pushing one another aside. Some received several kernels, others none at all.

Witbeck used these actions to generate more ideas for the class. Several phrases were placed on the blackboard:

Just as we grabbed the popcorn, people grab food and other items without concern for others.

Mankind struggles for survival.

Selfishness is an element in man.

Given the same amount of food, everyone gets less if the number of people increases.

"What has kept population in check?" Witbeck asked.

Pupils supplied ideas, including the "four horsemen"—conquest, war, famine, and death.

"Now that the 'four horsemen' are slowing down, do you have any suggestions for a solution to the world's population problem?"

Suggestions followed and were written on the blackboard:

Use the earth more fully.

Use outer space.

Control the birth rate.

Then, the bell rang and the period ended. Witbeck made his suggestions for the coming small-group discussions. "Find out what you can about Malthus and his ideas. Also, let's talk about this question: 'Have humans the right to control the lives of humans in order to save humanity?' "

Here was a teacher who knew how to create interest and stimulate discussion. With the help of relatively simple materials he drew from young students mature insights and provocative thoughts. Information was in the demonstration and the lesson, and more was to come, through the study of Malthus. Analysis was also evident throughout the lesson, as students thought about what they saw and analyzed its implications for people. Commitment and involvement were beginning to develop during this lesson, as students expressed their views.

Witbeck is in his late 40's. He came to teaching relatively late in life, after having been an automobile salesman in his father's agency. His interest in education has continued to grow over the years, and in 1965, he was completing his doctorate at the State University of New York at Albany.

Witbeck was selected as teacher and coordinator of the humanities program at Oneida by its understanding and energetic principal, Harvey Handel, who says, "Our purpose in the humanities program is to have young people come to grips with the burning issues of our time."

CONCLUSION

The three teachers whose classroom sketches have been given here are concerned with different subject areas, and their styles of teaching are strikingly different. Yet, they have in common an unusual skill in engaging their students in creative discussion. The objective in each of these classes was to guide students to discoveries of relationships between facts, concepts, and values.

In Mrs. Denz's class, students subjected commonly used words to fresh examination and grew in their awareness of how language is used to express values. In Sister Mercedes' class, students explored complex relationships between aspects of society and the interactions of these aspects. In William Witbeck's class, an imaginative analogy was used, much as a laboratory experiment might be used in a science class, to stimulate inquiry into one of the most challenging problems confronting society today. The social and economic consequences of the population explosion, as well as other implications, were demonstrated vividly.

Each of these teachers involved students actively in discussion and related their immediate experiences to larger issues. Information presented in such a way is likely to take root in a student's mind, where it can be used as a tool for understanding other situations. The artificial distinction between practical and theoretical understanding is thus removed, as information is used to uncover new information.

Civic education was not a compartmentalized aspect of these classes; it was the underlying focus that helped to make them successful.

*Education is a kind of
continuing dialogue and a dialogue
assumes in the nature of the case
different points of view.*

Robert Hutchins

CHAPTER 5

Developing an Analytic Citizenry

The two goals of civic education described in this chapter—development
of the student's ability to make value judgments for a changing world
and development of his receptivity to new facts, ideas, and ways of life
—stress the importance of an analytic citizenry.

GOAL 4: VALUE JUDGMENTS FOR A CHANGING WORLD

**Making Value
Comparisons**

At Mark Twain Junior High School in
Los Angeles, a basic issues program
gives students a 3-year sequence of
comparing historical and current issues.

The purpose of the basic issues pro-
gram is to offer students experience in problem solving through classroom study of controversial issues. Twenty basic issues have been identified and assigned, one to each unit, throughout the 7th-, 8th-, and
9th-grade social studies courses. The issue for each unit is presented in the
form of a question. Accompanying each issue are debatable propositions
that recommend a change in some law, policy, or citizen behavior. Before a debatable proposition is chosen for discussion with the basic issue

97

of the unit, the teacher polls the class; to be chosen, a proposition must have at least one-fourth of the class in opposition to the majority. Following is one of the 20 issues, with its debatable proposition, used in a 7th grade social studies unit.

The World As A Whole

Problem: How can world hunger be reduced?
Debatable propositions:

1. *Many of us should consider serving in the Peace Corps when we reach the age of 21.*

2. *U.S. foreign aid should be reduced.*

3. *Government price supports for U.S. farm products should be removed.*

Each debatable proposition draws upon current areas of controversy to give a contemporary dimension to the problem presented in the unit, which includes historical material. The debatable propositions used to spark discussion in 1965 were related to national and international concerns. In 1966, or 1967, some might be superseded as new events command public attention.

The basic issues program requires imaginative use of resources and creative communication in the classroom. The teacher has basic reading materials on the topic ready to distribute, and the library maintains vertical files with additional reference material. A questionnaire is distributed to students before discussion, and the opinions are tabulated. At the conclusion of class study and discussion, in which student discussion leaders play important roles, the original questionnaire is circulated again, to determine how many students have changed their opinions. Then, an analysis session concludes the unit. At this session, students evaluate their arguments, discuss reasons for their changed opinions, and try to identify the strong and weak points in their thinking. The study of each "basic issue" becomes a study of the process of analysis and critical thinking as well as an examination of a specific issue. The students acquire ability to deal with controversial issues as well as increase their information.

A further unique feature of the basic issues program is that students are guided to evaluate their own development of skill in handling controversial issues and to evaluate the skill of the class as a whole. Sometimes the teacher prepares study sheets based on the preceding day's discussion, such as the following:

Analyzing Arguments

Here are some of the arguments given yesterday in our discussion:

1. If tariffs are removed, our standard of living will go down.
2. If tariffs are removed, some industries will be forced out of business.
3. Tariffs have worked in the past. Why change the situation now?
4. Free trade may serve the cause of peace.

Which argument attempts to win support by predicting catastrophe?
Which argument contains a glittering generality?
Which argument needs more supporting evidence to prove the point?
Which argument wishes to preserve things as they are?

Which of the following pairs of arguments were most convincing to you?

1. If we had free trade among the nations of the world (a) countries would soon produce what they could make best and prices would go down; and (b) industries would be encouraged in the underdeveloped nations.
2. If we had free trade (a) taxes would go up; and (b) the standard of living would go down.
3. If tariff barriers were removed (a) U.S. wages would go down; and (b) we would sell more in the world market because the prices of our products would be lower in other countries and their people could afford them.
4. (a) Trade barriers do not cause any rivalry and trouble between countries; and (b) countries cooperating in trade seem to cooperate in other ways too.

Sometimes students are asked to complete checklists with questions such as this:

Did I let myself be convinced because someone spoke well?
Did I recognize which facts or statistics were relevant?

Did we let our thinking be clouded by our emotions?

Typical of this basic issues program at Mark Twain Junior High School is the 8th-grade social studies class of Mrs. Cradlock. At the beginning of the class visited by the project team, Mrs. Cradlock distributed a questionnaire to the students, asking them to mark 10 items with an "A," "D," or "U," for "agree," "disagree," or "undecided." The students approached the exercise with enthusiasm.

A D U *(1) The Federal government should set up safety standards for automobiles.*

A D U *(2) More national parks should be established.*

A D U *(3) Anti-smog devices should be installed in all cars.*

A D U *(4) Boys and girls should be permitted to fish without a license until they are 16.*

A D U *(5) All California beaches should be open to the public.*

A D U *(6) The Federal government should collect abandoned cars and sell them for scrap.*

A D U *(7) If damage is done to property by hillside sliding, damages should be paid by the government unit that issued the permit.*

A D U *(8) The Federal government should pay owners for the removal of billboards and junkyards from highways.*

A D U *(9) The Federal government should pay for removal of industrial waste from water supply.*

A D U *(10) National parks and government lands should be sold to private companies and individuals.*

While Mrs. Cradlock led a spirited discussion of the two items students were most eager to discuss (anti-smog devices on cars and fishing permits for youngsters), two students acting as tally clerks sat quietly in a corner, tabulating the questionnaire results.

When the results were announced, it was apparent that class opinion was most evenly divided on whether the Federal government should pay owners for the removal of billboards and junkyards from highways, so that question became the proposition for study and debate. In another class, the questionnaire tabulation might have resulted in the choice of another discussion topic.

After discussing reading materials distributed by Mrs. Cradlock, the students were again given the questionnaire. Several had changed their opinions. When asked why, one boy responded, "We didn't know enough about it before, so our first answers were just guesses." It is likely that these students will not be satisfied with guesses when they are asked, as adults, to form an opinion or to decide about an issue.

Students and teachers alike seem enthusiastic about the basic issues program at Mark Twain Junior High School. It was developed by Don Perryman, supervisor for Junior High English and Social Studies in Los Angeles schools and is being implemented at Mark Twain by Mrs. Marjorie Stokel, social studies chairman, and her staff.

There is a possibility that the stated issues may intensify the student's natural tendency to oversimplify, to see issues as black or white, to be voted for or against. But possible weaknesses exist in any teaching plan, and success depends on the wisdom and experience of the teacher. The values of the plan are many. Students deal with ideas and problems involving multitudes of facts to be organized, compared, and related.

Another example of development of the student's ability to make comparisons of values was found at Mount Hermon School in Massachusetts. In the U.S. history course, where the Declaration of Independence and John Locke's *Second Treatise* are studied together, students are required to compare ideas, discover similarities and dissimilarities, and in general, to sharpen their powers of intellectual discrimination.

Even questions in the course that do not require specific comparison of the two documents nevertheless demand comparison of ideas. Questions such as "Why does the Declaration of Independence refer to both the natural rights of man and the rights of Englishmen?" and "Do you think Jefferson intended to encourage revolution against oppression in other lands in other times?" provoke thought. They insist that students evaluate and compare, two actions that mark the beginning of establishing values.

A similar device is used in Darien High School in Connecticut, where students in the contemporary social issues course are asked to prepare book reviews of paired books, from a selection of 50 pairs. Titles include: Galbraith's *The Affluent Society* and Myrdal's *The Challenge to Affluence*; Mills' *White Collar* and Packard's *The Status Seekers*;

Humphrey's *The Cause is Mankind* and Goldwater's *Conscience of a Conservative*; Rossiter's *American Presidency* and Hughes' *Ordeal of Power*.

Thinking About Thinking　　At Denby High School in Detroit, students of high ability are encouraged to develop their analytic thought processes in a 12th-grade class structured around a few significant books. Mrs. Fleming's class, on the day of the project team's visit, had just read S. I. Hayakawa's *Language in Action*, and the discussion centered on the question, "How do we know what we know?" Mrs. Fleming asked students if they could explain what Hayakawa meant by intensional as opposed to extensional orientation. One student answered that a person has an intensional orientation when "he thinks in terms of words rather than objects," when for example, he talks about communism or capitalism from a definition he has given these terms rather than from the actual workings of the system. Another student expressed it differently; Hayakawa was interested in the "problem of people who look at life through their own personal map rather than through an understanding of the territory." Mrs. Fleming added, "Reality then becomes what is on the map. Is that correct?"

The discussion gathered momentum. A student asked, "Does this mean that no matter how intelligent a person is, his concept of reality is limited to the extent that his experience is limited?"

"What does Hayakawa say about this question?" Mrs. Fleming responded.

"He gives the example of the work done by WPA [Works Progress Administration] workers. A person who observed a WPA group working would insist that the men were working hard, but a person who had his own biased definition of WPA, a person who had an intensional orientation, might say that these men weren't working because WPA people never work."

"What's wrong with this kind of intensional approach?" Mrs. Fleming asked.

"If your orientation is something other than reality, you continually bring your own preconceived notions to the interpretation of events."

"How do you avoid this?"

"You have to have a kind of open-mindedness when you think about issues and about what is true."

"Can people look at facts? Can they gather different points of view and still have a closed mind?" Mrs. Fleming asked, urging the student to elaborate.

"Yes," the student answered. "Take the issue of fluoridating the water here in Detroit. Just yesterday the city voted by a small majority to allow fluoridation. Many people looked at the facts, but the vote was almost even."

"How do we screen these facts?" Mrs. Fleming asked. "Can we be completely objective? Aren't we all intensionally oriented in terms of our own image? What does Hayakawa say about this?"

The discussion continued, with students questioning, examining statements in the light of their own experience, and—with Mrs. Fleming's unobtrusive guidance—relating their ideas to Hayakawa's *Language in Action*.

The significant but not unusual feature of this class was its direct attention to problems of how we think. Formal attention to learning how to think—beyond the classic introduction to syllogisms—is commonly given in English and social studies classes. The topics may include, for example, evaluating sources of information, distinguishing between fact and opinion, evaluating the consistency of arguments and drawing inferences, and studying the nature of assumptions and the rules of logic.

Applying Critical Thinking to Current Problems

In some high schools, the contemporary problems course is organized largely as an extended exercise in how to think about contemporary problems. One such course, at West Leyden High School in Northlake, Illinois, begins with a thorough study of the nature and kinds of problems of man, from personal and family problems to national and international disputes. The course continues with an examination of some causes of problems, such as frustration and aggression, and then deals with scientific method, the problem of semantics, the dangers of assumptions, and techniques of clear thinking.

Other units in this course deal with propaganda techniques and defenses against propaganda.

Finally, students are given a series of case studies, modelled after actual situations. Students are asked to respond to the problems in writing, then to discuss their solutions, and finally, to compare their solutions with those of the experts in the actual case. Following are three examples from the series:

It is World War II. It is very important that you get American housewives to use cheaper cuts of meat. Fashions in food, however, are more stubborn and much more permanent than fashions in hats, and they express deep cultural prejudices developed very early. How will you carry on?

You are a "plant chairman" (a union official) whose job it is to settle local grievances. A complaint is brought to you. "Julie is making too many errors in stitching labels; her spoilage rate is high." You look over the record and find the complaint true. What procedure will you follow?

Your two children quarrel over their toys. "I want it," one says; "No, it's mine," says another. A fight follows, with yelling and tears. Reasoning and even punishment have little effect. What do you do?

"Critical thinking" does not bring the same connotations to all. To some it carries a suggestion of problem-solving, to others a permission to dissent, to still others an invitation to consider a wide range of alternatives. Critical thinking is too vast to be encompassed fully in any single lesson or any school course.

The student's encouragement to think is inevitably limited by the standards of the community, the school, and the particular classroom. The tone with which a teacher rejects a dissident thought can determine whether a student is likely to express a dissident thought next time. Students are quick to sense closed areas in any class. It is significant to note, however, that throughout the project team's visits, a comment of many teachers and students alike was, "We are completely free to say what we like and ask what we like. Anything that is in good taste and is related to what we are studying is acceptable."

Some teachers will make a point of telling their classes exactly what their own political affiliations are. They act on the assumption that it is impossible to be totally impartial; they tell students in advance what their commitments are so that their statements can be judged in that light. Other teachers, like James O. Cook, social studies department chairman at John Marshall High School in Richmond, Virginia, simply offer unbiased accounts of issues and parties, insisting on the right of privacy for their own political convictions.

Applying Critical Thinking to Historical Problems

Promotion of correct thought processes need not depend entirely on discussion or debate of current issues. Some of the most impressive examples of learning how to think observed by the project team were in ancient and medieval history classes. The 11th-grade students of Mr. Hunt's class in Medieval Europe at Germantown Friends School were learning how to think as they discussed readings in *Renaissance and Reformation, 1300 to 1648*, edited by Gene R. Elton.

Desks were arranged in a closed square, suitable for the give-and-take discussion based on the medieval readings. A lively discussion flowed from this quotation from Bruni, "For I would wish the understanding man to be both abundantly learned and capable of giving elegant expression to his learning." Throughout the class period, Hunt operated as leader and provocateur, constantly interjecting questions such as: "Of what does this remind you?" "What is the goal of the writer?" "Is this an acceptable goal?" "Does he state this?" "What would you infer?" "How do you know this?"

Similarly, Mrs. Edson at Wilbur Wright Junior High School in Cleveland also asks her students to look at each historical problem from different points of view. At the time of the project team's visit, for example, she asked two students to read accounts of the African slave trade. One student was given an account written by the captain of a vessel in the slave trade. The captain emphasized the humane treatment the slaves received, minimized the disease and death that resulted from the crowded conditions on the ship, and neglected to mention the slaves who attempted to starve themselves and were force-fed by members of the crew. The other student read an account penned by a clergyman who was a passenger on the same ship and who recorded a very

different version from the captain's. The class was then asked to reconcile these two accounts. Why had these two writers seen the same
conditions so differently? Or, had they in fact seen the same things?

When Mrs. Edson's class studies the Jacksonian period of American
history, at least one student reads a biography of Jackson's wife, Rachel,
and another reads a life of Martin Van Buren. Others read about John
Marshall and Amos Kendall, and everyone reads biographies to become
familiar with the life of Jackson himself. After the students have read
these biographies Mrs. Edson asks, "What would be your opinion of
Jackson as a person if you were Amos Kendall?" and "How would you
view Jackson if you were Martin Van Buren?"

**Developing Critical
Thinking through
Analogies**

A most impressive example of stimulating students to analytic thought was
seen by the project team at Yorktown
High School in Arlington County, Virginia. Here, Alex Anderson, Mack
Smith, and their colleagues in team
teaching used a simulated experience to guide their senior government
students to discover the basic principles of government and law. In this
class, 90 students were arranged in circles of 8 or 10 each. Leaders of
three of these groups went to the front of the room and led a discussion
based on conclusions reached in the small groups the previous day. The
class was evolving basic principles of law from study and discussion of
a concrete case that had been presented some time earlier.

The case involved 160 U.S. soldiers, all privates, who had been captured in the Battle of the Bulge and placed in a German prisoner-of-
war camp. They were imprisoned in a large, converted gymnasium with
bunks and tables. The men represented a cross-section of the United
States, and none had known any other in the group for longer than two
months. On the third day of their imprisonment, the prisoners were
told to choose a group leader to convey information and regulations
from their captors and to supervise general activities among the prisoners. With this description of the case, the students were given four
questions: (1) How would a leader be chosen? (2) What kind of self-
government unit would be chosen? (3) What sort of basic rules would
be necessary both for relations within the group and for communication

with the captors? (4) What method would be used to enforce these rules?

The discussion ranged widely from questions such as whether any rules could be established or enforced to how to handle the case of the murder of one prisoner by another. For the most part, the instructors allowed the students to contend with questions to which most adults would have ready answers. Occasionally an instructor intervened with a comment or suggestion, such as the reminder to think about power, right, and authority as three distinct terms. At one point in the discussion of the legal rights of the man hypothetically accused of murder, the teacher intervened, saying, "Suppose this individual is psychotic." The temporary student leader responded, "Your purpose in this discussion seems to be to confuse the issue." The instructor responded with complete composure and good nature, "Yes, the teacher's role is primarily to keep the issue sufficiently confused to make the students think."

Although these students seemed at times to be floundering, they were in fact struggling with basic questions of government, and after a period of several days a pattern of organized thought emerged. The students were creating group government and regulations at the same time that they were discussing how the captured American soldiers had handled the same problems. In examining and analyzing the situation of the war prisoners, students could observe how organization was established and maintained through periods of boredom and crisis and how rules of conduct and formalized controls were introduced. By the end of the introductory unit, students are expected to understand the components of a social control system, including common behavioral patterns of its members; the status system; rules of conduct; sanctions; services to members; conflict of interests (in other words, "politics"); systems of resolving these conflicts (in other words, "government"); and degrees of finality and decision.

The case of the prisoners of war was adapted from a study used at the University of Kansas and reported in a mimeographed pamphlet distributed to students after they had completed extensive discussion of this case. The students had assumed that they were dealing with a hypothetical case; instead it was the record of an actual situation involving captured American prisoners in a German camp during World

War II. Discussion became increasingly sophisticated and definitions became more precise as the class moved through the organizational experiences described in the case study and as they built backgrounds of understanding through reading. These students were learning to think critically and analytically.

In the Lebanon (Oregon) High School, Eston Way uses a method somewhat comparable to the prisoner-of-war case to help students to derive basic principles. He presented on a single mimeographed sheet the fable of Demokrita, Land of Change (borrowed, he said, from the Corvallis, Oregon, school system):

Demokrita, Land of Change

Demokrita, a land beyond the sea, was a small country of arid wastes dotted here and there by tiny havens of greenery—date groves growing around deep wells of water. A sparse grass formed patches of natural pasture. Since time began in Demokrita, the "People," as they call themselves, have made a bare living from their flocks and herds. As each scant pasture is grazed down, the "People" move their flocks to another and then another.

Once each year, the "People" come together with their brethren of the oasis to pay old debts, exchange gossip, settle disputes, and make decisions for the future of the tribes. Disputes and laws are discussed by a council of all the tribal chieftains. After deliberation, they announce their decisions to the assembled tribes. If the tribes agree, they announce their approval in a tremendous shout.

One of the most important of the yearly questions was the assignment of grazing routes to each tribe. A good route meant prosperity; a poor one, hardship. At the oases, dates were grown, dried, and packed to barter with traders from other lands and such of the herdsmen who would stop as they followed their flocks.

It came to pass that in Alta Hai, the hill country bordering Demokrita, a faranji persuaded the Haiwuns to build an electric-power dam across a great river. As the water was backed up, it unexpectedly found a new outlet and surplus water poured down on the arid lands of Demokrita. With the abundant water, the desert pastures have grown lush stands of grass in many areas. Since pasture is more abundant, the herdsmen no longer need to follow the grass. Many of the younger "People" have settled down. They claim ownership of plots of land; they fence these plots to save them for their flocks. Certain of them have discovered that cultivated crops bring a better living without the risk of keeping flocks. The older tribesmen find that their ancient pathways from pasture to pasture have been blocked by the new fences and their flocks grow thin.

Some of the oasis dwellers observe the change brought about in the desert areas and propose that water from the wells be pumped onto the land beyond the date groves. They suggest that more foods can be grown and that they will then be less dependent upon the traders from other lands. Other tribesmen of the oases declare in horror that if water be taken from the wells, the date trees will suffer, die possibly, and their way of life will be destroyed for ever.

In two months the Great Council of the tribes will meet.

On the blackboard Way had written some suggestive notes:

Is Demokrita a state? people? territory? sovereignty? government?
Youth (change) versus Age (status quo)
Kind of government
    A. Distribution of power
    B. Type of executive
    C. How many rules?

Discussion in this class flowed effortlessly, moving from one significant point to another without halting for consensus. Students considered certain problems suggested by the case description: Who owns the land? Should they have the right to build fences? Who would divide the land? What if they cut off the water supply? Later, the teacher turned the discussion to recognizable parallels in the contemporary world. Has Canada the right to shut off the water supply of the Columbia River? Should Oregon share its water resources with Arizona and California, and if so, who should pay for the pipe lines? Should we spend our money to educate people in the Congo?

What are the limits of our shifting sense of community? The students become aware of this problem and others related to it as they gave their attention alternately to the imagined problems of the mythical Demokrita, the current problems of their state of Oregon, and pressing problems of national and international scope.

Centennial Junior High in Decatur, Illinois, makes a unique use of analogies to develop critical thinking. Students meet once a week for a class that has no subject matter, offers no credit, and carries no grade. They willingly give up a study period to participate in this experimental class and find it the most exciting hour of the week.

At one session students saw a film showing a can with three holes punched in its side at different heights. The can was filled with water, which spurted out of the holes, making three sprays of different lengths falling at different angles. The film ended abruptly, with no explanation of why the spouts of water had different lengths or why they fell at different angles.

The teacher, Jon Rhue, did not explain, nor did he answer students' questions directly. If a student volunteered a solution, Rhue suggested that the volunteer think about it and obtain more evidence. At no time during any of the class meetings did Rhue confirm what is a right or good solution. He only encouraged the students to seek more evidence and allowed their spontaneous motivation to prompt them to do so.

Another session of this class was built around a short film which asked, "How can Fred drink boiling water?" Again, Rhue's technique was to offer no factual information, reassurance, or praise. Frequent periods of thoughtful silence occurred, and the lesson was given no structured conclusion. It was allowed to be a continuous, open-ended thinking exercise, based on the boiling-water problem.

This inquiry class is a pilot project conducted by Centennial Junior High School's assistant principal, Bill Williams, and Jon Rhue. The program, which Williams and Rhue hope to expand, aims at stimulating thinking by promoting curiosity, careful observation, and a method of attacking problems.

Williams and Rhue developed the program after becoming concerned about the intellectual lethargy of students. They began by recording sounds. They placed a paper in front of the classroom ventilator blower, for example, producing a noise that, when recorded, sounds very much like a buzz saw. Any sound can be played at different speeds on the recorder, so that a two-minute recording can consist of several problems.

The problem of identifying sounds motivated Centennial students to collect data energetically.

The content for inquiry learning may be drawn from any field. To date most of it has been adapted from science, but history and economics are potentially fruitful fields. However, the object is never to "learn" the subject matter, but to master an approach to thinking.

The inquiry approach used at Centennial Junior High School is based on techniques developed by J. Richard Suchman, of the University of Illinois. A report by Dr. Suchman makes clear the rationale:

Today the typical classroom fails to create the necessary conditions for inquiry. Many are downright hostile to it. The first step toward changing this is to create a teaching faculty that believes in inquiry, that is made up of active inquirers. Only a teacher who thinks open-endedly can maintain open-endedness for his pupils. Such teachers need an administrative climate that gives them the room to approach the teaching-learning process through the inquiry mode. Teachers who are forced by a rigid curriculum to "cover" a given set of materials are thereby barred from the open-ended approach. There is no sure way to produce powerful thinkers in the classroom, but this power does grow as children actively pursue understanding. The school can create the conditions that stimulate and sustain such pursuit. Open questions and challenging problems set the stage. Rich informational resources provide raw materials for inquiry; and freedom for the pupils to operate autonomously and attack the problems in their own terms opens the door to productive thinking.

Williams and Rhue concede that much of the success of the inquiry project derives from the Hawthorne effect; their inquiry class is regarded by students as new and exciting. This fact should not be used to discredit or discourage inquiry teaching, which holds promise of an unending series of new and exciting learning situations, each designed to bring out the potential of the students for whom it is judged most appropriate.

A more substantial caution might be advanced regarding the danger of destroying the values of inquiry teaching by institutionalizing it. All good teachers have always used some variation of "inquiry" or "discovery" methods of teaching, even when they have never heard these terms used. The purpose of programs such as that at Centennial Junior High School is to refine and perfect inquiry teaching and to extend its use to more teachers, especially by preparing appropriate materials for them. Prepared materials, however, should be accompanied by an appeal to teachers to use their own imaginations.

It is entirely possible that in-service training, perhaps in summer institutes that would expose teachers to a direct experience of basic inquiry learning, might influence many of them to adopt a discovery stance. This could be done without the usual prepared lessons and syllabi, which traditionally trained teachers might accept as something to be followed inflexibly rather than as a way of teaching.

Developing the Ability to Form Personal Values

Some critics assert that contemporary issues are unsuitable for the development of powers of reasoning, presumably because prejudices and emotions so often becloud the issues. This is the very reason why some teachers insist upon the importance of toughening students' thought processes on "real" issues. They believe students should experience the reconciliation of thinking with feeling and come to recognize that great decisions are not made by robots but by human beings. They learn to appreciate that feelings are facts of life, even as they strive to understand and control their feelings and reach towards the ideal of the rational goal—where thought and feeling are integrated to create a compelling commitment.

Robert Clifton at the Abraham Lincoln High School in Denver actively encourages his students' expressions of opinion, and uses an abundant supply of films, speakers, lectures, student reports, and discussions to provide provocation and stimulation of thought.

Clifton teaches a senior course in psychology in four parts: (1) basic principles; (2) the nature of love; (3) the nature of man; and (4) the search for identity. In the unit on love, he has used outside speakers, including a case worker from a hospital for unwed mothers and an expert on venereal diseases. For a unit on the nature of man he invited a minister, a priest, a rabbi, and an attorney. He has taped for class use a number of commercial broadcasts, including the play *Inherit the Wind* and a documentary about the Ku Klux Klan. These presentations are prepared for the reaction, reorganization of ideas, and presentation and defense of conclusions that are important to learning.

Asked about the source of his inspiration for his teaching, Clifton replied, "It was a revolt from an early exposure to a doctrinaire outlook on life and morality." He was pleased because a day or two earlier one of his students had brought in a picture of a Vietnamese mother and baby she had clipped from the paper and asked, "Isn't this what Michelangelo's 'Pieta' is all about?"

The project team visitor talked with a senior boy enrolled in this psychology class. The student said, "You can't tell someone what the nature of love is, or the nature of man. You have to let him find out for himself. This method of teaching brings up many things you wouldn't normally think about but which are important. Compromise is the only way to learn. How can you possibly get acceptance of ideas through force? No one can teach me anything by ramming it down my throat."

If the course offered as Bible IV at Mount Hermon School in Massachusetts were introduced into public school, the title might have to be changed. This course offers seniors at Mount Hermon a choice of three sections: Religous and Moral Problems in a Contemporary Society; Religious Dimensions in Literature; and Living Religions.

On the day the project team visited the class in Religious and Moral Problems in a Contemporary Society, the instructor was lecturing on the works of Tennessee Williams, describing him as an author concerned with "man and the universe at war." Williams' plays, according to Duane Estes, teacher of this class, depict crises that have a shattering effect on all the characters. His plays are vehicles for showing diverse and bizarre escapes from reality. On the one hand, Estes pointed out, he uses a dead past and on the other, a depersonalized man in a technological age. Tennessee Williams sympathizes with these doomed characters, said Estes, and his plays also carry a message for theology.

Estes suggested that there are other alternatives. Many other views, which, although not religious in origin have high moral value, are provided in this course. Because this is a class in the Bible, Estes also suggests that students examine some of the answers provided by religion.

On the day of the project team's visit, Estes asked his students, at the end of the lecture, to consider answers to the specific problems of the place of man in modern society and of the loss of a human center described by Samuel Miller in *The Dilemma of Modern Belief*. The students left the class with a number of thought-provoking questions on their minds.

The stated purpose of this course is to examine some of the religious and moral problems facing modern man. Among the problems discussed are the tensions between doubt and faith, Christianity and Communism, and Protestanism and Roman Catholicism. A final section is devoted to specific personal, social, and ethical problems such as sex, vocation, economics, and race relations. Particular attention is given to the moral dilemmas of students. The course attempts to combine lectures, active discussion, and reading (including plays and novels) to assure coverage of the issues.

Much of what went on in this class in religion in an independent school could well be adapted for public school use. Although Estes would argue that he was not trying to indoctrinate his students into Christian beliefs, others might say he was. This, of course, could not be done in the public schools. But to consider the ideas raised in the works of Tennessee Williams and other secular writers studied in this course along with the basic doctrines of Judaism, Christianity, Confucianism, Islam, and atheism could be an experience that would add much to the civic education in public schools.

Among the civic responsibilities which the 20th-century American school has frequently assumed is the promotion of a sense of family responsibility. As higher divorce rates testify to the growing instability of the American family, many communities agree that their high schools should provide youth with the information and orientation that might contribute to more stable marriages.

At Denver's East High School, Mrs. Alice Call teaches a course called "Girls' Social Problems." On the day of the visit, the class was viewing a film, titled "Worth Waiting For," which argued against teenage marriages. During the same hour boys, in a similar class, saw the film, "How Much Affection?" At other times, such as when a priest, a minister, and a rabbi are invited to discuss inter-faith marriages, boy and girl groups have a joint class.

Both Mrs. Call and Robert Sims, who teaches the boys' classes, report that community response to the course has been uniformly positive. Many parents have indicated how pleased they are that their own son or daughter had the opportunity to take the course.

A great deal of time is given to discussing the power of emotions and the usefulness of admitting to the quirks of one's own personality. The course outline includes attention to dating, teenage marriages, elopements and secret marriages, unwed mothers, narcotics, alcoholism, prostitution, and homosexuality. It appears to be a promising practice to provide straight answers on these topics, which are of real concern to youth.

Asked if any topics were taboo in this course, Mr. Sims replied, "Yes, two. These are sex techniques and techniques of birth control. Aside from these, any topic dealing with social problems will be fairly and fully discussed."

Perhaps a notion of the tone of this course can be gleaned from one of the many supplementary information sheets distributed to the students. The example deals with parent-teenage relationships:

Parent-Teenage Relationships

Understanding is a two-way street. Parents are expected to understand teenagers; teenagers should try to understand parents. Parents show love as much by saying "no" (sometimes even more) as by always saying "yes" to their children's requests. "Growing up" requires that we accept the love which limits as well as the love that permits from the same source—our parents. It is often difficult for parents to be firm—to say "no"—because some parents fear rejection.

A few "do's" for young growing-ups

1. Share with your parents—your interests, your activities. It might be a pleasant surprise for you to show an interest in their activities. A good family sharing time might be the evening meal—only don't bring up requests or argumentative topics.

2. Assume responsibility—but don't take on more than you can handle. Be willing to admit a "goof," because parents should expect some mistakes.

3. Show understanding of their problems and have patience with their quirks of personality, just as you expect them to tolerate your fads in hair and dress. Accept them as people who are normally intelligent adults. Try to understand their attitudes on dating, homework, etc. "Do unto others—"

4. Communicate with them—let them know how you feel; talk things over with them—their expectations and yours. Ask their advice and occasionally take it. You still need your parents even though you also need freedom.

5. Give them a little attention and time. Show in small ways your gratitude for their judgment, good taste, restraint, and—most of all—their love.

A few "do's" for parents

1. Remember always that a happy home is a happy husband-wife relationship and this spills over onto your children. They are affected by this just as much as they are affected by husband-wife arguments.

2. Give your child unconditional love and as much sympathetic understanding as you can muster. Exercise your sense of humor in viewing your adolescent.

3. Set high standards and humanitarian attitudes and give them a working code of conduct and the proper guidance necessary for their growing up. Your own stability and security will help. Respect for you as a person generally causes your child to accept your values.

4. Discipline and punishment are not synonymous. Discipline should be aimed at eventually attaining self-discipline; punishment can foster resentment. Have rules which are fair and agreed upon—then stick by them. Adults are by nature conservative; young people, radical and adventurous.

5. Do be tolerant, forgiving, patient, and compassionate. Searching for identity and selfhood is not easy, and teens needs TLC often and in large doses. You must be honest and logical if you expect your child to listen to you.

6. Value your child—not as an extension of your self but as a person in his own right. Let your love illuminate his path—no hovering, for this causes him to cast his own shadow—but leading and allowing.

In the Oakland Technical High School in Oakland, California, a comparable opportunity for students to obtain information and under-

standing of sex and marriage is offered as an elective for seniors by the Homemaking Department. The course, officially known as "Home-making IV" and unofficially called "Marriage and the Family," enrolls boys and girls together. The class visits places such as divorce courts and child care centers and listens to speakers on various specialities related to family life. A senior, Paul Elms, summed up his reactions to the course with, "I think this course tells the truth. It shatters the myths. It breaks the stereotypes." Another senior, Roy Costa, said with obvious sincerity, "This course has taught me to be a human being."

Summary

The project team believes that the ability to make sound value judgments—about controversial contemporary issues as well as past issues, issues of personal as well as societal importance—can be developed. In some of the classes described above, students dealt directly with the same issues that will call for their informed and analytic judgments as adults. In other examples, the topic used in the class was of secondary importance to the stress on the methods of reaching informed and analytic judgments. Both approaches are valid. Both, when pursued by competent and imaginative teachers, help students to form habits of thought that can be used in dealing with the crucial concerns of adult citizenship.

GOAL 5: RECEPTIVITY TO NEW FACTS, IDEAS, AND WAYS OF LIFE

The ability to subject one's beliefs to continual reexamination, adjusting them as much or as little as needed, is an essential element for responsible citizenship in an age of change. If a school is committed to the objective of fostering receptivity to new facts, ideas, and ways of life, and if it approaches this task with energy and imagination, its students are likely to enter adulthood with resilient values.

Reexamining Historical Truths

Studies in Modern History is the relatively conventional title of an unconventional collection of readings prepared or compiled by Timothy Tomlinson, Kenneth Kieffer, and Krastyu Krasteff, teachers at Horton Watkins High School, Ladue, Missouri, for the school's 10th-grade world history class.

On the day of the project team's visit, the class was discussing one of its readings, an excerpt from "Last Lecture," by E. J. Harbison, which had first appeared in the *Princeton Alumni Review*. This article was the imagined record of proceedings of the Celestial High Court of the Next World, May 19, 1972. On trial were seven men famous in historical annals: King Philip IV of France; William of Occam; Alexander Borgia; Niccolò Machiavelli; John Calvin; Nikolaus Copernicus; and Antonio Antonelli, merchant. All were charged with contributing to events which led to the destruction of the world. In his opening statement, Sir Thomas More, prosecuting attorney, declared he would prove "that these defendants, individually and by their common action, undermined and sapped the foundation of man's one truly great idea, the Medieval ideal of an ordered and organized society—one in language, one in culture, one in government, and one in allegiance to God—an ideal which, had it been preserved intact, would have rendered impossible and unthinkable the recent catastrophe." The proceedings continued:

MORE: *I call to the bar Philippe Capet, fourth King of France of that name. (Philip the Fair rises slowly from his seat, trips over the corner of Calvin's gown, and walks slowly to the prisoners' stand facing Dante. He is a handsome figure, with an air of easy dignity about him, but he has the wary look of a balky witness at a Senate committee hearing. He gives the impression of being something between a master of men and a television vice-president.)*

MORE: *Philippe Capet, I charge you with a crime of incalculable import to humanity—that of fathering the totalitarian, national state— the most perverted and ignoble ideal of human association ever devised by the mind of man. I charge you with being the parent of that mass egotism, that national exclusiveness, and that soulless imperialism which has recently helped to destroy human civilization. I charge you with the destruction of that Medieval ideal of the brotherhood of man and the fatherhood of God which once held all western humanity in willing allegiance to the Vicar of Christ. I charge you finally with the destruction of the organic ideal of society, with the atomizing of the social organism. Have you anything to say in your defense?*

PHILIP: *I appeal to the Fifth Amendment.*

MORE: *You forget, sir, that there are no amendments in this place.*

The celestial constitution is perfect and needs no amendments. You have no right to silence here. You must defend yourself.

PHILIP: *Well, I can't say as I understand the accusation—not exactly, that is. Big words always bother me, and you use a lot of them. I needed money—that's all. They told me a king ought to live on his own, but how can a king live on his own when prices are going up and rents are not? I needed money, my people wanted security, and my ministers told me how to get the money and give the people efficient government at the same time.*

Each of the six other defendants appears before the court to answer to More's charges. One is charged with promoting nationalistic chauvinism, one with immorality, another with imperialism. All are accused of encouraging some evil condition which contributed to the downfall and eventual destruction of mankind. Copernicus, for example, is accused of participation in a conspiracy to undermine faith. The presiding judge, Dante, proclaims:

You, Copernicus, are the true traitor to mankind. God made man a little lower than the angels; you and your followers made of him an insignificant worm, clinging desperately to a whirling second-rate planet of a fifth-rate sun moving at incalculable velocity out of nowhere into nowhere. You turned the universe into a mathematical machine and man into a fortuitous conglomeration of polarized abstractions. You and your fellow scientists taught man that, in the words of one of your philosophers, he was "the product of causes which had no prevision of the end they were achieving, that all the labors of the ages, all the devotion, all the inspiration, all the noonday brightness of human genius, are destined to extinction in the vast death of the solar system, and that the whole temple of Man's achievement must inevitably be buried beneath the debris of a universe in ruins."

This new view of long accepted historical "facts" produced animated discussion. No indication of disinterest or boredom could be seen. Students seemed dismayed and fascinated at the same time to learn of the wide range of interpretations to which historical "truths" can be subjected.

The new approach is reinforced by three summary questions related to the imaginary trial:

(1) *What accusation is brought against each of the individuals on trial? From your own knowledge of the "long 16th century," how valid are the charges?*

(2) *If the charges are valid, did they, in fact, contribute to the decline of the Medieval world? In what ways?*

(3) *After analyzing the manuscript of the trial, which of the defendants would you find guilty?*

In a further step to promote individual and original thinking in this world history class, the new materials were followed by an essay examination asking students to react to a provocative hypothesis:

(1) *Take a position on the following basic hypothesis: The Renaissance as a movement was interested in this world, not the after-life.*

(2) *Take a position on the following basic hypothesis: The Reformation was successful because of the personality and ability of Martin Luther.*

(3) *Take a position on the following basic hypothesis: The Renaissance and Reformation were conflicting movements.*

Ingenuity in stimulating openmindedness about historical interpretations is also found in Ladue's experimental American history honors course.

In an exercise for this course, students were shown slides of five different paintings of the Battle of Lexington. The first had been painted immediately after the battle; the others, presented chronologically, had been painted at later periods in history. George Glass, teacher of this class, explained the purpose of the exercise as follows:

We hope they will come up with the idea that events are changed by society in the retelling or the revisualizing of events because of patriotic fervor or for other reasons. After they see these five paintings, we hope that at least some of them will come up with hypotheses about how propaganda can be used and is used. If students formulate such hy-

potheses with no more information than we have given them, they will have developed a facility for reformulating ideas that they will never derive from listening to lectures.

A girl from one of the history classes admitted:

> I haven't decided whether I like the course or not . . . but it's good to be aware that things aren't just the way they appear to be and probably this course has helped me to think that way. Of course, I feel myself growing up and maturing intellectually and perhaps thinking straighter and more logically, but how can I tell whether it's because of this course or not?
> Here you have to think it out for yourself. Before, it was told to you and told that it happened just that way . . . Just recently we were studying the American Revolution. The British account and the American account are entirely different. So you can't say which one is right, because they both wrote the facts that they thought were accurate, but they interpreted differently.

The student was learning to be receptive to new ideas. One idea—that human emotions have colored the writing of the history of mankind and that history, therefore, must be evaluated in the light of all possible information—was new enough to her that she was still uncomfortable with it. She was learning, however, that an open mind and willingness to alter previous convictions in the light of new evidence are of primary importance in understanding history. The objective is to help every student in this Ladue honors class to recognize that it is important to learn to think and that it is wrong to assume that one's own interpretations constitute absolute truth.

Learning About Government

When Frank J. Hammer, psychologist-mayor of Mountlake Terrace, Washington, and Dean D. Hunter, Jr., the town's city manager, sought ways to help the general public become better informed citizens, they formed the idea of having high school seniors attend school in City Hall. With the cooperation of the high school principal, A. C. Christiansen, and a steering committee composed of interested citizens, the municipal government workshop was begun in September 1963. Students come to City Hall two afternoons a week for lectures given by city staff members and for on-the-job training in several departments of their choice. They also attend City Council and Planning Commission meetings and Municipal Court sessions. They write term papers, take examinations, and receive course credit for their work.

The goals of the program are three-fold: (1) to stimulate students to select careers in municipal government; (2) to create informed citizens even if the student chooses a career unrelated to municipal government; and (3) to benefit any student with career interests in business or industry.

Results of the first semester indicated that the program had such value that it was continued as a permanent part of the city and school district operation. After the second full semester, this program was awarded a $10,000 grant from the Edgar Stern Family Fund of New York so that results could be documented and details of course content, problems encountered, and suggestions could be published for the benefit of other cities and schools.

The following outline of class topics suggests the scope of the course. These topics are for the weekly lectures and demonstrations offered by department heads and other local government specialists. Alternate class meetings are devoted to on-the-job training.

MUNICIPAL GOVERNMENT WORKSHOPS CIVIC CENTER
Training Schedule—Mountlake Terrace High School

SUBJECT

Orientation to the class
Tour of the city and Civic Center
Orientation to Mountlake Terrace City Government
Historical background of cities
Legal and theoretical background of city governments
Functions of the Mayor and City Council
Responsibilities and duties of the City Clerk
Responsibilities and duties of the City Manager
Purchasing and Contracting Department

Responsibilities and duties of the City Treasurer
City financing, bond issues, LID's and financial advisors
Examination on course material covered through October 8, 1965
Organization and functions of the Police Department
Responsibilities and duties of the City Attorney
Municipal Court and responsibilities of the Municipal Judge
Animal control activities
Duties of the County Prosecuting Attorney's Office
Responsibilities and duties of the Public Service Director
Responsibilities and duties of the City Engineer
Functions of Board of Adjustment and Building Inspector
Functions of the Planning Commission
Functions of the Mountlake Terrace Planning Commission
Examination on course material covered through November 17, 1965
Library Board and library activities
Intergovernmental cooperation
Relationship of Chamber of Commerce to City Government
League of Women Voters and their activities
Activities of Snohomish County Hospital District No. 2
Panel of newspaper representatives
Park and recreational activities
Discussion of term papers
Review of didactic material
Job opportunities in municipal government

Lectures and demonstrations by department heads and other local government specialists are supplemented by extensive unpaid on-the-job training. Usually each student works in two or three departments of his own choosing, rotating assignments throughout the semester, although a student may be permitted to spend all his work time in one department if he has a special interest or major project in that field. Every attempt is made to minimize routine tasks. Department supervisors select activities or projects which will stimulate the student to learn about the functions of the department and how these contribute to the overall operation of the city government and the welfare of the citizens. A second phase of the workshop is the 40-hour per week summer experience, in which participants, selected from among volunteers who have completed the regular semester course, work for 10 weeks at a minimum wage in preparation for other jobs.

A major value of the government workshops is the opportunity they give students to work with adults at adult jobs. Learning about real situations at first hand is not a common school experience. Here students study the operation of city government at first hand and in some detail. There also appears to be a carry-over to the rest of the student body. The image of the police force, for example, is reported to have improved throughout the school. The program has also vastly improved relations between school and government officials. Finally, city officials have looked more carefully at their own programs as they have prepared lectures for the workshop, and the result has been to sharpen operating efficiency throughout the city.

Students, teachers, and government officials alike are pleased with the program and agree that it should be continued and expanded. Even officials who were apprehensive at first, feeling that the students might be in the way, are completely sold because of the enthusiasm the boys and girls bring to the job and because of the quality of their work.

Seniors in the workshop have worked in these areas: the public library; the police department, making an analysis of traffic violations; field engineering, observing the installation of sewers and fire hydrants; city hall clerical service, analyzing city purchases; water department; park and recreation departments, doing clerical work and registering children and adults for a recreation program; city manager's office, indexing city ordinances; city pound, analyzing dog control laws in various communities in the hope of developing a uniform law.

This successful program would have been impossible without the time and personnel for thorough, careful planning. Alan McLeod, administrative assistant to the city manager, devotes one-fifth of his time to administering the program. The two most difficult problems have been finding appropriate work opportunities for enough students and adequate text material for the course.

The Mountlake Terrace municipal government workshop appears to be a promising practice not only in providing well informed citizens for tomorrow's cities, but also in making young people aware of career opportunities in municipal government, and in giving them work experience.

Studying Cultural Changes The introductory social studies course in Atlanta, Georgia, and the surrounding Fulton County schools is prepared by a teacher committee and is titled "Changing Culture." The course is designed to help 8th-graders to understand a society and its culture and to prepare them for social studies work in high school. The stated assumptions of this course, which emphasizes Georgia history, are these:

1. *Students are affected by the forces of time, physical environment, and cultural surroundings.*
2. *Conflicts and combinations of these forces produce the questions which the student will face in making decisions.*
3. *Students learn best when they are involved in an inquiry which appears to have direct relevance to their questions and decisions.*
4. *These questions are not likely to be answered in a final form, and they require an attitude of inquiry as part of the student's learning.*
5. *History and the social sciences are the most appropriate tools of such an inquiry.*

Essential materials, prepared locally, are two booklets, *Economic Concepts: Case Studies—Anthropology*, and *Man Looks at Man: An Introduction to the Social Studies*. These booklets highlight the changes which unite and separate the culture of Georgia at three epochal periods, the 1770's, the 1870's, and the 1960's.

Members of the project team visited the Sylvan Hills High School where the class discussion in Mrs. Margaret Mahan's class moved from "What is history?" to "Is there a caste system in Atlanta?" The class had just completed a unit on colonial economy. For contrast, the students had prepared a booklet on the economy of the school, including sections on the cost of maintaining the band, finances of the concessions, the audio-visual program, the cost of textbooks, taxes for school support, and salaries and wages, all under the general heading "Our school is big business."

The committee which prepared the course visualizes it as "not one-fact-after-another political history, nor a flag-waving course in modern Georgia, but a study of Georgia as a social scientist would study Georgia." These teachers know that 8th-graders cannot operate like social scientists, but they are convinced that they can be led by an alert teacher to engage in the process of inductive reasoning. They hope this reasoning may lead students to an understanding of certain key ideas in political science, economics, sociology, anthropology, geography, and history.

Examining Biases   Young people are much more likely to develop receptivity to new ideas if they are encouraged to examine and discuss openly their own biases and prejudices. In two government classes at Woodside, California, high school students are encouraged to do exactly that in a week-long unit on tolerance of nonconformity.

On the first day of the unit, Miss Joyce Fulton's students are asked to record anonymously their responses to a poll Louis Harris gave to a carefully drawn cross-section of the adult population. The students do not see the distribution of responses by the general public until after they have given their own responses. Then, they compare the responses of the adults polled by Louis Harris to the tabulation of the classroom responses. In Figure 1, student responses are shown by paired numbers. The first number in the pair indicates the students response at the beginning of the unit; and the second number represents the percentage who held that view at the conclusion of the unit, after analysis, reading, and discussion.

After the students recorded their own answers to the poll, Miss Fulton distributed a second sheet revealing the distribution of responses by the general public. She asked the students for their comments. Several reacted spontaneously:

"These are adults?"

"Some of these guys are out of step."

In both of Miss Fulton's government classes, students were especially surprised that so many adults feel that a person who does not believe in God is a bad influence on his country and, second, that such a large percentage should feel that a lawyer who defends a notorious criminal is also a bad influence. Their comments indicated their feelings. "If a

Figure 1. Excerpts from responses of the general public to the Louis Harris poll on intolerance, compared with student responses at Woodside, California, before and after a class unit on intolerance.

"America has many different types of people in it. But we would like to know whether you think each of these different types of people is more helpful or more harmful to American life, or don't they help or harm things much one way or another?"

RESPONSES

POLITICAL OR PROFESSIONAL BEHAVIOR[1]	General public, as polled by Louis Harris			Students at Woodside, Calif. (paired figures show response before and after class study and discussion)		
	More Helpful	Doesn't Matter	More Harmful	More Helpful	Doesn't Matter	More Harmful
American Communist Party members	1%	10%	89%	23–33	18–30	59–36
People who don't believe in God	1%	27%	72%	24–30	60–56	16–14
Anti-Vietnam-war pickets	5%	27%	68%	52–62	17–19	31–19
Civil rights demonstrators	16%	16%	68%	92–83	3–12	5–5
Student demonstrators at colleges	7%	28%	65%	54–59	23–26	23–15
College professors active in unpopular causes	6%	36%	58%	41–41	28–41	31–18
Working career women with young children	8%	42%	50%	21–16	50–56	29–28
Lawyers who defend notorious criminals	18%	48%	34%	49–78	38–20	13–2

[1] The public poll also called for views on social behavior, such as reactions to homosexuals, "beatniks," gossiping women, and young people who like "rock 'n roll" music.

person fears a Godless society, then he is likely to limit the freedom of non-belief," said one student. "Who is anyone to say what anyone else should believe?" said another.

The teacher emphasized the need to defend the constitutional safe-guards of right to counsel and the presumption of innocence until guilt is proven. "This is a constitutional issue on which 100% should say that it is more helpful to have our lawyers willing to defend a notorious criminal," explained Miss Fulton, "while the other items on this poll are actually matters of opinion on which differences of response are to be expected."

On the third day of this unit, the students receive a third sheet, this one giving the breakdown of the respondents to the Harris Poll showing the levels of intolerance by key groups in the population. This leads to further discussion and additional generalizations.

As the fourth and concluding step of the unit, Miss Fulton distributes reprints of Louis Harris' commentary on the poll results, as reported in the September 28, 1965, *San Francisco Examiner*. Harris drew attention to two points he considered particularly significant, as revealed by the poll. "First, there is little doubt that the more educated and affluent people become, the more tolerant they are of off-beat behavior. The massive pressures toward conformity are rooted in the less articulate and less privileged sectors of society. Second, it is perfectly apparent that American beliefs in the right to be different are not nearly as firm as some have claimed." Although these conclusions appear to be descriptive of the responses made by the adult population polled by Harris, it is equally apparent that the students in Miss Fulton's government classes are receiving an education that emphasizes tolerance of differences and open-mindedness.

Summary

In showing the variability of historical interpretations, the contemporary operations of municipal government, the evolution of Georgia's culture, or the distribution of prejudices, the classes described above also prompt students to subject old beliefs to new examination and to approach the unfamiliar with an open mind.

CLASSROOM DIALOGUES

Like the dialogues presented at the end of Chapter 4, the following sketches of classes are intended as examples rather than absolute standards of creative teaching. In different ways, each provides an atmosphere conducive to developing the student's ability to make value judgments for a changing world and to be receptive to new facts, ideas, and ways of life.

American Studies at Euclid High School

The American Studies course at Euclid High School near Cleveland is taught by James W. Lindsay, a quiet, scholarly-looking man of perhaps 35 years. He is a graduate of Baldwin-Wallace College and received his Master of Arts degree in teaching from Wesleyan in Connecticut.

When his class of slow students in the junior-senior year American studies course entered the room, he greeted them in a friendly and relaxed manner. "Nick, how are you?" "Jerry, are you awake?" "Sam, how are you feeling?" His first announcement was, "If you can, I would like you to watch Channel 8 tonight. This program will be broadcast all over the country. Some of you saw the National Driving Test. Now, the purpose of this program is to discover what you know about the rights and duties of a citizen."

He then said, "I asked you to read this article about the immigration law in *Scope*. I am disturbed about this business of allowing more immigrants to come into this country."

One student quickly rose to the bait and said, "Yes, we should allow more Italians, only as long as they are not peasants."

Lindsay then asked, "What is a peasant? You mean we should only let in the rich and educated Italians? Frank, what do you think?"

The boy replied carelessly, "I don't care."

"But where were you born?"

"Germany."

"Suppose the law had forbidden you to enter this country?"

"I don't care."

"You mean it doesn't matter where you live?"

"No."

A short discussion followed about the opportunities and privileges available to citizens in various parts of the world and certain advantages of living in this country. One student digressed by saying, "The Russians make everyone study about rockets at about 10 years old. Why do they want rockets? Why bother the moon?"

Lindsay admitted that this was an interesting view and worthy of discussion at another time, and then said, "Back to immigration. Should your grandparents have been admitted into the country?"

Soon students were offering their opinions about possible immigration standards. "I think immigrants should be admitted only if they have a job. All these Cubans are willing to work for a dollar an hour, and they are doing us no good. We should limit the number and only admit those with a job waiting for them."

Lindsay reminded them of the origins of our nation and the theme, "Americans all, immigrants all."

"But it was different then. There was lots of room and lots of jobs and we needed people. Today it's different."

Another student suggested that any immigrant who comes to the United States today would be leaving his home and perhaps his family. He would have to have powerful motivations. These ambitious people, the student said, would have a bad opinion of us if they weren't wanted. Another boy contributed, "We've had many outstanding immigrants, like Wernher von Braun, who provided better jobs and more jobs."

Lindsay then said, "Here is Doug, who opposes immigration except for those with jobs. Here is Jack, believing just the opposite, that immigrants can make jobs. To get a policy, we must reconcile these views. What is the picture on the cover of *Scope?* The Statue of Liberty. What do you know about the Statue of Liberty?"

The students read the description of the Statue of Liberty and recalled details of how France gave this symbol of our liberties to the nation. Lindsay then drew a time-line of immigrants to the United States, beginning with the English in 1607, and adding Negroes, more English, Irish, Germans, Swedes, Poles, Russians, Italians, Czechs. "Does anyone know why I stopped the time-line at 1924?"

"Quotas," a student said. A discussion followed on the meaning of the word "quota." Lindsay took time to be sure the students understood the meaning of every technical word. They discussed the annual limits of 150,000 immigrants and the operation of the 1924 quota system.

"Don't you think this is fair?" Lindsay asked.

"No," said a student, as the class ended. "It should be the same for all countries."

Lindsay keeps his students thinking, even though they are not bright students. They are aware of their limitations and they lack confidence in their verbal and intellectual abilities, but they are realists, and they respond to Lindsay's realistic appraisal of them. He is friendly and spontaneous with his students, but one can sense in his deliberate selection of each word that he is concerned for the effect it will have. Toward the end of this period, for example, he said, "You know from many things I've said that I think the United States is the greatest country in the world, but I do not claim it is perfect. I think we have made mistakes."

This teacher's manner is always accepting. Slow learners do not have the feeling that they are regarded as second-class citizens, for they are treated with the full dignity and acceptance they deserve. With this understanding teacher, the slow learners seem to have the self-respect necessary for a wholesome concept of citizenship, a concept that is all too often associated only with more academically capable citizens. With confidence in themselves, they are encouraged to enlarge their views of the world.

Lindsay believes that every social studies teacher should be knowledgeable enough and flexible enough to teach the brightest and the slowest students. He rejects the notion that a high school teacher should specialize in teaching fast students or slow classes. He teaches both, as does every teacher in his department.

7th-Grade Geography in Washington, D.C.

Isaac Jamison, chairman of the social science department at Paul Junior High School in Washington, D.C., stood next to his desk talking informally to one of his students. Among the objects on Jamison's desk were a large plastic globe, a vase with two red roses, a small statue of Rodin's "Thinker," and several books.

Sixteen students entered the classroom and promptly took their seats. "All right!" said Jamison, speaking in a loud, crisp voice. It was clear that the class was about to begin.

"How many saw the program on television called 'It's a Small World'?"

Several students indicated that they had seen it.

Jamison, twirling the large plastic globe on his desk, continued, "What do you think is meant by 'It's a Small World'?"

"It means that we are getting closer and closer to each other."

"Is that important?"

"Why, yes! Because if we're getting closer to each other, what one person does can affect all the rest of us."

"Can anyone think of a word or words to describe this closeness of man to man?"

"We are all *connected*."

"Connected?" Jamison asked.

"We are all *related*."

"If what you say is true, we might state that 'It's a Small World' and *we are all related in some ways*. Let's examine how much closer we are to each other today than men were years ago. How long did it take Magellan to travel around the world?"

"A little over three years," a student answered.

"How long did it take Columbus to cross the Atlantic?"

"A few months."

"And what about today—by ship?"

"Nine days."

"Nine days? Do we all agree?"

"No, I don't agree," said one student, who had taken a trip to Europe recently. "It takes only five days on a fast ship."

"You say five days," Jamison said, addressing that student. "Let's see. You actually made the trip yourself, didn't you? You left France and made a stop in England before you came to the United States. How long did the entire trip take?"

"Five days in all."

"That's interesting," Jamison remarked. "You know, they once timed the 'United States,' the fastest of all ships, and they found that it could cross the Atlantic in three days and a few hours—if it travelled at maximum speed. What can we conclude from the information about Magellan, Columbus, and ships today?"

"That there has been a big change."

"Can you explain that a bit more?"

"Well, I mean that men can get there a lot quicker today than in earlier times."

"All right. And is there any *relationship* between the men of Columbus' time and men today? Do we owe them anything?"

"Yes," a student said forcefully.

"Go on," Jamison urged.

"We learned how to do things from them—I mean about boats and sailing—and then we did them better."

"I think you have helped us to understand one of the jobs in this class—to see the *relationships between past and present*," Jamison said. Wrinkles formed on his forehead just above the eyebrows and he said, "You know, we've left out something. We haven't mentioned the role of the airplane yet. Let's do so now. What is the advantage of an air route over a sea route?"

"The airplane can go directly."

"All right. Anything else?"

"The airplane can get there faster."

"Speed and a more direct route," Jamison summarized. "Then are science and technology—specifically, the development of the airplane—related to our study of geography and the social sciences?"

"Yes, they are."

"How? Can you develop your answer?"

"They have a lot to do with the way we travel—take jet planes and space ships."

"Are scientific discoveries and inventions related to us only in connection with means of transportation?"

"No, they affect us in many ways—in everything we do," a student said. "They're part of us."

"You've made things clearer for us on this point. All right. Now turn to page 25 in your book. We are going to start our study of the solar system."

Jamison started to read, " 'The solar system is made up of the sun, the earth and other planets, and . . .' " Then he called on a student to continue the reading. The student read a section that referred to man's "probing" of the universe.

"In the section we just read, what have we learned?" Jamison asked. "How extensive is man's probing? Is there any place on earth that man has not yet probed?"

"We still have not been able to explore the bottom of the oceans."

"All right. Anything else?"

"Man knows more about the moon than he knows about Greenland!"

"Is that a fact or an opinion?" Jamison asked.

"I'm not sure."

"Think about it for a moment."

"It's an opinion, that's what it is—an opinion."

"Now is there any *relationship* between fact and opinion?"

"Well, I guess we could say a fact is what 'we know,' but an opinion is what we think we know."

"That's an interesting answer," Jamison said. "We'll explore the whole matter more thoroughly a little later."

Jamison then called on other students to take turns reading. He did this as a means of providing students with material with which to make stimulating interpretations. The students read carefully, and, if they made an error in pronunciation, Jamison corrected them—kindly but firmly. The class examined the solar chart in their books, discussed the nature of planets, and related progress in space science to social science problems involving the United States and the Soviet Union. Jamison summed up this part of the period by saying, "You have mentioned the word 'relationship' several times now; and, indeed, never before have men and the universe been so closely bound togther."

There were still a few minutes left in class time so Jamison now made dramatic and effective use of the plastic, air-filled globe on his desk. He detached it from its holder and tossed it to a student. The student took it, and a grin on his face indicated his pleasure.

"You have the whole world in your hands now," Jamison said. "Do you realize how powerful you are? Move it around like a Hercules. Now come up here before the class and tell us something about it."

The student with the globe, as he walked toward the front of the classroom, said, "The earth's surface isn't smooth. See, it has mountains and other land formations jutting from it. Here—" he touched a spot on the globe, "here, here, and here."

"All right, Hercules, you've held the world long enough," Jamison said. "Pass it to someone else."

All of the students in the class had their arms up now, eager to receive the globe. A few said: "Here, here, give the world to me!" The student tossed the globe to another member of the class who came quickly to the front of the room.

"What can you tell us about the earth that you're squeezing like an orange?" Jamison asked with a smile.

"I'm stronger than I thought to be able to squeeze the world. Yes, sir! Well, there are continents on it. Here's one—"—he pointed to it carefully—"and here and here and here. There's another one over here where my finger is pressing down." Then, on Jamison's signal, the student tossed the globe to the back of the room. Another student took it, laughed, and hurried up before the class.

The next student began, "There are also many rivers on the earth. Here is the Nile. And here—let me see—yes, here is the Amazon. And here is the Mississippi."

Jamison and the students continued the "geography game." The students demonstrated a real knowledge of geography, and the use of the plastic globe made them eager to talk about their knowledge.

"One more person," Jamison said as the class period drew to a close, and the globe was passed to another student.

"Look here! If you were a pilot and you wanted to go from London to Seattle, this is a good air route to take." The student showed it on the globe.

"And now one final question," Jamison said. "You've been passing the world around like professional basketball players and rattling off a number of facts. Someone once said that isolated facts of geography are not important in themselves. Do you agree?"

"Yes, I do," answered a student. "Separate facts are important. But it's even more important to see the relationships between them. That way we can understand them and use them."

As the bell rang for the next class, Jamison smiled, pleased that his class had understood the point.

Among the outstanding features of Isaac Jamison's class was his

Robert Fatherley, at Germantown Friends School, also makes effective use of a globe.

ability to strengthen his students' appreciation of the importance of relationships. He helped them to see the relationships between past and present, between science-technology and social science, and between fact and opinion. Further, he made imaginative and effective use of a visual aid—a moving plastic globe—in teaching of geography. He motivated his students to express their knowledge of the earth. Finally, he increased his students' knowledge of geography and thus contributed to their development as good citizens.

CONCLUSION

James Lindsay and Isaac Jamison's classes are illustrative of the quality of teaching that can help students to form sound value judgments and an open-minded approach to the issues of citizenship. The students in these classes are gaining information, analyzing opinions, and enlarging their views of the world. Like the other teachers whose practices have been described in this chapter, Lindsay and Jamison place great importance on the value of permitting the student to make his own discoveries as the teacher guides unobtrusively. Through their discoveries, students acquire habits of informed and analytic thought that can guide them in making value judgments as adult citizens.

In the following chapter, other aspects of civic education will be explored, with emphasis on the use of information and analysis for the objectives of committed and involved citizenship.

> *I don't know what your destiny will be,*
> *but one thing I know: The only ones among*
> *you who will be really happy are those*
> *who have sought and found how to serve.*

Albert Schweitzer

CHAPTER **6**

Developing a Committed and Involved Citizenry

Developing the student's ability for informed and analytic thought, as vital as this objective is, does not end the school's responsibilities in civic education. Equally important is development of the student's ability and desire to participate in society effectively and in ways consistent with democratic values.

In this chapter, goals of civic education directed toward constructive social action will be discussed. The project team found abundant evidence that schools are giving attention to these goals. Some efforts by schools, often in cooperation with the community, are recorded here; other accounts will be found throughout this report.

GOAL 6: PARTICIPATION IN DECISION-MAKING

Direct Participation

In Detroit, after the 38 students in Denby High School's Great Books class completed their study of Plato's *Republic*, their teacher, Robert Donaldson, suggested that they analyze a non-Utopian society and write papers describing aspects of it that could be improved. Some students questioned the value of the assignment, doubting that any good could

139

result from writing and talking about conditions they were powerless to change. Donaldson convinced them that although "You can't beat city hall" was indeed a hallowed aphorism, it might be worth the effort to put it to the test. The obvious need of their community was for better facilities at the Receiving Hospital, a city-owned and operated institution.

The students had heard that facilities at this hospital were inadequate, so they visited the hospital and interviewed administrators to satisfy themselves about the facts. They saw as many as 500 patients crowded into wards designed for 100. They learned that the hospital handled 300 emergency cases a day with facilities planned for 100. They found that the emergency psychiatric services were able to treat only 25 percent of the 2,000 children who annually attempt suicide or homicide. The hospital had requested a $300,000 budget for expansion and improvement of its services. The mayor, in his budget, requested only $130,000.

The more the students inquired, the more committed they became to the fortunes of the Detroit Receiving Hospital. They organized themselves as SPACE (Students for Practical Action through Community Effort). They interviewed the president of the Detroit Common Council, the City Planning Commission, the Wayne County Board of Health, and the Detroit Bureau of the Budget, and gathered more information from officials of the hospital.

The students explored the frequently repeated statement that the real need was for a new hospital (apparently out of the question because of the unavailability of funds). When the president of the Council told the students that funds simply were not available, they replied that it was common knowledge that $50 million would be found to build a stadium and other facilities for the Olympics if Detroit were selected as the site for the games. The students pursued the matter of alternative sources of funds, inquiring if the city could use its bonding authority to begin a new hospital if Federal aid could be secured, or if some of the $60 million surplus in the state budget could be made available.

SPACE adopted the motto, "If we can afford to put a man in space, we can afford a space for man." It extended its organization into other schools, enrolling several hundred students, and when the Common

Council convened for a budget hearing, 500 students appeared. They prepared a fact sheet to share the knowledge they gained about conditions at the hospital and the imperative need for relief. All of this activity led to newspaper feature stories and radio accounts, and this in turn helped to concentrate public attention on the plight of the hospital. As a result, the Council appropriated not the $130,000 the mayor had requested, nor the $300,000 the hospital had requested, but $550,000.

The knowledge these students gained—about hospital administration, municipal administration, budgets, political processes, the press, and public relations—was impressive. The experience they gained in consulting adults in a completely unstaged setting about a real problem, was valuable. And the confidence they gained in themselves and in the democratic process, by succeeding when their parents and other adults had warned them they would not, is beyond computing. As their teacher happily pointed out, "They learned that you *can* fight city hall and win. They used power in the real sense."

Few student action programs achieve such dramatic results as this one in Denby High School, but many schools do have action-oriented groups that are equally dedicated and active, and probably equally valuable in providing experiences in decision-making.

Norwalk, Connecticut, for example, has its Action Project, organized in 1962 by about 40 students from two public high schools and a parochial high school. The Action Project evolved from an outdoor education program jointly promoted by the social studies and health education departments. Its original aim was to provide a youth center. Now it is a fund-raising group for both the youth center and the United Fund.

By 1965 the Action Project had $430 in the bank. It had not yet developed the momentum to achieve dramatic results or to make a terrific impact on the community. Its members, however, were getting the week-by-week benefits of cooperative working and planning for goals with civic value. One girl, asked about the value of the project, said, "It gives me an opportunity to express my views and show that teenagers are not giddy kids." The student president said, "We do it because we like to do it. It gives us a chance to exercise our leadership abilities."

In New Hampshire, juniors and seniors in the Sociology-Economics class at Henniker High School participate directly in the political affairs of their community through a class project. The project, "Consolidation —A Study," was granted an award by the New Hampshire School Citizenship Project with the support of the Sears Roebuck Foundation. It is designed to "enlighten the voters of Henniker as to the many advantages of a consolidated school with the hope of reversing their 1961 decision against it," and it has had considerable impact on the community. By 1965, attendance at the annual town meeting increased from the usual 150 to more than 400, and the meeting appointed a committee to study consolidation, which had previously been rejected without serious consideration.

The students, teacher, and principal cooperated in the selection of the topic, which was chosen because of its importance to students and the community and because it offered an opportunity to achieve a positive result. The students first heard a speech on the advantages of school consolidation, delivered by a member of the State Department of Education. Then they went to work to gather information and to inform the community. Letters were sent to local, state, and national education associations requesting information. Polls were conducted of the local citizenry to determine community sentiment. Questionnaires were sent to large schools, small schools, and consolidated schools to determine the advantages of school consolidation. A fact sheet was prepared for local distribution. A second community poll was conducted to detect any shifts in public opinion as a result of the study. Conclusions and analyses were made and a report of the project was written.

The teacher, Mr. Willoughby, and the principal, Theodore Gladu, share the conviction of the students that the project was exceptionally valuable. The students state it this way in the conclusion to their report:

This project, which began as an exercise in citizenship for our sociology and economics class and as an attempt to destroy the apathy we knew was present among the townspeople concerning a subject about which we were personally involved and concerned, has had its desired effect. We have learned about the problems of citizenship and the workings of a small town government, along with the economic factors governing a school system. There is no doubt as to whether we achieved our purpose. Through the various polls conducted and the information passed out, we certainly have increased the knowledge of a substantial number of people in our town on the topic of consolidation. That we revised their 1961 decision is equally clear. Finally, that we eliminated at least some of the voter apathy in Henniker can be proven by the records. There are ordinarily about 150 people at the town and school meetings. This year the figure was in excess of 400. Yet, the only significant change in either the school or town warrants from last year was the article concerning consolidation. The attendance record is proof in itself of the increased interest in town affairs generated by our project.

In every section of the nation some schools are helping their students achieve maturity and independence by providing opportunities for direct participation in political affairs. Student council leaders at the Ingraham High School in Seattle, for example, report with pride that their testimony helped persuade the City Council to reverse a decision to locate a garbage disposal plant near the school. At the De Witt Clinton High School in New York, varsity athletes, student government leaders, and other students participated in an educational campaign that reduced losses from vandalism in school busses from $180,000 a year to a negligible amount. At West Leyden, social studies teacher Herbert Paske encourages initiative by suggesting that his students write letters to the editor. Many of these letters are published in the local newspaper, and some have appeared in the Chicago dailies.

Another example of student activity directly related to adult citizenship decisions occurred in Detroit. It is best described in the first part of the principal's report to his superintendent:

A highly successful Civil Rights Sympathy March was held by approximately 1600 students at Central High School on Friday, March 19th, 1965. . . .

During the entire course of the Civil Rights March the 1600 students were absolutely orderly. . . . In my opinion they were a credit to Central, the Detroit School System, and they proudly proclaimed their feelings in participating in the national Civil Rights Movement. . . .

The entire March was completed and the students back in their fourth hour classes by 10:25. Thus, only one complete class period was missed, and, frankly, I feel that this experience was perhaps the greatest

demonstration of living social studies that this school has seen in a long time. To me, at least, it was a valuable learning experience.

Model Experiences Of considerable value in preparing students for decision-making responsibilities are the simulated action programs which have been popular in some schools for many years. These include mock elections, model congresses, student courts, and youth courts.

One of the largest in scope of these is Detroit's city-wide mock election in grades 6 through 12, that takes place during election time for adults. Some junior high schools are permitted to schedule their election on the day preceding the actual election, and many senior high schools hold theirs a week earlier to use the city's voting machines.

This 45-year-old tradition in the Detroit schools is an important contribution to education for civic participation. The central administration's social studies office prepares thorough memoranda for all teachers,

Civil rights sympathy march at Central High School, Detroit, on March 19, 1965.

underlining the importance of the experience and the need for instructional as well as physical preparation for the election. It provides fact sheets on the candidates and issues that appear on the ballot.

It is significant that student involvement includes more than simply studying about candidates and issues and then casting a ballot. Students are responsible for most of the mechanics of the operation. Under the direction of social studies teachers they appoint election officials from the student body; number the ballots for use on election day; prepare poll lists and registration books; prepare voting booths for the casting of secret ballots; and arrange for the tallying of ballots and reporting of returns.

For some students this is the first experience related to voting. For others it is the last before they become adult voters. For all, the teacher's responsibility is the same: to transmit to the student an awareness of the importance of the voting process and the necessity for engaging in it with the fullest possible information and the keenest judgment.

At the time of the team visit, students at Christopher Columbus Junior High School in Detroit had been preparing for the election for three weeks. Social studies department head, John Yoskovich, feels that the toughest job is to overcome voter apathy (so prevalent in local elections). He added that an apathetic citizen is likely to say, "They washed my street today because this is the day before election, but they won't be back for another year."

A spirited discussion in Mr. Yoskovich's 9th-grade class revealed that these students were well acquainted with the issues and had convictions at least as well supported as those commonly held by their elders. Attitudes towards law enforcement had been a major issue in the mayoralty campaign, and this became the focus of the class discussion. Following is a sample of the comments of students in the class:

Since Chicago initiated reforms in its police department, the crime rate has gone down 17 percent.

I don't think changing the police force is going to make much difference. We should work on the causes of crime. Putting on more policemen won't solve the problem.

I think maybe police should be given more support. They are criticized all the time. For example, if a policeman shoots a criminal, it is the policeman that gets the blame. I think maybe policemen should shoot a few criminals. My father says this might reduce crime.

I don't think that adding to the police force would make much difference either. They ought to pay the policemen more. This would enable them to get better men.

When they asked Mr. Cavanagh why he didn't pay the policemen more he said they were public servants; yet he accepted a raise. I think policemen deserve a raise just as much as the mayor.

I don't agree that the police do more work than the mayor and are therefore just as deserving of a raise. He has the executive function. He is responsible for many more areas than the police department. But I agree that we should have higher standards for policemen. In California they raised the requirements to a minimum of a college education. And even with the higher standards, California is able to get more policemen than it had before.

It was refreshing to note that the teacher did not enter this debate, although he admitted later, "I could scarcely keep from joining the discussion."

The hazards involved in bringing controversial current election issues into the school can easily be exaggerated. The guidelines set by Christopher Columbus Junior High School for its teachers suggest how the hazards can be avoided:

If a teacher expresses himself on a particular candidate or issue (and this is proper if it is related to the course of study), it should be clearly labelled as his opinion. Even in this area teachers should be careful to exercise good judgment, for we all know what a tremendous influence teachers may have on the minds of young people.

A mature graduate of the Detroit schools asserted, "I can never fail to vote at any election because the voting experience I had in school was so real. I can't fail to evaluate candidates, because for so long candidates were my friends and I had to learn how to evaluate them carefully."

Another—and controversial—example of a model experience that provides a close link between high school students and the adult world of government is the so-called youth court, in which students preside over a quasi-judicial body concerned with juvenile offenders. The Southwest youth council in Kansas City has existed since 1940, and since 1956, it has had a youth court.

The youth court, consisting of a foreman, clerk, bailiff, and 12 jurors who are members of the youth council, meets on alternate Wednesdays if there are any cases to be tried. Each school is permitted to fly a green safety flag below the American flag on its school standard during the time when that school has none of its students brought before the court.

When apprehended, a teenage traffic violator is taken to the regular Municipal Court, where his case is tried. If convicted, he is usually fined; and, if he attends one of the schools which participates in the youth courts, he is sentenced to one day in jail, which can be satisfied by an appearance before the Southwest youth court.

At the Southwest youth court the violator and his parents are told of the youth court's history and purposes. Then a letter from the Munici-

pal Judge explaining the offense is read to the court. The student jury
acts according to the seriousness of the offense, and may suspend the
driver's license of the violator for a period of not less than two weeks or
more than six weeks. The offender is then asked to sign an honor pledge
which states that he will comply with the decision of the youth court.

In 1965, the court heard 72 cases; of these, 57 offenders signed the
pledge that they would not drive during the time determined by the
court. In eight cases, no suspension of driving privileges was decreed,
and in seven other cases the accused did not sign the pledge.

Valuable legal assistance is offered by the junior section of the
Lawyer's Association, which sends one or more lawyers to each session
of the youth council and youth court. A Municipal Court Judge, in an
attempt to develop some statistics, estimated that the youth court has
reduced traffic violations in the area where it operates by 75 percent.
Officers of the Kansas City Police Department express amazement at
the continuous improvement in the driving habits of teenagers and their
attitudes toward law enforcement.

Perhaps the success of the Southwest youth court and other youth
courts which have grown out of this venture can be explained by saying
that a youth court is an organization under which teenagers are pun-
ished by young people their own age who understand the situation and
are able to assist in a manner beneficial to both the traffic violator and
the community.

A number of schools, including the Fresno High School in California, still maintain student courts as model student government ap-
paratus. These student courts are not as common as they were a generation ago.

The Fresno student court, which has operated for 17 years, exercises
authority over hallway traffic cases throughout the school. Two courts,
each with a chief justice and four associates, handle cases arising during
the two lunch periods. The courts are assisted by a chief prosecutor, a
defense staff headed by a chief defender, a clerk of the court, and a
bailiff.

When a student is given a citation, the court holds a preliminary
hearing to determine whether he should be tried. Preliminary hearings
are held at 8 o'clock each morning, to give the student who has been
cited a chance to plead. If he pleads guilty, the preliminary hearing

judge, together with any other judge present, sentences him. If he pleads not guilty, a hearing date is set and a panel of judges hears the case. The trial may be held with as few as three judges, but typically all five judges are present. The usual sentence for students found guilty is time in the detention hall. Appeals from the decisions of the court may be made to the administration, and finally also to the board of education. Consistently, the administration and the board have upheld the decisions of the court.

Perhaps less common than student courts, but not necessarily less valuable as model experiences to promote an inclination to participate in decision-making, are student congresses. Among impressive model congresses is that convened every January at Edison Junior High School in Wheaton, Illinois.

The 450 8th-graders who make up the model congress spend three months in preparation. Each student plays the role of some actual senator or representative and is given a certificate of membership, which reads: "Be it known that _____ is in fact an official and duly recognized member of the Senate of the United States in the 89th Congress first session held at Edison Junior High School, Wheaton, 1965." One of the new congressman's first duties is to research the person and the state he represents, becoming as knowledgeable as possible concerning the man and his constituency. This job is made easier by the careful accumulation of materials received in previous years and filed by state and legislative area in one of the social studies rooms, labelled "Library of Congress." Here are filed 80,000 letters and pieces of literature, the result of student letters to the legislature, accumulation of newspapers, and material from Chambers of Commerce.

The success of the model congress rests on careful planning and preparation. It is preceded by instructional units designed to equip the students for confident and competent participation in the mock congress. A government unit emphasizes legislative procedure and basic political terms. A unit on debate in language arts prepares students for parliamentary protocol. A refresher unit on library methods speeds research. Students write to the Congressmen they represent or to newspaper editors in the district they represent, and the students' letters are analyzed, corrected, and rewritten before being mailed. Copies of the

U.S. Senate and House handbooks, all state constitutions, and *The Congressional Record* are available and are consulted frequently.

Each student is required to prepare a bill and personally introduce it, with a summary of the arguments in support of it. Every bill is duplicated and distributed to all members of the model congress. The president pro tempore of the senate and the speaker of the house refer all bills to the appropriate committees.

Students rapidly become involved in their roles and in competition to get their own bills passed. They become sophisticated in tactics, arrange unexpected caucuses, and call for votes at unexpected times. Party whips do their best to enforce party loyalty, and students experience the dilemma of being caught between party loyalty and personal conviction regarding the bills. They quickly learn that if they do not support the party, the party, in turn, will not support the bills they sponsor. The extended discussion and revision of proposed bills teaches students that many issues involve competition and compromise.

Of the 450 bills introduced, four or five are likely to survive the process of committee hearings and passage by both houses. The school principal plays the role of president, with authority to veto a bill. In 1964, he vetoed two, neither of which was passed over his veto.

The informal evidence of success of this unit, as reported by the teachers, suggests that, as a result of the model congress, students show more interest and enthusiasm in reading newspapers and some students talk of going into politics as a career. Students are reluctant to leave this unit, and high school students frequently return just to attend a session of the congress. Conversation with senior students in the high school confirmed the fact that four years later students are still enthusiastic about the model congress as the highlight of junior high school.

A Schoolwide Commitment to Political Participation

"Some of our youngsters went to a ward committee meeting. Nobody asked them to go; they just decided they would like to see what a ward committee meeting was like. They wandered in and nobody questioned them. The ward leader was explaining tactics, 'Now, you should all know you are not allowed to display party literature inside the polling place. It's against the law. Here is how we do this.' And he explained to his ward workers how they could break the law and get away with it. Well, the youngsters were fascinated and stayed for four or five hours at this meeting. That's how my history students became involved in political affairs," explained Mrs. Robert N. Reifsnyder, a teacher at Germantown Friends School in Philadelphia who is also advisor to the school's civil rights committee.

Students at Germantown Friends School are encouraged to feel a high degree of involvement in political affairs. Mrs. Reifsnyder said:

We had over 100 youngsters at the polls last election day with a big sign, "One Man, One Vote in Mississippi," and then they collected money to help in voter registration. We collected almost $500 that way. Other students who couldn't participate in that activity wanted to help, so the dance committee gave a dance netting $650, which they gave to the Student Nonviolent Coordinating Committee to be used for voter registration work in Mississippi. That got the junior high students excited about voter registration, so they sold fruit cakes at Christmas time to raise money for the same cause.

In her own history classes, the attention given to politics appears to have considerable influence on students. She said:

My students work in the election every year, so we have been able to formulate a most interesting set of statistics for the 59th ward, the ward in which the school is located. This year Fred Wilson, a brilliant mathematics student, is doing a statistical analysis of the returns over the past four elections in this ward. Incidentally, students who have graduated often write back saying, "Please send me the 59th ward voting statistics. I have to write a paper for college on some political division, and I want to do it on the 59th, which I know."

The faculty of Germantown Friends School is unusual. As Mrs. Reifsnyder described:

Our faculty members are deeply involved in politics and social concerns. Many of us are Quakers and devoted to the peace testimony, so

our youngsters are not surprised when they see us in picket lines. Therefore, they have reason to believe that we mean what we say in the
classroom. We have people in this school who have gone to prison for
their beliefs. The students know that, not that we hang a sign on the
teacher saying, "I am an ex-convict," but they know who these people
are and what they stand for, hence they can judge what the teacher is
speaking about.

Because we are an independent school, we probably don't have to be
quite as careful as a public school might have to be about our youngsters
participating in politics under the direction of the teacher in school.

GOAL 7: BELIEF IN EQUALITY AND LIBERTY

Important to the development of a citizen's commitment to the principle that all citizens have a right to share in the Constitutional guaran-
tees of our democratic system is understanding of the contributions
made by various racial, ethnic, and religious groups.

**Appreciating Varied Racial
And Ethnic Contributions**

In the 1960's, as the movement for
civil rights for Negro citizens has gained
momentum, an increasing number of
schools are reevaluating the role assigned to Negro history in the curricu-
lum. Nevertheless, inadequacies are apparent. Some schools simply do
not mention the Negro's contributions and changing position within
national history; this is true even in some schools that have Negro
students. In other schools, particularly those with large numbers of
Negro students, a special unit on Negro history may be found. This
approach, often described as a "stop-gap," has serious weaknesses.

A teacher in Philadelphia expressed strong concern about the distor-
tions that occur when Negro history is treated apart from other elements in our national past:

I think we should teach American history and, because Negroes contribute to it, mention this. If they are not a part of it, we don't try to
force them in. I wouldn't teach Negro history as such—I consider that

an inversion of values. To point to Crispus Attucks, who was killed in the Boston Massacre, and to make a big deal of it because it is believed he was a Negro seems to me completely false.

This teacher might be accused of intolerance by some who misunderstand her remarks, but her convictions instead are part of her concern for possible injurious effects when groups of citizens are isolated and treated as an adjunct to, rather than a part of, the American heritage.

Her reaction is confirmed by several Negro students in Detroit's Central High School, where Mrs. Annie Wilkins teaches a one-semester elective course called "The Negro in American History," covering the period from 1619 to the present. Mrs. Wilkins explained the pupose of the course:

It is to show our students that others have overcome obstacles and made significant contributions; to help them realize that they can do it, too; to convince them that if they have the ability and the stick-to-it-iveness, they can't be held down. The course exists primarily to help our students raise their image of themselves.

At the same time, she admits that the course is a temporary offering to meet an immediate need. She says:

We certainly hope that it will be incorporated into the regular American history course. In a sense, the course in Negro history is a stop-gap to indicate what can be done in this area and to encourage curriculum planners and textbook publishers to include the history of the Negro. Some students ask why no white teachers are teaching about Negro history. Is this just something that Negroes teach to other Negroes? Other students—and parents—would rather not concentrate on the past, with its inescapable emphasis on slavery and degradation.

A dedicated teacher such as Mrs. Wilkins, who is simultaneously devoted to raising the aspiration level of her students and aware of the limitations of a separate course in Negro history, provides a good yardstick for measuring reactions of students. When the project team asked her students, who all expressed respect and admiration for their teacher, to comment on the course, they gave mixed responses:

I elected this course because I thought it would be something different, and my advisor said it would be good for me. And I've learned about people I never even heard about before.

I like the course. But unless it's done right, it might lead to more prejudice. It would be wise if material about Negroes could be included in regular American history courses.

They ought to combine the two histories—American history and Negro history. If a Negro did something important, we should say it was a Negro. The books haven't done this in the past.

We've learned about many famous Negro people, and I've been very interested in that.

I found out a lot of things I didn't know—and I realize that the things Negroes can do are just as great as those anyone else can do.

I think everyone should have Negro history—but it would be good if American and Negro history were combined.

Recognition should be given to all groups—Negroes, Italians, Poles, and others.

Other schools are making an effort to recognize the contributions of non-white minorities by featuring books on this too often neglected area of our national life.

In Cleveland, every junior and senior high school is encouraged to enlarge its holdings of books on human relations. Funds have been made available to the schools for this purpose and annotated bibliographies have been prepared and distributed. To advance intra-city understanding, Cleveland also fosters exchange meetings of teachers, human relations clubs, and student councils. The Human Relations Office of the central administration plans in-service programs to improve teacher skill in an inter-cultural situation and distributes inspirational material for weekly bulletin board use.

In New York City, teachers wrote a series of 48 biographies of local citizens—people from minority groups who made good—which were published under the title *Call Them Heroes*. Although these biographies were written on the 6th-grade level, it is expected that they will be used by selected reading groups in all grades. The assumption is that many children of minority groups will face conflict situations and may find support by identifying with these models from their own community, whose achievements are not beyond the reasonable aspiration level of the students.

The New York City Board of Education has long recognized that "the problem of improving intergroup relationships remains one of our urgent challenges." Its 1960 statement on textbooks pointed out areas for improvement:

> . . . textbook illustrations rarely reflect the varied ethnic components of American society. The role of minorities as groups, particularly in the process of industrialization and urbanization in the 20th century, has not been adequately treated in the texts. It is not sufficient to list the contributions of a few prominent representatives of these groups to the development of American culture . . . Current conflicts involving the changing status of the Negro receive scant treatment, as does the significance of the Supreme Court decision on school desegregation and the continued resistance to the implementation of that decision.

The report concludes by requesting textbook selection committees in the city to apply these questions to all instructional materials being considered for adoption:

1. How adequate is the space and treatment given to the roles of various minority groups in our culture?

2. Do the illustrations, both photographs and sketches, reflect the pluralistic nature of our society?

3. Does the treatment reflect the findings of recent historical scholarship?

4. Does the treatment avoid reality by ignoring or glossing over the present-day tensions of inter-group relations and the efforts made to relieve those tensions?

5. Does it help to promote the goal of a pluralistic society, free from the social ills of discrimination and prejudice in areas such as education, employment, and housing?

Improving Human Relations

In Rochester, New York, one of many cities where racial imbalance persists, students began to learn the meaning of equality through a series of exchange meetings between city schools. James Madison High School, located on the south side of Rochester, had 801 non-white students, who constituted 50.2 percent of the school's population; John Marshall High School, on the north side of the city, had only one non-white student. Charlotte High School, also on the north side of the city, had no non-white students.

The first of the series of inter-school seminars was naturally the most difficult. When the Marshall contingent arrived at Madison at noon, they were brought to the dining room, where students drew numbers assigning them to their luncheon seats. Then, with much of their reserve broken by conversation during lunch, the delegates assembled for the conference. A brief keynote address reminded the students that many American ideals of democracy came from the frontier, where every individual was judged solely on his merits as a person. During the discussion period, one group attempted to analyze civil rights; another deliberated on what constitutes an ideal form of government. Both groups reflected serious thinking; and courtesy, tact, and willingness to consider differing views were outstanding features. Following the first meetings in Rochester, a questionnaire showed almost unanimous agreement among the participating students that cross-cultural conferences should be continued and extended. One student noted that "a feeling of tension at first" had dissolved before the end of the second meeting.

The same conditions that led to the Trans-Urban Conferences in Rochester sparked the formation of the Los Imperiales Club in the Fresno High School in California. Los Imperiales is the only club in the school that Mexican-Americans feel free to join. These students often feel that other school clubs welcome only students who get good grades, who are well dressed, or whose parents are wealthy.

Denancio Gaona, Mexican-American faculty sponsor, hopes that Los Imperiales will acquaint its members with the procedures of club organization so that they may feel more comfortable in other clubs. Los Imperiales members want to demonstrate their ability to contribute to school and society. They have collected money for Thanksgiving baskets for needy people. They have made holiday gifts for the men of an Army unit. To let teachers know that they "appreciate the value of teaching in their lives," they gave a cake for the teachers at Christmas time.

One of the difficulties encountered in helping Mexican-Americans to become integrated into school and community is a tendency to try to make them "100-percent American," to insist that they abandon the Mexican elements of their heritage. This is virtually impossible, according to Mr. Gaona, because Mexican-Americans retain so much of their native culture—a fact that some Californians fail to understand.

Darien, Connecticut, a town of 20,000 on the shore of Long Island Sound, is described as "almost exclusively white, predominantly Protestant, and overwhelmingly rich." Of the 5,200 children in the public school system, not one is Negro. This fact once caused Superintendent Gregory C. Coffin to say, "Our children are culturally deprived; when they go out into the real world of social change, they will not be as fully prepared as they ought."

To break out of this insulation, Coffin began a program of civil rights education, the first such program in the history of Darien schools. A part of it called for the exchange of six Darien teachers with six Negro teachers from the New York City School System for a period of three weeks. In another part of the program, a group of Darien students attended New York City schools while several dozen New York Negro students went to Darien classes and participated in Darien school activities.

The success of the Negro teachers in destroying stereotyped thinking in Darien classrooms was evident. A particularly talented New Yorker, for example, after leading a discussion on civil rights for several days, was asked by a Darien student, "Are you really a Negro?" The "culturally deprived" youngster had never before thought of a Negro as having the competence that this teacher displayed.

The National Observer says of the Darien exchange plan:

Teacher and student exchanges to promote better understanding of someone else's problem are not new; they have been used internationally for years. What is new are the programs aimed primarily at understanding the social revolution in this country. Among the communities of its size and type, Darien is taking a lead. It is not easy. In his office, Dr. Coffin has a drawing of a turtle with this message: "Behold the turtle. He makes progress only when his neck is out."

Teaching About The Bill of Rights

"What Bill of Rights has the teenager got?" "Can a cop stop your car and search it, without a warrant, when you haven't been doing anything?" "How far can a school go in enforcing conformity of dress?" "What are my contract rights in buying a car or a house if I get married at 18?" "Do children have legal rights against their parents?" "What are the divorce laws in this state?"

Can a teacher effectively teach an understanding of and respect for the Bill of Rights if he is unable to help students find the answers to questions like these—or unwilling to discuss them seriously? Concern over national attitudes toward the Bill of Rights and the lack of commitment by the American people to the principles underlying these classic safeguards of civil liberties seems to increase with every public opinion poll. A number of public officials have stated their belief that the Bill of Rights could not pass in a referendum of the American public today. As a result of this concern, many high school teachers are devoting more attention to this important aspect of civic education and are devising more effective ways of presenting the complex principles behind the Bill of Rights.

A few years ago, the California State Board of Education recognized the importance of teaching about the Bill of Rights by urging all superintendents to give this subject the highest priority. The Board expressed its concern by creating an advisory panel which agreed upon the need for a substantial teaching contribution and for strengthened preservice and in-service education of teachers in this area. As a result, the State Department of Education prepared a curriculum publication, *Teaching the Bill of Rights*, which treats both its historical and contemporary aspects. It presents a teaching outline, suggested learning experiences and activities, appropriate audio-visual and published materials for both teacher and student use, and court cases in which the Bill of Rights has been tested. Emphasis is on activities which place the

Bill of Rights in a contemporary setting and assist the teacher in making this area of learning come to life.

Another organization in the state, The Constitutional Rights Foundation, contributed to the interest in improved teaching about the Bill of Rights by inaugurating an annual statewide contest for the best teacher presentation on the subject. The winning presentation, by Joyce Fulton, government teacher at the Woodside High School in California, was based on an article titled "The Due Processing of Asbury Howard" in *The Reporter* (April 16, 1959). The article described the arrest and beating of Negro Asbury Howard and his son for their activity in behalf of Negro voter registration.

Miss Fulton explained how she introduced the unit on the Bill of Rights:

My first question is the obvious one: "What is the Bill of Rights?" Even customarily vocal students become suddenly silent. Each student "feels" what the Bill of Rights is, but he does not know. Cautiously, a few students volunteer ideas, usually those contained in the First Amendment. With prodding and pointed questioning, most students arrive at the judgment that the first ten Amendments protect individuals from State action, as well as Federal action. We look at the First Amendment, which begins "Congress shall. . . ." Uneasily, the students squirm. Leaving them in doubt, I turn to a carefully timed reading of "The Due Processing of Asbury Howard." Near the end of the class period the reading ends in shocked silence. The bell rings and the students remain seated. Quietly, they begin to leave, shaking their heads. "Tough" boys look grim, a few girls have tears in their eyes, and though I've read the simple description a dozen times or more, I have trouble keeping my voice firm. One student says, "I can't eat my lunch after that." "Sick, I'm sick," says another. And they all leave the room in twos and threes.

She then described the second class period spent on this unit:

Armed with their first work sheet, a copy of the article, and an excellent pamphlet on the Bill of Rights prepared for the Senate Judiciary committee, the students are ready to ask questions and seek answers.

The class bristles next day; first questions reflect doubt and suspicion: "Who is Jeffrey Fuller and how do we know he is giving us the truth?" Inevitably, a student refuses to accept the evidence given or feels that part of the story was deliberately omitted. One boy, particularly hostile to me, claimed that the whole story was a fraud perpetrated by me to wring an emotional response from my students. I learned of this from another teacher who reported that he made the statement in her class and was promptly challenged by several of his peers, who argued that he was "blind, naive, or ignorant" if he didn't admit that such injustices exist.

The project team asked Miss Fulton to describe some of the difficulties she must overcome in teaching effectively about the Bill of Rights. She said:

The greatest difficulty in teaching about the Bill of Rights is in getting students personally involved and in removing the document from its aura of abstraction. This is why the description of Asbury Howard's experience becomes significant. It is a specific, concrete violation of "fair play." The notion that "a man would be arrested for such an innocent poster is outrageous," as one student put it. The fact that Howard is a Negro is important, but as the days of discussion follow it becomes apparent that my all-white classes identify with his plight, including those students who were rigidly committed in favor of Proposition 14 (a ballot proposal in which California voters in 1964 rejected a measure to forbid racial discrimination in housing).

Miss Fulton also drew attention to the time required to develop the unit in class:

I once thought it would be possible to complete the discussion in three days, working from three worksheets. The first is aimed at a general understanding of the Bill of Rights, with particular emphasis on the Fourteenth Amendment. The second is concerned with a specific examination of due process. The third is designed to cover equal protection of the law and the nature of the Negro revolution. I now find this time limitation is inadequate.

This semester, for example, we spent nearly a period discussing one worksheet question on police powers of the State and the need to maintain order. As an example of the State police power, I introduced a newsclipping of a recent California case of a Jehovah Witness mother who refused to grant permission for a blood transfusion for her dying three-day-old baby. This provoked a vehement argument among students about freedom of religion and the rights of the State. Further discussion of relevant Supreme Court decisions postponed completion of the worksheet guidelines to the point that one student muttered, "I'm losing sympathy for Asbury Howard, Miss Fulton. When will we get to the end?" After 11 class sessions, in spite of the compulsion some have for checking off items and feeling immediately satisfied, I believe that my students become simultaneously involved in two things: an analysis of Negro Howard's case—and an application of broad principles to their own liberties. By using the worksheets for tangential discussion of human rights and liberties, even the habitually shy and silent students will argue and debate with vigor. It is not often that one finds 30 to 35 young people squirming and arguing, totally absorbed in a single problem. But it happens throughout this study.

In Portland, Oregon, the case study approach to the Bill of Rights developed from cooperation between the Portland schools and the Oregon Bar Association over a period of several years. The Bar Association, concerned by the low level of understanding of legal principles evidenced in public opinion surveys, wanted to do more than merely sponsor the traditional Law Day for the schools. A committee of teachers and lawyers pondered possible ways to make the Bill of Rights come alive for students and settled on a program of case study units and an in-service program to prepare teachers to use them effectively. Sixteen lawyers assisted in the construction of the units, each of which includes historical data, an analysis of principles, and related court decisions, especially those handed down by the Supreme Court.

Jonathan U. Newman, chairman of the lawyers' committee, feels that the units should be unscheduled and used at any appropriate time when the legal principle involved is highlighted in the news. He said, "One day the papers may be full of news about the arrest of an accused for a crime about which there has been a great deal of pre-trial publicity. The teacher can then take out his material on free press and fair trial and use it as a basis for studying the issue." He continued:

> During our 10-week in-service program, again and again the press seemed to carry a write-up relevant to the very issues we were talking about. Before the free press-fair trial issue, we had a number of releases about the Sheppard case. Before the search and seizure unit, there were stories about a police roadblock just two days earlier. When we studied citizenship, the papers were headlining the case of a native-born American of Japanese ancestry who was about to be denationalized because she had voted in a foreign election. And argument in the press and elsewhere ran high about Vietnam protests at the time we were studying the principles of freedom of speech. Because the Bill of Rights is vital, it is constantly being invoked and it is always easy to demonstrate its relevance.

Units prepared for this course are: right to counsel; procedural due process; search and seizure; self-incrimination; freedom of expression; flag salute; church, state, and education; free press and fair trial; citizenship; segregation; and martial law.

At the Community High School in Naperville, Illinois, K. A. Kruse has prepared a 100-page booklet containing summaries of the decisions in 18 key civil liberties cases heard by the United States Supreme Court.

The 18 cases involve aspects of the application of principles from the Bill of Rights to criminal court procedures in the states. They are used to demonstrate that many basic safeguards are included in state constitutions. They also illustrate that if the safeguards are abridged, and no remedy is offered by the state, then appeal and possible remedy may be obtained in the Supreme Court of the United States. To help each student make his own discovery of the facts, the class was divided into groups of no more than four members each. To each group was assigned a particular guarantee, such as right to trial by jury or right to counsel. Group members, individually, were required to examine the cases and decide which ones hinged on the assigned group topic. Again individually, they briefed the related cases and one member from each group made a summary report to the class, explaining the Supreme Court's decision and evaluating the current status of the guarantee in question.

Evaluation of this method of handling case study material is not yet possible. Preliminary results seem to indicate that the material thus used is easily mastered by high school seniors. It must be coupled, however, with an introduction which explains state and Federal court structures and defines common legal terms that will be encountered in the decisions. It also appears that effective use of the case study material, with textbook, reference materials, class lectures and discussion, requires at least 15 class sessions.

Other schools interested in using the case method to teach about basic legal principles have elected to use the series published by the National Council for the Social Studies under the title *Judgment.* Eight of these case-study pamphlets are now available: Bible reading and prayer in the public schools; Congressional reapportionment; the right to counsel; the privilege against self-incrimination; the security of citizenship; the role of the press in a defendant's right to a fair trial; state loyalty oaths; and poll taxes. Each pamphlet gives background explanations, including brief references to classic court cases, but primarily, it reports on a single recent case.

At the Miami Beach High School, Sidney Cooper goes into much more factual detail in teaching about the Bill of Rights than do most teachers. In addition to citing and analyzing separate court decisions, he guides his students through careful organization of legal generalizations. They prepared, for example, a lengthy chart showing the relation between the Bill of Rights and the due process clause of the Fourteenth Amendment, listing in one column each specific right detailed in the Bill of Rights and in the second column the degree to which that guarantee was made to apply to the states by the Fourteenth Amendment.

In this class, the teacher did a great deal of lecturing, in a rapid-fire, machine-gun tempo which kept the students alert. Students interrupted, however, whenever they felt the need for clarification; and they were given the opportunity, as well, to organize and express their thoughts at a later time.

Another class which tackled the same subject was observed in Webster Groves, Missouri. The teacher was Department Chairman P. Kenneth Boulding, who began teaching in the Negro school in Webster Groves before integration.

His first question might seem off the mark. He asked, "To what extent should one conform to the group?"

After the class had responded to this question with various answers, Boulding continued: "Now let me read you a case." He read a brief summary of the case involving the right of Jehovah's Witnesses to disseminate their views by broadcasting loud-speaker recordings on public street corners.

Immediately the students became involved in the kind of discussion that highlights the complexity of social issues and the absence of absolute answers. The discussion centered on the conflict between social organization and individual freedom. It was brought to an end, near the close of the class period, with summaries by three students. The summaries, although widely different, indicated a general class awareness that there are no quick answers to this central problem of democracy.

Although discussion in the Webster Groves class seemed freer than it did in many others, the careful listener—even without benefit of the unit outline, which Boulding was inconspicuously following—could discern a thoughtful, step-by-step approach.

At the DeWitt Junior High School in Ithaca, New York, a unit on civil liberties emphasizes the difference between fact and opinion, and the concept that majority acceptance of a point of view does not necessarily mean it is correct. The project team observed the teacher, John Bozzone, conduct an effective class discussion based on students' responses to the following 19-item query about civil liberties, presented as a true-false quiz:

1. *Any private individual should have the right to criticize any government or governmental official anywhere in the world.*

2. *Congressional investigations into "un-American activities" are essential to our nation's security.*

3. *Segregation in public schools violates the equal protection of the laws guaranteed to all Americans by the Constitution.*

4. *A trade union member should be permitted to advocate "right-to-work" laws without jeopardizing his union membership.*

5. *Belonging to the Communist Party should be punishable by fine or imprisonment.*

6. Everyone who invokes the privilege against self-incrimination must be guilty as suspected.

7. Religious exercises, such as the Lord's Prayer and Bible reading, should be barred from public schools.

8. Books such as Tropic of Cancer should be banned from news-stands and libraries.

9. States' rights clauses in the Constitution justify efforts by certain states to prevent Negroes from voting.

10. Communist leader Benjamin Davis and Birch Society head Robert Welch are both entitled to make public speeches.

11. Movies, books, and plays presenting an offensive characterization of a particular racial or religious group should be suppressed.

12. Everyone should have the right to travel to any country, and be permitted to return to his own country.

13. In their war against crime, policemen are entitled to listen in on private phone conversations.

14. Parochial school pupils are entitled to free bus service, financed by public funds.

15. Those accused as security risks under the Federal security program should have the right to confront and cross-examine their accusers.

16. Students receiving financial aid from the Government should be required to swear that they are not members of the Communist Party.

17. Racial discrimination in housing, public and private, should be prohibited by law.

18. Police are entitled to hold and interrogate arrested persons as long as 24 hours before arraigning them in front of a magistrate.

19. To "emancipate the American Indian," reservations should be closed and Federal services terminated—without regard for the tribes' wishes.

GOAL 8: NATIONAL PRIDE AND INTERNATIONAL COOPERATION

Symbols of National Pride

Attention in our high schools to American institutions and to our national history has been a dominant and uninterrupted feature of public education. The traditional view of the school as an agent of civic education has

meant to most people fostering pride in our country through a study of its heroes and their achievements.

With slightly altered emphasis, the symbols of patriotism remain important. If fewer students today have committed the National Anthem to memory than was true two generations ago, and if students are less dedicated to the proposition of "our country right or wrong," it does not necessarily mean that they are less devoted to their country and its ideals. Many of this generation of youngsters are more concerned with the process of democracy than with the symbols. But the symbols have not been abandoned.

The daily patriotic exercise at Miami Beach High School is similar to those of many other schools. A recording of a bugle playing "To the Colors" is followed by the Pledge of Allegiance. Each student in the homeroom stands and follows the lead of the voice on the public address system. Then a girl reads a thought for the day: "Every act that we perform helps or hinders the progress of the world. Each thing we do or fail to do counts and helps to determine the final outcome. Every act we perform is planting a seed even though the harvest we may never see." The voice then asks, "Will you join me in silent meditation?" A 30-second period of silence concludes the exercise.

The South Dakota Young Citizens' League has published a mimeographed handbook of patriotic materials that should provide ample reassurance that the traditional evidences of pride in country have not been forgotten in the schools.

The booklet begins by quoting President Kennedy's ". . . ask not what your country can do for you, ask what you can do for your country." It continues with proposed activities, "to be used during any period of the year," based on materials covering these areas: patriotic quotations; the American's Creed; the Pledge to the Flag; flag etiquette; the Great Seal of the United States; milestone events in our national history; Arlington National Cemetery; Valley Forge; the United Nations headquarters; patriotic songs; and the concepts of patriotism, duty, courtesy, good health, sportsmanship, truth, and reliability.

The United States And The World

Our schools have continued the tradition of pride in country, although with less pomp and pageantry and more intellectual commitment, and they have also extended the curriculum to increase the student's knowledge and appreciation of other peoples. Both emphases are important, although they are not always easy to reconcile. To be comfortable with both commitments requires a broad education and a thoughtful outlook. It is to this difficult challenge that many of our schools are addressing themselves.

A fine example of recognition that wholesome pride in the United States can arise from an understanding of her role in relation to the rest of the world is found in the Core Course of the summer program at Mount Hermon School in Massachusetts. The school curriculum bulletin describes the course this way:

> The Core Course. (All students participate in this course.) The great experiment of the American Republic was not designed as a part of an international political system, much less as a venture in empire. Yet it is a fact that in the second half of the 20th century there is an international political system, and the United States of America plays the dominant role in it. And it is also a fact that there are many who feel that this role is a selfish and self-righteous one, and call it "imperial." As great as the difference between the isolation of United States in the 18th and 19th centuries and the global involvement of America in the 20th century has been the discrepancy between what America, and Americans, have actually done in dealing with other nations, and what they have often honestly thought they were doing.
>
> The World and The United States: The Dilemma of Power will consider the history of American attitudes and actions toward the rest of the world since the days of the founding fathers. The effort will be not so much to narrate the history of American foreign policy as to analyze the development of the awareness of the American people of the role of their nation as a world power, and to study some of the problems of conflict and contradiction between ideals and the realities of power. Two weeks will be spent on establishing the major lines of thought about America's involvement with the world, from Washington's Farewell Address to Senator Fulbright's "Myth" speech in the 87th Congress. The remaining four weeks will be devoted to case studies of the dilemma of power in Berlin, Korea and China, Latin America (Cuba), and Vietnam.

The role of the United States in world affairs is better understood by the student who is well informed about other parts of the world. Increasingly popular are elective courses in area history, especially the Far East, Latin America, and Africa.

The course in African Studies offered in the Darien, Connecticut, High School uses an interdisciplinary approach which includes the tools of the historian, political scientist, physical anthropologist, social anthropologist, sociologist, and the economist. Miss Georgia Hale, the teacher, spent two years in Africa working in community development and teaching refugees. She hopes the course will produce the "cultural sensitivity" important in achieving better inter-group relations.

This course was constructed by the teacher from her own knowledge, experience, and convictions. In her introduction to the course outline, Miss Hale says:

Since World War II, Africa has become one of the major areas of the world that has captured almost universal interest. Every day we read in newspapers and periodicals of African nationalism, political agitation, economic development schemes and military bases. Race relations in South Africa and uprisings in Central Africa have become matters of worldwide concern. We are increasingly conscious of African problems and argue their possible solutions. Yet today many studies of the "dark continent" concentrate solely on political developments of the emerging African nations. This, however, can be a frustrating enterprise, for it is not unlikely that at the end of such a course the political structure of African nations could be radically different than it was at the beginning. This course, then, will focus on traditional societies and cultures and the rapidity and success with which these societies are being converted to the new western way of life, rather than on a systematic study of contemporary political institutions.

The eight units in this course in African studies follow a well planned progression:

1. Geographic settings
2. African history
3. Traditional societies: African anthropology
4. The role of the cities
5. Sub-Saharan economics
6. The problem of race
7. African education
8. Africa and the world today

She lists a bibliography of several hundred titles and a required reading list of six: John Beattie's *An African Kingdom*; Fred Burke's *Africa's Quest for Order*; Alan Moorehead's *No Room in the Ark* and *The*

White Nile; Simon and Phoebe Ottenburg's *Cultures and Societies of Africa*; and Herbert Spiro's *Politics in Africa*.

International Relations Programs

Pride in our country, coupled with an appreciation of the backgrounds and aspirations of other peoples, is frequently fostered in school international relations programs, sometimes sponsored on a regional basis by a community organization such as the World Affairs Council. Sixteen of Philadelphia's high schools cooperate in the Council's programs, which during a year include a leadership workshop; high school council meetings; Saturday morning high school forum meetings; and trips to the United Nations headquarters, to the annual model UN General Assembly meeting, and to Washington, D. C.

One of the schools involved in the Council's Philadelphia program is the George Washington High School. During the team's visit to George Washington, students were preparing for the coming Saturday's forum meeting, in which about 40 students from the school were to participate. The printed announcement of the meeting, which was to feature talks by two persons who had lived in Vietnam, included six study questions designed to give background information on that country. The students used the study questions, listed below, as guidelines for their week-long preparation for the forum:

1. *Trace the origin of the commitment of the United States to South Vietnam.*

2. *What are the objectives of U. S. policy in South Vietnam?*

3. *Describe the official position of South Vietnam.*

4. *What are the arguments against the current policy of the United States?*

5. *Discuss the arguments pro and con for a number of alternatives to current U. S. policy, excluding the two extreme positions, i.e., assumption of complete responsibility for the conduct of the war or complete U. S. withdrawal.*

6. *What are the essential elements of the U. S. AID program in Vietnam?*

**Student Exchanges
And Travel**

Some persons believe the most effective method for promoting an appreciation and acceptance of other cultures is through a direct, person-for-person exchange between the countries. Certainly student comment, in school after school, was loud in its praise of student exchanges and convincing in its claims of their value. In this connection, students at Webster Groves, Missouri, spoke of their experience with the American Field Service student exchange program:

First of all, it makes you realize that people are basically alike in their attitudes and their emotions. At the same time, it makes you realize that cultures are different; people are brought up with very different backgrounds and environments, and this affects them as people.

Last year I was fortunate because I got to know our German exchange student very well and we both learned to look at things from the other person's point of view, not only politically but basically. He has gone back and is now in charge of the exchange program where he lives. He has told a great many people about America and has changed many misconceptions. So I think this is important in breaking down the barriers between countries. The world we live in today is going a long way toward being unified because of the rapid transportation and instant communication we have. We know so much more about other countries and this affects us much more than it used to, so we can't ignore the other countries and their problems. I think this getting to know people from other nations helps to further good relations.

Dr. J. R. Yerby, the director of guidance at Webster Groves, is in charge of the program. A student council committee on the American Field Service is in constant contact with the guest student, who is an ex-officio member of the student council. The student committee also works with the adult committee, whose responsibility it is to select the American family with whom the visitor will live. A major responsibility of the student council is to raise $1,200 annually to finance the exchange. A spaghetti dinner followed by an appeal for contributions has become a tradition, well supported by the community and consistently successful in providing the needed funds.

Most of the Webster Groves students who have gone overseas with the Americans Abroad program have done so for only a summer, partly because of the expense involved and partly because of fear that a whole year away might interrupt the regular academic program and imperil college admission.

Frequently, the major problem in connection with the AFS or other student exchange program is how to insure that the benefits reach the entire student body, and not just the student leaders, host family, selection committee members, and others immediately involved. This means establishing more direct contact between the visiting student and the American student body and more reporting by the returned American exchange student to his classmates. Many schools plan assembly programs at which foreign students from neighboring schools come together to present a variety of cultural offerings for the benefit of the entire student body.

Exchange students to this country are selected as rigorously as are the American students who are sent abroad. Consequently our students are frequently impressed, if not awed, by the high caliber and maturity of the foreign students, and especially by the fluency in English which some of them possess. Yerby, at Webster Groves, believes the presence of these exceptionally mature foreign students in our schools has a sobering and wholesome effect on our students.

Student Clubs For International Understanding

At Lebanon, Oregon, the 75-member International Relations Club seeks to increase understanding of other cultures through a wide variety of activities. The club lists as its objectives the following seven goals:

1. *Help identify and define the principal issues in current international relations.*

2. *Acquaint students with a wide variety of resource materials on international topics.*

3. *Encourage student initiative in studying and discussing international problems.*

4. *Help students to develop an appreciation for the interpretations that other individuals give to international affairs.*

5. Provide among American students a greater degree of empathy for people living in different parts of the world.

6. Facilitate communication and understanding between people living in different parts of the world.

7. Encourage students to take an active part in promoting better understanding of international affairs among more members of their community.

In 1964, this group scheduled 30 activities, nine of which featured presentations by non-Americans, including one student each from Pakistan, Norway, the Netherlands, and Cuba; one from Ethiopia; four from other African countries. Other activities included a teachers' panel, two college-sponsored symposia, sponsorship of an orphan under the Foster Parents Plan, and an international relations program presented for the Rotary Club. In addition, the students raised funds for the American Field Service program; contributed to CARE; maintained an international relations library; participated in regional and state conferences and a governor's reception on United Nations Day; and handled an AFS banquet, an awards banquet, and an exchange meeting with other clubs.

Jenifer Ziegler, vice-president of the International Relations Club at Lebanon, offered her candid view of the value of the club meetings:

Some of the student panels are excellent and some of them aren't so good. It just depends on the students themselves. . . . We don't expect 100 percent responsiveness. If they just learn one thing about the relations of our country with the rest of the world, if they just learn the importance of citizen participation in international affairs, then it is worthwhile. They're bound to get something out of it. We have certainly learned a lot about Germany, Ethiopia, and Japan. Those are the countries our exchange students come from. One of our girls went to Germany last year, and when she returned she gave us a very good picture of that country.

In another example of increased international understanding, 52 members of a choral group at Seattle's Ingraham High School experienced an intensive, direct exposure to Japanese culture when they traveled to Kobe, Japan.

Several years ago this school had been asked to host a visiting Japanese choral group, the Japanese National Choral Champions, which visited Seattle for a three-day concert tour. At that time, the 40 Japanese students and five adults lived in homes of Ingraham students. Later the invitation came from Kobe asking Ingraham to send a choral group there. Apparently, the students at Ingraham had taken some initiative in inquiring about the possibilities of a return visit and, in effect, soliciting the invitation to visit Japan. The objectives of the trip were to raise the image of American youth abroad, to demonstrate the quality of an American high school choral group, and to take traditional American entertainment, especially folk song and square dance, to Japan. The large Japanese community in Seattle encouraged this trip.

Great pains were taken to prepare the choral group for this experience. The 52 students selected for the trip, who had been highly impressed with the quality of the Japanese choral performance, took without credit an eight-week summer session of three hours a day of rehearsal to try to do as well. They also enrolled in the school's regular choral course and rehearsed two hours daily during the entire year prior to the visit to Japan, again without credit, to prepare for a superlative performance.

Preparation for the trip included orientation conducted by Miss Suguru, a Japanese counselor at Ingraham High School who spent several months explaining forms of Japanese culture to the 52 students. The students learned a basic vocabulary of dozens of polite phrases for every occasion, including the commonly used expressions that would be found in a commercial phrase book as well as courtesy phrases used among family members in Japan. They were taught several Japanese songs and the Japanese words to a number of western songs, including some of Stephen Foster's, which seem to be very popular in Japan. Miss Suguru later proudly reported that Japanese oldsters said, "Your youngsters are more polite than ours and your students sing the Japanese songs better than our own students."

Students in the choral group undoubtedly profited, especially in learning to appreciate Japanese culture. The project also led to intense interest in Japan by other students in the school and wider horizons for them and their parents. The following summer, two Ingraham students went to a student leadership conference in Kobe and six Japanese students were scheduled to make a return visit. When Governor Kanai of Hyogo province visited the United States, he came to Ingraham High School and spoke to the assembly with Miss Suguru serving as interpreter. Mr. Takiyama, principal of the Kobe school, now sends many Japanese visitors to the United States to visit the Ingraham High School, thus continuing the international contacts begun when a Japanese choral group visited this country and the Ingraham chorus returned the visit. Ingraham High School has become a focal point of continuing exchange between the Kobe area and the Seattle area.

It was not easy to raise the $65,000 necessary to finance the trip of the chorus to Japan. The parents of the 52 students agreed that each should pay $450, which would cover about one-third of the total cost. Another third was raised by donations solicited by the sponsors, and the final third by various student projects.

Although financial restrictions limit opporunities for foreign travel for high school students, this promising practice is spreading. Inspired by the trip of the Ingraham High School chorus to Japan, for example, another Seattle high school has completed plans to send a choir and band on a privately financed trip to England. Similarly, a 28-voice choir from the Germantown Friends School has toured Europe on a number of occasions; on a recent trip it gave concerts in France, England, Germany, Switzerland, and Denmark. Increased interest in foreign travel by students, heightened support, both moral and financial from many parents, and the lure of attractive group travel rates may produce a substantial increase in this kind of contact by students with the culture of other lands.

Other secondary school student groups, mostly from independent schools, have sought inter-cultural understanding through trips to Mexico and to Europe. Among the most impressive examples are the student field trips to Mexico and to Indian reservations by the Verde Valley School in Arizona. The students travel to Mexico in specially constructed buses, complete with electrical power, drinking water, food supplies, and camping gear. They camp by the road each night and, once there, divide into groups to live with Mexican families for eight days. On trips to an Indian reservation, some students are guests of Indian families and others are assigned in pairs to a Navaho Boarding school or to a U. S. Public Health Hospital on a reservation.

A Verde Valley student gains a new friend.

Hamilton Warren, founder of the Verde Valley School, described an incident which occurred in placing students in an Indian home. On one trip, two pairs of boys were assigned to stay in Indian hogans. When one pair reached the first Navaho hogan, no one came out to greet them. The teachers went back to check the next day and found the students in a hogan of their own, and with nothing to eat. The students explained that the family with whom they were to live had not invited them to join them at meals. For some reason, no one had told the students that the Navaho does not give invitations to meals; the prospective guest simply goes. After the students acquired this information and acted upon it, everything went smoothly.

The students live with the Indian families and help them construct and plaster hogans, plant fields, and perform other tasks. They have worked much harder than the Indians expected. In so doing, these young people developed tremendous pride in their own accomplishments and also gained considerable respect from the Indians. They are also acquiring awareness of the diversity and yet unity of all peoples.

**Sister Schools And
Other Exchange Programs**

Another device for promoting intercultural exchange between students is the so-called sister school or school affiliation. Ingraham High School, like 39 others in the state of Washington, has adopted a Japanese sister school. A scrapbook received from Fukiai High School was circulated in Ingraham homerooms and placed in a corridor display. Ingraham has sent copies of its school paper and several volumes of American history and poetry to the Japanese school, and students from both schools enjoy a lively pen-pal correspondence. A calligraphic kakemono was sent to Ingraham by Fukiai with a translation, and Ingraham High School has sent student mathematics papers to the Japanese school as well as drawings and paintings.

The affiliation of the Germantown Friends School with a sister school in Falaise, France, has continued uninterruptedly ever since shortly after the Nazi occupation ended in November 1944. At that time, the Religious Society of Friends offered to sponsor the rebuilding of the school in Falaise. The offer was accepted and the affiliation has grown. Letters and gifts are exchanged regularly between students of the two schools. Germantown students send some of their French papers to

Falaise students for correction, and Falaise students send their advanced English compositions to Germantown for criticism. There is also an annual exchange of a student and an occasional exchange of faculty members.

When the project team arrived at the Germantown Friends School, the students were just going into an assembly to be addressed by Mr. Machary, a teacher from the French sister school who had been visiting for three weeks. The extended and spontaneous applause by students at the end of Mr. Machary's talk demonstrated the appreciation that has developed in these students for their sister school in France and for this informal ambassador.

Similar affiliation is being developed with a school in Rhodesia, which was visited by one of the Germantown Friends faculty members last summer on a mission for the American Friends Service Committee. Two teachers from Rhodesia, one an art teacher and the other a history teacher, later came to Germantown Friends School for three months. The junior high school still exchanges art with the Rhodesian school.

Another intercultural opportunity, provided by the Germantown Friends School, is an annual summer mission of six students on a work-camp experience to Britain. Because only six students may go in any one year, careful selection is made by a faculty-student committee from among those who apply. The cost per student is $850 but lack of funds is not a barrier, because the school wants to send its most deserving students and those who might profit most from the experience. Entering 11th-graders are sent so that they may return to share their experiences with fellow students for at least a year.

Another kind of exchange has been provided at the Middlesex Junior High School in Darien, Connecticut, by geography teacher Coleman Alexa, who plans an annual Pupils' Geography Project. Recently he designed a cultural exchange with the pupils of the Agordat Boys' School in Agordat, Eritrea, Ethiopia, with the cooperation of one of his former pupils, now a Peace Corps teacher in Eritrea. The 9th-grade Darien students asked the Peace Corps teacher what would be most useful to further his work and help give his Ethiopian students a better education. The Peace Corpsman requested books, especially the textbook *English Today*, and the students in Darien then provided 100 copies of this book. Each student earned and contributed $1.50.

A goal of this project was to introduce students to the concept of global interdependence. Alexa emphasized that people working in different environments contribute different products, commodities, and cultures to the total life of mankind and each contribution has its value.

In addition, the students gained specific geographical knowledge in a meaningful setting. The correspondence they carried on with the Peace Corps headquarters in Eritrea, the Ethiopian Mission to the United Nations, and the various air lines to arrange for shipment of the books involved learning geography through action. The students also prepared a booklet, that was shipped with the textbooks, which described their own town and school. Further cultural exchange took place when the First Secretary of the Ethiopian Mission to the United Nations visited the school and talked with the students. An unexpected satisfaction occurred when, in the course of negotiations for the purchase of the textbooks, a publishing executive became interested in the project and offered to donate additional volumes for an Ethiopian school library.

"International Eating" Students in a world history class in Sarasota, Florida, have been encouraged to broaden their cultural horizons by joining a voluntary experiment in "international eating." This program was planned by the teacher, Sister William Marie, in the hope that it will lead to increased respect for what is "different"—and possibly even enjoyment and appreciation of it—and greater willingness to try the unknown. She explained:

Sarasota has quite a variety of restaurants and it has not been difficult to plan the meals. I call the restaurant, speak to the manager, and explain what it's all about. To date all have been willing to offer a student rate. We plan a typical menu and each student is served the same thing. The restaurants get into the feel of it fast and offer all the extras they can to make the atmosphere authentic. For example, we ate our sweet-sour pork with chopsticks. Next week we are going to an Italian restaurant. Of the 35 students in the class, from 22 to 28 attend each dinner, along with two or three parents who asked if they could join us.

On the other side of the continent, at San Carlos, California, 120 adults and 65 students come to high school one evening to enjoy a

Russian dinner prepared by student members of the Russian Club. About 40 of the 60 members of this club are studying the Russian language with its sponsor, instructor Don Richardson. Ninety students in the school are enrolled in Russian language, two sections in beginning Russian and one each in second, third, and fourth years. Richardson feels that a serious study of the language leaves no time for becoming acquainted with the culture, so this he reserves for the club.

The Russian dinner has become an annual event, attended by club members and their parents. Some girls and a few boys interested in the art of cookery provide an authentic menu cooked in Russian style. The dinner includes stroganoff, borscht—everything except vodka—and it creates an atmosphere that encourages talk about the Soviet Union.

In 1964, a member of the club presented a program of Russian piano selections and talked on trends in Russian musical composition. Another member gave an excellent analysis of some Russian short stories and a third delivered a talk on the function of the artist in Soviet society. A knowledgeable military man talked to the club about military aspects of the Soviet Union's participation in World War II, and a college instructor was scheduled to lecture on Sino-Soviet tensions.

Richardson is confident that the activities of this club have contributed to the improved attitude in the school and the community about the study of the Russian language. Before the club started, Richardson and his students were sometimes regarded with something akin to suspicion. Today, Russian is accepted as an important language and has an established place in the curriculum; and the club, the teacher believes, has helped the community to become more sophisticated about the Soviet Union.

**Promoting Commitment
To International Peace**

A few schools provide learning experiences aimed directly at studying the problem of peace through international cooperation. For example, the Maine Township, South, High School in Illinois received a Leadership and World Society (LAWS) grant for its Social Studies Forum to enrich the curriculum with material on the topic, "Dispute Settlement in the American Democratic Framework." The proposal was to "develop the idea of national sovereignty and world peace through a specific analysis of the American governmental framework and the impact of world problems on it." A major attraction of the program was the participation of university professors who presented and discussed specialized areas. The result was an elective fourth-year course with an abundance of speakers, telelectures, and forum meetings from which many students benefited.

Other schools devote attention to the dilemmas of peace in their study of the United Nations, both in government classes and in international relations clubs. These efforts are frequently supplemented and reinforced by regional UN conferences sponsored by groups such as the World Affairs Council. Some of the area conferences are entirely school-administered, without the co-sponsorship of any outside agency. Examples are the High School UNESCO Conference of Kansas City and the High School Council for the United Nations in New York City. In addition to sponsoring city-wide or area-wide conferences, forums, and model UN meetings, these groups usually provide bibliographies, newsletters, and other literature.

Schools which launch these efforts do not presume, as some impatient critics assert, that students will find solutions to problems that have baffled mankind throughout history. They are convinced, however, that a serious introduction to problems of war and peace can establish important attitudes in students' minds, especially the attitude that persistent social and political problems are amenable to thoughtful study and perhaps eventually to rational solution.

GOAL 9: THE CREATIVE ARTS AND HUMANISTIC AWARENESS

Many high schools have always offered elective courses in music, drama, drawing, painting, and a variety of crafts with a dual objective of providing professional instruction and encouragement for students who will seek careers in the arts; and offering organized exposure to the arts for other students whose talents are more modest but who will benefit from a constructive hobby or avocational interest. To these dual objectives now is added a third.

Some schools today are deliberately giving to some of their arts programs what can be identified as a humanities emphasis. This emphasis transforms the music or painting class from an exercise in crafts-manship to an experience in relating observation and interpretation to basic human emotions and to the expression of those emotions through the arts of many cultures down through the ages. Excellence of performance or technique by students is not slighted; it is made meaningful by being related to the superlative artistic expressions of others—native and foreign, contemporary and past—that provide a powerful link with the rest of humanity.

At Labette County Community High School in Altamont, Kansas, students have unusually ample opportunities to enrich their lives through learning to play a musical instrument. Pressures for professionalism are minimal, and the school loans practice instruments to students and has several practice rooms as well as 14 pianos and an organ.

Another imaginative approach to music is found in the Contemporary Music Project of the Music Educator's Conference. This 10-year project, financed by the Ford Foundation, places selected young composers in public secondary schools for a year in residence to compose music suitable for performance by school musical organizations. More than 70 different school systems have benefited by having a composer in residence, bringing new vitality to the musical life of the community and of the school.

At the Fieldston School in New York City, national and international understanding are strengthened through songs sung during all-school assemblies, according to John Anthony Scott.[1]

One history assembly is given each year at this high school. It lasts for approximately an hour, and deals with specific aspects of American history. Among the assembly topics have been the Civil War, the New Deal, the Negro people, Irish immigration, and whaling. A narration gives the outline of the story, and dramatic episodes and appropriate songs are also used.

All history students in the junior and senior year are entitled to take part in the assembly, which from beginning to end is entirely voluntary and extra-curricular. Each year the total number of participants has

---

[1] Mr. Scott describes the music assembly in his article, "Folksong and the Schools," in *Teaching and Learning*, 1965.

been about 110, a majority of all students studying history during the year. They sing in the chorus or take parts as narrators, soloists, or instrumentalists. Talent is also in demand for assistance with posters and sets, lighting, staging, and directing.

The purpose of the assemblies is not to "cover" a subject, but to provide, through a dramatic enactment, an opportunity for students to convey an aspect of history in a way that will arouse the curiosity and interest of others. "An awesome chemical change seems to occur when you put people on bare boards and have them act and sing out an historical drama," says Scott.

Concerning the availability of folksong and folklore material for the teacher who wishes to adopt this approach, Scott said, "Much can be contributed by the joint efforts of the school library and the music department. The possibility of building up reserves of such material is very great, notwithstanding the fact that the systematic recording and analysis of historical song is only just beginning. There is a fine range of excellent songbooks and many useful commercial recordings."

At Fairmont Heights High School, in Maryland, students have developed a strong interest in drama. Every year many groups from the school travel to nearby Washington and a few go to New York to see plays. These students are making a serious effort to understand theatre, as is shown by the number of students who go to see a play a second time to catch something they missed at first. Some students seek interviews with leading actors and actresses to inquire about the deeper meaning of a scene or an act.

The outstanding feature of dramatic presentations at the Oakland Technical High School in Oakland, California, is the freedom engendered by a policy that imposes no limitations—and thus no stereotypes—in the plays selected for presentation or the actors selected for roles. Plays such as Ionesco's *Rhinoceros* have been produced, as well as *Macbeth* with a modern jazz accompaniment and a Negro girl as Lady Macbeth. Thomas Wayne, in charge of dramatic productions, gives even his least experienced actors some opportunity to perform.

Oakland Technical School in Oakland, California, produces a number of plays under Thomas Wayne, director of drama. Shown at right is a scene from Oakland Technical High School's 1965 production of Macbeth.

The Visual Arts

Cartooning is an art form too seldom used in the classroom. At Glastonbury High School in Connecticut, however, art teacher Robert Manning uses it frequently, not only to stimulate interest in art and develop students' talents but also to increase their political awareness. "In no other place," says Mr. Manning, "do we discover more about politics and political symbols than in cartoons."

During the 1964 Presidential election, Mr. Manning conducted a school-wide contest, with 15 prizes for the most effective cartoons on the Presidential campaign and its issues. The political cartoonist for a leading daily newspaper came to the school to talk to the students about the role of the cartoonist in a democratic society and selected winners from 300 entrants.

In the same school, the cultural arts committee, essentially a fundraising group, is dedicated to promoting the arts. With $1,300 per year raised through the efforts of the committee in selling individual and class photographs to students, the school stimulates artistic activities. It brings painters to assembly programs to discuss art; it also rents films, and has produced an experimental film using a surrealistic approach. This 20-minute color film, titled *Apparitions*, was produced in three months at the remarkably low cost of $85. Twenty students, under the direction of Manning and with the assistance of a professional cinematographer, were involved in the production.

Glastonbury High School also conducts an annual Cultural Arts Night. The program for 1964, for example, included a one-act play written and produced by students, choral singing, and the experimental film *Apparitions*. Following the program, the audience went to the gymnasium to view an exhibit of student work in the visual arts.

Other Applications Of The Arts

The five-man art department at Maine Township South, in Park Ridge, Illinois, is convinced that an active relationship should exist between art instruction and the aesthetic environment of the school. At the time of the project team's visit, students were involved in three beautification projects for the school library:

1. A circular mural for the large kiosk in the library. The design will be chosen by a competition among Art IV students.

2. Another mural for the library, to be executed in foam glass, portraying a boy and a girl reading.

3. A brass hawk, symbol of the school, to be done in thin brass.

Joseph Stilip, head of the art department, believes it is important to take art from the studio into every part of the school. He feels that art, like any other school subject, makes its fullest contribution to civic education when it has some visible relationship to areas and activities beyond classroom boundaries.

The faculty at Germantown Friends School sees evidence of substantially increased awareness of art since 1962, when they introduced an art-oriented humanities course. This voluntary non-credit exposure to music appreciation, art appreciation, and studio work enrolled half of the senior class for regular attendance and another fourth for periodic participation. The testimony concerning the effects of the course came from Miss Mary Brewer, a teacher who regularly accompanies the choral group on its European concert tours. In 1956, she said, before this course was offered, the touring students showed little or no interest in the art treasures of the European cities they visited. In 1962, the year the course was begun, the group displayed some interest, although it still included a number of students who were relatively apathetic. By 1965, however, all members of the choir were so genuinely involved that only reluctantly would they leave the museums and cathedrals.

The Detroit Children's Museum is a significant extension of the learning environment of the Detroit Public Schools, offering experiences in areas ranging from science and social studies to music and painting. This unusual resource, which is supported solely by the Board of Education, is one of the first children's museum in the United States and owns the largest lending collection of its kind in the nation. It serves elementary, secondary, and college students, but a particularly important part of the work of its five-man staff is the production of puzzles, games, and other attractive learning materials for elementary school children.

According to Miss Beatrice Parsons, director, the Children's Museum contributes to civic education by helping students understand the customs and beliefs of other people and by tracing these customs and beliefs as they fit into our own cultural pattern. Through exhibits, the Museum makes students aware of how natural resources and contributions of various peoples have enriched life today. It also provides a place where children of different ethnic and economic backgrounds may meet —perhaps the only such opportunity they have. And, finally, the Museum's planetarium helps students understand the universe and the earth's relation to it.

Another Detroit school program provides supplemental Saturday morning art classes for talented students from all the city high schools. For 22 weekly sessions, these students are given the opportunity to draw and paint in various city galleries. The classes, organized through the cooperation of the Detroit Institute of Art with the Board of Education, are taught by high school art teachers, and special exhibits of student art work are occasionally placed on public display at the Detroit Institute of Art, to give recognition to talented students.

GOAL 10: A COMPASSIONATE CITIZENRY

Hospital Volunteers

At West Leyden High School in Illinois, 100 student members of Mental Health Organization (MHO) visit the Chicago State Hospital to bring companionship to human beings who desperately need it. The student volunteers are given a brief orientation and then make regular trips to the hospital. They talk to the patients, play chess or cards with them, dance or give skits, and serve coffee and cookies.

MHO, which was organized by Malcolm Berd, a teacher, is regarded by its members as the most significant activity at West Leyden High School. MHO service allows students to learn about the problems of the mentally ill, and also something about themselves, about their capacity for compassion, for tolerance, and for understanding. The teachers recognize the value of such experience and agree that youngsters learn more in MHO about the needs and life of their fellow man than they do in hours of classroom work.

Even students who are themselves slightly unstable profit by the experience; in helping others less fortunate, they gain assurance; in watching others get help, they learn that such help is available. According to Berd, MHO service forces such youngsters to face a reality of life at a time when, seemingly, they would prefer to look the other way. It may stimulate such students to seek the counseling they need.

The MHO annual publication, titled *What is Man?*, contains students' work in prose, poetry, drawing, and photography. Recently, one student wrote: "Man is a conformist. To some degree, this is necessary. When carried too far, it is harmful. When conformity becomes his way of life, man loses his identity. He becomes only a grain of sand on the beach of society. Individuality is necessary lest he lose his self-respect."

MHO, like many other high school service groups, sometimes has difficulty recruiting boys, not only because many boys consider this kind of activity unmasculine but also because they have already committed their time and interest to athletics and other activities. Some persons would prefer MHO to be more formally structured in order to provide instruction in the mental health field and possibly stimulate consideration of this field as a career. Such redesigning of the club, however, could result in switching the emphasis from the personal involvement and spirit of service which have characterized the hospital visits.

School and hospital administrators have the highest praise for this program, which brings students into an elemental relationship with others, demands a giving of self in the relationship, and later encourages a thoughtful expression of feeling as a result of the experience.

Week-end Work Camps   In the Philadelphia area, as in several other parts of the nation, students take their sleeping bags and go for week-end camping trips—not to the green countryside but to the gray inner city. The experience includes a full day of physical work in a home of an underprivileged family, cleaning, painting, repairing, and doing something to improve the family's way of life. The students also attend a session of the Magistrate's Court and a service in the neighborhood church.

These students are aware that the major value of the experience is gaining knowledge of how others live and learning to understand people whose backgrounds are very different from their own. Learning to communicate with people having different cultural values and to work with them rather than simply for them are the objectives. Students are expected to work with the householders. If the latter are reluctant, the students try to encourage them to participate in the work. One boy, who admitted that his team's members had worked by themselves because the hosts were old and semi-incapacitated, nevertheless understood that the real value of the work was coming to know the family. The program's purpose may be described as an attempt to narrow the gulf between privileged and under-privileged through mutual understanding.

The young people involved include about one-third of the senior high students, which means that over the three-year period nearly every student goes on at least one week-end camping trip.

This program is operated by the Germantown Community Council, formed by eight private schools and one public school to help them do what each cannot do alone in the way of community service. This inter-school agency has a faculty advisor from each of the nine schools. There are monthly meetings, a talent show, an annual dinner, and scheduled tours of the United Fund Agencies, as well as inter-school visits. For the latter, one day is set aside by each school to receive students from other schools, in order to promote better understanding between public and private schools.

The overall purpose of the Community Council and the work-camp program is to acquaint youngsters with the total community. In much the same way that a good teacher in an academic course may require the students to have contact with primary source material in his subject, the community project requires that students have first-hand contact in their community setting.

Fund-Raising And Collections

The difference between a nagging, high-pressure appeal for everyone to contribute to a charitable drive and a spontaneous, student-directed collection that simply goes ahead with a project because it seems worth doing also marks the difference between conformity and compassion. A genuine concern for others seems to characterize the SHARE Program at Miami Beach High School. It appears to be as free of impersonal "collection" and as full of the spirit of giving as any large-scale campaign is likely to be. Students say of SHARE, "It's a great program because the students have the feeling that they are doing something worthwhile for the community. It gives the community a favorable picture of the school. The students like it very much."

The SHARE Program is an annual effort to have students share their material well-being at Christmas with the needy. The overwhelming majority of the students are of the Jewish faith. That people of one faith should contribute to the true spirit of the highest religious holiday of another constitutes an especially valuable element of the program.

The annual money collection for SHARE conducted in the homerooms produces more than $5,000. Student council members purchase $4,000 worth of toys from a wholesale house and establish a school store from which the homerooms purchase toys for their contribution. Some funds are saved by the homerooms for purchasing food. The campaign is climaxed by a ceremonial program in which each homeroom brings its toys to the stage of the Municipal Auditorium. The art and music departments cooperate in bringing dignity and importance to the season and the gifts.

The same school demonstrates its will to promote the spirit of service and interpersonal concern in a dozen other programs. These include *Operation Amigo,* in which visiting students from South America stay with families in the community, and *Operation Gateway,* which offers miscellaneous social services to exchange students on their way to or from their home school. The school also works with the American Field Service, which receives exchange students from other countries; the Sunshine State Tennis Championships, in which 40 countries are represented; and Books for Freedom, which in 1965 collected and sent 40,000 books to South America.

Collection drives for books or for money, food, or clothes for the needy of a community, for flood victims, war victims, or the poverty-stricken of Asia and Africa, are so numerous and for the most part so similar that no substantial purpose would be served in describing or enumerating them all. A few of these outstanding school drives are included here.

A 9th-grade geography class in the Middlesex Junior High School in Darien, Connecticut, taught by Coleman J. Alexa, collected clothes for the needy in Appalachia. This project had the virtue of involving students in a variety of supplementary activities: recording on tape requests to other groups; planning an assembly at which a priest aroused the enthusiastic support of the whole student body for the collection drive; and packing the 2,900 pounds of clothing collected into 32 cases for shipment. Albert Benson, principal of the school, said, "The greatest value was in helping the students to understand that there is another part of the world, really many different worlds, many ways of living. The students were exposed to a real problem and assumed responsibility for making a contribution."

The Welfare Drive at Mather Junior High School in Darien is organized with parental cooperation. The school sends letters to the parents explaining the drive and recommending that on a stated Saturday, designated as Junior Work Day, youngsters be paid for performing enough chores to fulfill their pledges to the Welfare Drive. As part of the preparation for this drive, all 8th-grade students compete to produce the most convincing themes related to the Welfare Drive.

One of many "special" drives was conducted by the De La Salle High School in New Orleans to provide 25 cases of soap to be sent to Viet-

Fund-raising at Cleveland's Lincoln High School.

nam. This drive was in response to a plea by an alumnus stationed in Vietnam, who asked for donations of soap to help alleviate the boils, infections, and abscesses that plague the children there.

A noteworthy example of student collections is the United Fund Drive in Kansas City, where for the last several years one of the leading contributors has been the Lincoln High School, located in a culturally deprived and economically depressed area. Here, principal Harry Harwel and fund director Archie Weaver are determined that students living in a neighborhood accustomed to receiving charity should learn very early the importance of carrying their share of the load whenever possible.

Human Relations Clubs

In an assembly program at DeWitt Clinton High School in New York City, a slide was projected on the screen, depicting different nationalities and races. At a given signal a student, who was on the stage with his back to the picture, turned and viewed the picture for exactly five seconds. He was then asked to describe briefly what he had seen to one of six boys who had not been permitted to view the picture. Each of the six, in turn, passed the description along orally to the next one. By the time the last of the six described the scene, inaccuracies and discrepancies were apparent, and the final description was obviously inaccurate and misleading. Part of the distortion resulted from the unconscious introduction by the narrators of their own stereotyped images. With this as a starter, the school's human relations assembly proceeded with student presentations on topics such as "causes of prejudice" and "stereotyped attitudes."

This program was presented as one of many projects of the Human Relations Club at DeWitt Clinton. Other activities include an annual toy drive for the benefit of a local hospital and the Kennedy Foundling Home; a collection drive for books to be distributed through CORE to underprivileged children in Mississippi; and participation in the Panel of Americans, which goes from school to school to familiarize students with the problems resulting from prejudice and discrimination.

A comparable group at East High School in Cleveland calls itself the Junior Volunteers. In 1965, 55 students offered their services and averaged two hours per week of contributed time. Each of the 55 was interviewed by the director of the Volunteer Bureau of the Welfare Department, and 30 were accepted and assigned to the service most appropriate to their talents. Some worked in a settlement house in charge of 8-year old children, some served as clerks, and some as general aides in the city hospital. The Junior Volunteers is especially popular with girls who are contemplating careers in social service work or nursing.

Many schools now operate human relations clubs with similar programs of volunteer work. A wide variety of other service clubs, under a multitude of names, also offer opportunities for volunteer service to the unfortunate and underprivileged. The Key Club at the DeWitt Clinton High School, which can serve as an illustration, concentrates on providing equipment for the nearby Veterans' Hospital, to which it has already donated a color television set, a pool table, and an electrocardiograph. It has also provided the funds for two Seeing Eye dogs for the Sight Foundation, substantial amounts of clothing for the Save the Children Federation, and books for collections to be shipped overseas. Perhaps even more important to the future citizenship of these boys have been the hours they have spent reading to blind patients in the Veterans' Hospital.

Tutoring

A different but equally service-centered program at DeWitt Clinton takes place in the school cafeteria at the close of the regular school day and in the homes of students on Saturdays, when academically advanced 9th-graders tutor academically deficient 7th-graders, usually from economically and culturally deprived backgrounds. James Campbell, in charge of the program, believes that the 30 tutors and their 60 charges have all benefited greatly. The most important outcome was that the children from underprivileged homes were exposed to books and ideas and to other young people who liked books and ideas, in a new and meaningful way. Such stimulation often is lacking in the home and difficult to provide in the classroom.

This program operates with minor variations at hundreds of high schools across the country. In one such project, at Darien, Connecticut, the tutoring program recently included 12 junior high school girls who were driven weekly by their parents to nearby Norwalk, where they tutored a group of young Puerto Rican girls, thus combining service with an intercultural experience.

At the Germantown Friends School, three separate student-tutoring programs are in operation. Two afternoons a week students go to a nearby settlement house where they help younger children in regular studies. A second volunteer group works on Saturday mornings at a Baptist Church under the auspices of the Germantown civil rights committee described earlier in this chapter. A third group goes regularly to the neighborhood elementary school to assist in the kindergarten and the lower grades with games and physical education. As a supplement to this, many school athletes organize teams of elementary school pupils and become very proud and very fond of their young charges.

GOAL 11: DEVELOPMENT AND APPLICATION OF DEMOCRATIC PRINCIPLES

In a sense, the eleventh goal of civic education identified in this report —fostering principles consistent with our democratic heritage and the application of these principles in daily life—is also implicit in each of the other ten goals.

The three illustrations that follow are of schools that appear to provide integrated preparation for citizenship, each keyed to different ob-

jectives. The first example is a public high school in Virginia with emphasis on quality performance, based on pride in the traditions of the school and the nation. The second example is a private school in Arizona whose objective of understanding self and fellow man is built on the study of anthropology and the experience of living with people of differing cultures. The third illustration of concern for developing the student's commitment to democratic values and his application of these principles to daily life is found in the school system of Detroit. The distinguishing feature of these three illustrations is that the dominant objective is a persistent quest for a civic ideal, shared by the entire staff and caught to some degree by the entire student body.

Tradition And Order A unique aspect of the tone of civic education at John Marshall High School in Richmond is the fact that it is partly based on the existence of a military cadet corps, an institution seldom applauded in a democratic public school system.

It is generally assumed that there can be little democracy in military life. In this school, in a state where racial adjustment still poses substantial problems, one observes Negro officers giving orders to white and Negro cadets, and white and Negro cadets showing apparent goodwill and comradeship. It appeared that the military corps was in the vanguard of education for basic human acceptance in John Marshall High School.

The Corps has existed in this school for 50 years. Although only one-fifth of the boys in the school are enrolled in it, it seems to be as highly respected by many non-members as by the members. Of the boys who enroll for the first two years of military corps, 95 percent continue for the final two years. The Corps contributes to the entire school, with its emphasis on pride, precision, neatness, and respect for authority and tradition.

The commandant of the Corps, Lt. Col. William E. McLain, and the principal of the school, Fred B. Dixon, agree that the purpose of the Corps "should not be to train soldiers, but to educate citizens in the qualities that will make them useful to their peacetime community as well as to their wartime country."

The influence of the Corps on high civic performance is based on several factors: (1) its dedication to the traditionally respected virtues of obedience, courtesy, respect, and neatness; (2) its many public services, such as ushering at public functions and providing color guards at civic programs, marching units for parades, and buglers for funerals; and (3) the high visibility and emotional appeal of the military symbols, the uniform, flag, salute, bugle calls, and attendant ritual of the Cadet Corps.

Membership in the Corps serves as an alternative to physical education and provides a full program of physical development. Physical and health education is second only to leadership, drill, and exercise of command in the amount of time devoted to it.

The sense of pride and tradition prompted by the military corps at John Marshall is manifest in many ways. Portraits of John Marshall, Robert E. Lee, Woodrow Wilson, and Walter Reed adorn the walls of the front lobby and likenesses of other illustrious Americans hang on the walls in corridors and classrooms. Special display cases throughout the school are filled with facsimile copies of historical documents, maps, and artifacts. In the social studies office stands an elaborate stone and bronze dais containing copies of the Declaration of Independence and the Constitution of the United States displayed in a manner to stress their dignity. Almost every student in the school has signed a volunteer honor code. Several pamphlets with titles such as "Leadership," "Traditions," and "Political Thinking," have been prepared by the administration for the students.

To some, the formalism and the stress on tradition in this school might seem excessive. Some might say that the punctiliousness and uniformity, coupled with the military air, are bound to work against freedom and a spirit of equality. They might insist that the formalism tends to invade the intellectual sphere and operates against creativity. These persons might reject an assignment such as memorizing the Preamble to the Declaration or the Constitution, preferring instead a discussion or an interpretation or application of the ideas in the Preamble. A John Marshall teacher might respond by asking how any student can intelligently analyze or apply a statement with which he is not thoroughly familiar. Let students learn the basic message first, they would say, and then attempt to analyze, discuss, or criticize it.

**Moral Commitment
To Humanity**

In the Arizona desert, 2,500 miles west of Richmond, is a school whose approach seems to contrast sharply with the one stressed at John Marshall. Here, instead of addressing their teachers as "sir" and "ma'am," students call their teachers by their first names. This small private school, with fewer than one-tenth the number of students at John Marshall, has had a far shorter span of school history during which to build up its institutional traditions. Yet, dating from 18 years ago, when the school was opened by Hamilton Warren, it has maintained a distinct and influential school tone.

Verde Valley is a coeducational, college preparatory school, founded to promote responsible citizenship and to further understanding among people of different cultural, racial, religious, and economic backgrounds. Its unique program includes field trips to Mexico and to Indian reservations as well as a required course in general anthropology.

The school believes in giving students as much responsibility as they can carry; it further believes that an important criterion of responsible and worthwhile student government is the degree of enthusiasm with which the elected student representatives actively further the basic principles of the school.

Zdenek Salzmann, the headmaster, is a teacher of anthropology who makes a strong case for the role of anthropology in the development of character—which he regards as the primary requirement of good citizenship. He expressed to the project team his belief that respect for man is the basis of a number of desirable personal qualities and added that anthropology potentially can play an important role:

To develop character by teaching respect for man an anthropology course must go far beyond the mere recital of the likenesses and differences among men. It must be deliberately fashioned to strengthen the intellectual and moral foundations of our students—foundations which they must have if they are to become enlightened citizens of a country designed to play a crucially important role in the affairs of the world.

His argument for the importance of anthropology to civic education continues:

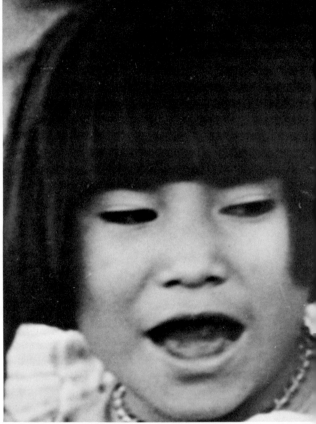

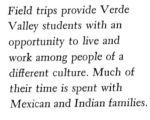

Field trips provide Verde Valley students with an opportunity to live and work among people of a different culture. Much of their time is spent with Mexican and Indian families.

We are dealing with a startling paradox in contemporary American education. For example, we see to it that our students understand thoroughly the nature of combustion and the scientific principles underlying the action of fire extinguishers. But why should we then expect them to overcome whatever racial prejudices they have acquired if we do not carefully examine with them the cultural nature of prejudice and expose them to modern scientific findings concerning the nature of race and racial differences?

Salzmann objects to the trend towards increased technical specialization among high school students, especially when such specialization renders it impossible to provide students with courses such as anthropology. He points out that few secondary school students are exposed to anthropological concepts. The Verde Valley anthropology course is unique not only because it brings anthropology to the high-school level, but also because it has as its goal the same objectives that the entire school emphasizes—to promote a better understanding of man.

About one-fifth of the course is spent in discussing the concept of race, and that part is followed by a consideration of language, especially of the relationship of vocabulary to the cultural world of its users. More than half of the course concerns cultural anthropology, an essential area, as Clyde Kluckhohn reminds us, because "anthropology holds up a great mirror to man and lets him look at himself in his infinite variety."

In addition to the formal course in anthropology, the school sponsors several activities, required for the entire student body, which effectively supplement the classroom teaching. On Sunday nights, students are made familiar with the major religions of the world. This program either brings in speakers representing various faiths or draws on faculty contributions. Among the topics covered in one semester were Hinduism, the Bahá'i Faith, Judaism, Quakers, Buddhism, the Bible, science and religion, religion and art, the Navaho religion, and others. An attempt is made to provide the students with authoritative information on these subjects. Following the formal presentation, the assembly is adjourned for discussion. The school feels that this sort of exposure to religion should not weaken one's religious beliefs, but should on the contrary strengthen personal religious principles by generating tolerance and respect for the faith of others.

On Wednesday nights, the so-called International Hour program is presented. At least once a month, this program features foreign and occasionally American films noted not only for their thought-provoking themes but for their outstanding aesthetic values as well (e.g., "The Last Bridge," "The Forgotten Village," "The Maya Through the Ages," "Ordet," and "La Strada"). Speakers are scheduled on subjects of current world importance or of general anthropological interest. The function of this program is to acquaint the students with other cultures in a compelling fashion.

Finally, there are the school's annual field trips to Mexico and the Indian reservations. The former takes half of the student body into Mexico for three weeks of study and work. Students are divided into small groups to become acquainted with aspects of Mexican culture such as family life, village or town life, and archaeology. During other trips students live with Zuñi, Navaho, and Hopi families, help in reservation schools or hospitals, or study the relationship of the Federal government to the Indian.

Student evaluations of the program are uniformly thoughtful. One student wrote:

The field trips had the obvious effect of making me feel at home in Mexico and on the reservations and I have been back to both since, always with the feeling that I was returning to places which I knew and understood. That is really the long term effect of the trips, the understanding of the existence of life in different ways or in different terms from middle class Americans. This is a fact perfectly obvious to the intellect. But I think it has to be lived to be known and at their best the field trips allowed us to come pretty close to living it. With the background of field trips, the romanticism is gone. But identification, which is to me the basis of understanding, is there. It is this quality of identification which, incidentally, I find incredibly absent in white Americans in their dealings with and thinking about the Negro situation in this country. Perhaps the solution is to send the whole country on field trips.

Another student said:

You have to know yourself in order to know other people. Verde Valley helps the students to know themselves better. This whole field *trip we are talking about is a lesson in living together. So is the life in the dormitory. We have to learn how to conduct our own lives within the bounds of the few rules that we have. We have a great amount of freedom.*

Another girl added, "Our own communities scare me. Verde Valley life is so ideal. All sorts of people here come to think pretty much alike, but in any case I don't intend to be buried in some suburb going to bridge parties and giving teas. I expect to bring up my children in Verde Valley ideals."

This school recognizes citizenship education as a primary goal, to which college admissions and other practical goals are subordinated. Verde Valley School helps its students to develop principles and habits of daily action consistent with the highest ideals of our heritage.

The high quality of Verde Valley's program may reflect in part the selective admissions policy, impossible in a public school, which creates a student body for whom this program is uniquely appropriate. This fact, however, in no way reduces the value of the program for these students, nor does it eliminate the possibility that other schools can borrow adaptable features.

A City-wide Concern For Civic Education

The schools of Detroit should be mentioned along with John Marshall and Verde Valley as a very different example of a successful effort to permeate an entire school system with an overriding concern for civic education. The schools of Detroit, like John Marshall and Verde Valley, do not limit responsibility for civic education to a civics class or even to the social studies department. The entire school is involved.

Because the Detroit public school system is a vast organization of more than 200 elementary schools and nearly 100 secondary schools, it is clearly impossible to create singleness of purpose and unity of philosophy in every one of the city's schools. At the same time, this large system does achieve a high degree of district-wide operation of the principle of applied citizenship. Detroit wants its young citizens to know, to care about, and to participate in the democratic process. Under the superintendency of Samuel Brownell the system extended the school-community cooperation to immerse high school students in the realities of a democratic society.

The mock elections that take place in Detroit schools each year were described earlier in this chapter. A companion program sends students on trips to the courts each week. Because of logistical problems, this experience cannot be shared by all, like the voting experience, but annually some 1,300 students (about one percent of all the high school students) do see a court in action. The voting experience is real to the student because he personally participates; he must make decisions before casting his ballot. The court visit, although more passive, requires students to report in detail to their own classes on the day following the visit.

On the morning of the project team's visit, 25 students from six classes at the Henry Ford High School visited the Recorder's Court. Because the Court was hearing misdemeanor cases, for which no jury is used, some of the students were permitted to sit in the jury box during the hearings.

"Hear Ye! Hear Ye! Hear Ye! The Recorder's Court of the City of Detroit is now in session." Judge Gillis, substituting for Judge Brennan, took several minutes to explain to the students the working of the Court before hearing the first case. This Court is limited in misdemeanor cases to sentences with a maximum of 90 days or $100. For the visiting students the greatest value may rest with the preparation and follow-up for the Court visit. The actual visit to the Court has its greatest impact as a means to dramatize and personalize the complex abstraction of the law.

Another Detroit program to develop responsible future citizens is the Student Volunteer Service of the United Community Services, directed by Mrs. Barbara Stone. The school system provides the organizational link between the teenage volunteers and the community agencies that utilize student help. Of all Detroit's city, suburban, and parochial schools contacted last year, 87 percent cooperated with the program. In each of the 216 cooperating schools, a coordinator publicized the program and directed student queries to the central agency.

The program, for students 14 years of age or older, is intended to organize student volunteer work during the summer months. In 1964,

24 interview stations were established and more than 1,000 students were interviewed. Other students performed volunteer work without going through the central agency, applying directly to a neighborhood agency with which they were familiar. In Detroit's city schools during 1965, 1,355 students gave 82,000 hours of volunteer work. It is probable that most of these youngsters developed a larger sense of citizenship as a result.

Just as this service brings students to work in the community, another Detroit school agency places the community at work in the schools. This Volunteer Service, headed by Mrs. Aileen Selick, handles the services given by adults who assist in public school programs. This service, which began in the spring of 1964 as a tutoring program organized for public school children by the Kennedy Memorial Fund, has mushroomed as school-community cooperation has increased. It now offers four types of volunteers: (1) volunteers for auxiliary services, such as transportation and lunchroom aides; (2) clerical and technical helpers serving as teacher aides; (3) community resource people, including the neighborhood policeman, the judge, the retired businessman, or the labor arbitrator—anyone who is available to tell about his specialty; and (4) the tutorial aides which include hundreds of high school students who work regularly with thousands of elementary school students needing help. This volunteer service serves the double purpose of enriching the lives of students by bringing a variety of community-resource people into the school while educating these people into the aims and problems of the school. It now has over 2,000 registered volunteers regularly scheduled for assistance work in 137 different schools. The service also offers advice in advance to newly formed groups wishing to assist in education.

These services, directed toward school-community cooperation and richer civic experiences for students, are supplemented by other programs, including the human relations clubs established recently in many high schools and the annual student government day. On student government day, 400 delegates from all the city schools—public and parochial—meet to select student officers. Each school sends a delegation of as many as eight members, depending on the student population of the school.

Effective educational programs seldom mature overnight. Usually they must be carefully nurtured over a period of years before they can be expected to bear solid fruit. It is not surprising, therefore, to learn that the Human Relations Program of the Detroit schools (now organized in the School Relations and Special Services Division) is the direct descendant of a program that began in 1943. It has been in continuous operation during the subsequent 23 years under a number of different names, each reflecting a broader concept of its scope and responsibility. It is important to note that the program is carefully organized at the building, the region, and the city-wide level.

Equally significant in the city-wide effort to provide civic education at a level consistent with democratic ideals is the attention that has been devoted to obtain text materials which give adequate attention to the contributions of minority groups, and especially of the Negro American. A 1962 statement by the Board of Education announced:

The Detroit Board of Education calls upon publishers of books used in schools and the makers of audio-visual and other instructional materials to recognize this concern as they revise or develop books and materials. The Board re-affirms its position that materials purchased for use in the Detroit schools shall be consistent with its stated objectives and policies with regard to fair and adequate treatment of all groups in the American culture.

At about the same time, the Board approved the writing of new supplementary texts to fill the gaps in the currently available materials. This action has resulted in the publication of *The Struggle for Freedom and Rights; The Negro in American History*, for students' use in the junior high schools; and *A Guide for Unit 1: A Great Crisis*, a teacher's guide for Grade 8B United States History.

This positive program to produce culture-fair textbooks, added to the continuing provision for human relations clubs, court visits, volunteer services, and city-wide school elections, places Detroit among school systems with a commendable concern for translating democracy from textbook words into school and community actions. With programs like these, emanating from the central administrative offices, Detroit school leaders try to insure that the 150,000 secondary school students will make contact with the realities of democratic society in a metropolitan environment.

A CLASSROOM SKETCH

Most visitors to Julie Stindt's sociology classes at Detroit's Denby High School are impressed immediately by the number of books in the classroom. Near the front of the room, two oversized bookcases contain more than 400 paperbacks, including Eric Fromm's *Escape From Freedom*, Bruno Bettleheim's *Truants From Life*, and C. Wright Mills' *White Collar*. These books, bought through a $2 contribution by each student at the beginning of the school year, are loaned to any who want to read them. Some of the reading is done as background for independent study projects, but a large share of it is promoted simply by intellectual curiosity.

Other books, with titles such as *The Book of Cowboys* and *Funny Bunny*, are at the rear of Miss Stindt's classroom. These have a different purpose; the books, as well as clothes and toys, are given to the children in the city who have been adopted by Miss Stindt's students in a Big Brother and Sister volunteer program.

The two collections of books reflect the dual emphasis in this unusual sociology class, an approach that simultaneously requires rigorous study of major social issues and active participation in the life of the community. No textbooks are used. Instead, each student selects a significant social problem for independent study; his research includes background reading and discussion with the class. In his final report, he is asked to present a possible solution to the problem he has studied. To receive a grade of "A" or "B," he must test this hypothesis through personal participation in a social action project. It is apparent, however, that these students are motivated in their community work by genuine concern for others rather than by a desire for higher grades. Miss Stindt seems to have succeeded in channeling the natural idealism of her students while she guides the development of their minds.

The Big Brother and Sister program pairs Miss Stindt's sociology students with children from families in the Brewster Douglas Public Housing Project. "We place our students almost entirely on their own," Miss Stindt says. "The only regulation we have is that all their work must be done during daytime hours."

"We find," she continued, "that our students take these children to the Art Museum, to parks in Detroit, to historical museums—places these children might never have had a chance to visit. The students play with them and read to them. Sometimes a Big Brother or Big Sister will take the child to a movie." The students themselves evolved the idea of a book collection for their "Little Brothers" and "Little Sisters," she explained, after they found that many of the children came from homes that did not contain a single book.

Miss Stindt's students, most of whom come from middle class families, are warned to avoid condescension in relationships with the children and their families. "They are instructed not to act like 'Lady Bountiful,'" as Miss Stindt describes it, "but to give of themselves in some way to help these kids become something better than they otherwise would."

A good example of this positive approach occurred at Christmas time, when the students discussed what they might do with their "adopted" children. They rejected the traditional Christmas party with presents in favor of another idea—helping the children to make their own Christmas gifts for their parents.

An exchange program between students of Denby High School and those of a predominantly Negro school also originated in Miss Stindt's classes. The program began in 1962, when some of Miss Stindt's students wanted to find out more about the quality of education and the interest in learning in schools where the majority of students are Negro. An exchange program with Eastern High School was arranged, with Miss Stindt's students attending Eastern for a day while Eastern students attended Denby. In 1965, exchange day involved 120 students from each school. Before the exchange program began, there was considerable friction between Denby and Eastern students; now, relations are noticeably improved. "We don't expect miracles after one day of exposure," Miss Stindt explained, "but at least we have planted a seed of doubt concerning the unfounded prejudices of many of our students."

The Big Brother and Sister activities and the student exchange program are not the only social action projects in which Miss Stindt's students apply what they learn about sociology to actual situations. Three times during the semester, each student attends some kind of community meeting dealing with his area of interest. The student is asked to take an active part in the meetings, whenever this is possible, and this may lead to participation in the organization's projects.

Numerous resources are used during class periods. A Negro minister, for example, has spoken to the class, and an official from the Detroit school system presented a report on the effects of increased educational opportunities for Negro students.

A film was shown to the students on the first day of the project team's visit. "The Eye of the Beholder" deals with an artist, Michael Girard, as he is viewed by those who came into contact with him on the day he supposedly committed a murder. A taxi driver thinks of him as a gangster, and Girard's landlord thinks he is a lunatic. Girard's mother sees him as a good but inconsiderate boy. A waiter in a restaurant believes Girard is a ladies' man, and a cleaning woman views him as a monster. Then, after each of these points of view has been presented through flashbacks, the film shows Girard as he saw himself.

Before the film began, Miss Stindt prepared her students by saying, "When we look at social problems, our point of view influences what we regard as fact." She gave several analogies, such as the cube that seems to multiply to several cubes as it turns and ink blots used in psychological testing.

Midway through the film, after the students viewed Michael Girard through the eyes of others and before seeing him as he saw himself, Miss Stindt stopped the projector, turned on the lights, and asked the students for their reactions to the first half of the film. A lively discussion followed.

Miss Stindt asked provocative questions: "Did Michael Girard believe in reality?" "Does the fact that he was an artist mean that he could feel more deeply about matters?" "Is there any such thing as an artistic temperament?" One student's reply indicated the candor with which topics are discussed in this classroom, "I think his painting is just a front to get girls into his room," the boy said.

"What do you think?" Miss Stindt asked the girls in the classroom. "On the basis of what you've seen, would you go on a date with him?"

"I would be curious to see if he is really what they say he is," one girl responded. "You would have to find out for yourself."

"Do you mean that you must know a person to make a realistic judgment about him? Is a personal relationship the best basis for judgment?" Miss Stindt asked.

Several students commented. "You still may not know the real Michael," said a boy, who continued, "He might hide himself from you just as he apparently hides his real self from the rest of the people in this film." Another student added, "You ought to be able to profit from other people's experiences too. You can't though; you have to find out everything for yourself." A third student took a different view, saying, "If you have to know everybody personally, how can you vote? Sometimes you have to take other people's word for things."

The film resumed, and after it was finished, Miss Stindt asked the students to use the last few minutes of the period to write down their first impressions. "What was the purpose of the film? What was the editor's point of view? What is he trying to do for you? Try to show relationships between the film and what we have been trying to do in sociology up to this time."

For the next class period, the students discussed the film in greater detail. Miss Stindt also took time at the beginning of class to publicize one of the meetings that class members might attend to meet the requirement for attendance and participation in a community meeting. It was a meeting sponsored by the Detroit Human Relations Council, dealing with organizations such as CORE and NAACP.

She frankly stated, "I am going to give a commercial." She remarked that most of the students' parents belonged to the homeowners group. "What is the purpose of the homeowners group?" she asked rhetorically. "We all know that in addition to keeping our homes beautiful, the main purpose of this group is to keep Negroes out of the district." The Human Relations Council, she explained, was trying to offset the homeowners group. "This might be a good meeting for you to attend, and it might also be useful to take your parents. After all, no matter what opinions we have, it's a good idea to know what 'the enemy' is doing."

The question might be raised about how a teacher such as Miss Stindt, who makes no attempt to conceal her convictions while she encourages independent thought by her students, can feel free to discuss any topic of significance without regard to community conservatism, social taboos, and other restrictions. A part of the answer can be found in Miss Stindt herself; she is a teacher of unusual ability and conviction.

Sol Elkin, assistant principal at Denby High School, also drew attention to the role performed by the man who was principal of Denby High School when Miss Stindt's sociology classes began. "Mr. Wolf, who retired in 1964, built such an image of educational statesmanship in his school community that people have complete confidence in the school. He provided the setting in which unusual things could be done," said Elkin. "Mr. Wolf was not a liberal politically, but he was liberal in the sense that he gave teachers considerable autonomy to plan and carry through on the assignments." Elkin also feels that the school board deserves credit for supporting good teaching such as that of Miss Stindt.

SURVEY OF STUDENT OPINION

This chapter has related some of the school activities that help motivate students toward six goals of civic education: participation in political processes; belief in constitutional liberty and equality; pride in United States along with commitment to international cooperation; sensitivity to the creative arts; compassion for one's fellow man; and development of democratic principles and their application in daily life.

The main justification for these activities is the influence they may exert on the civic behavior of the students. This cannot be measured precisely, and perhaps it can never be measured at all, because of the difficulty of isolating the influence of the school from other influences on the life of the child.

Although this project was not designed to assess the results of instruction, an informal effort was made to secure student responses to current civic issues, to see what level of interest and involvement students displayed and what principles they evoked to substantiate their convictions. What commitments have high school students today accepted or absorbed? What has priority in their list of values? Papers written without forewarning by students in several schools may offer clues.

Student demonstrations at Berkeley and elsewhere and civil rights demonstrations throughout the nation were on the public mind at the time of the project team's visits. Because these activities represented a significant complex of public issues centering around the basic dilemma of order and freedom, the project team asked students at one midwestern high school to write about their reactions to persons who participate in public demonstrations: "Is a person who participates in a demonstration a good citizen? What is your source of information and opinion?"

It was apparent in the responses that students were not parroting a pat answer learned from someone else. Each response was different, and each appeared to be based on at least one substantial point. These comments should be read in the light of what they reveal of the student's knowledge, thoughtfulness, and commitment.

In my opinion, a person who does participate in a demonstration is not necessarily a good citizen. First of all, this person may be participating for reasons other than supporting a cause. He may have such reasons as wanting publicity, or simply just going along with a crowd or a general opinion. On the other hand, though, he may actually believe in this cause and through demonstrating be fighting for the cause he believes in. Marches for civil rights are an example of what I've been saying. Many people demonstrate and truly believe in this cause, whereas others are just demonstrating to go along with the crowd. Another example would be recent demonstrations by college students against the action that President Johnson has been taking in Vietnam. In my opinion, these students do not have enough knowledge of the situation to demonstrate or to know what other course of action should be taken.

*   *   *   *   *

A good citizen is one who not only voices his opposition to a government policy or government actions, but also supports his opposition with logical reasoning, voices this opposition in a manner becoming to an educated citizen, offers a better solution, and finally accepts the reasons behind the government policy—accepts its good points and looks objectively at these reasons. In order to look at these reasons objectively, the good citizen must be educated not only in the single issue at hand but also in the principles, values, goals, and mechanics of the American government. If after such education, the citizen reviews his entire outlook on the policy he finds objectionable and still maintains and can support his objections, then he is justified in participating in demonstrations against government actions.

*   *   *   *   *

Demonstrations have a purpose. This purpose is to get an idea across to anyone or any group of people who might help the cause. If the demonstrators believe honestly that they are achieving a goal and that their actions will help them, they are not showing bad citizenship. But, when the demonstration leads to violence it becomes an uncivilized act.

American citizens are supposed to act for the welfare of the entire country, not on an individual basis. Therefore, if they are placing other people in danger, they are being poor citizens.

In other schools, students were asked if they would personally engage in a demonstration. Their responses—which show the nature of their reasoning and their commitment—may offer a useful clue to the quality of their civic education.

A student in a small California high school in a mountain community replied, "No, because I believe in what our government is doing. I believe that the government has enough troubles without people adding to them." Another said, "I might if I thought it would do any good and if it was an issue I felt very strongly on. It must also have some organization. But I doubt an instance like this will ever occur."

Students in an all-Negro high school in Selma, Alabama, responded predictably affirmatively to the same question:

I would march because I would like to have all of my people get their rights, to vote, to have their voice in government, not because they are black, but because they are free people of the United States.

*   *   *   *   *

I would take part in a demonstration only when it's necessary to protect actions or things that cause community disturbances and prevent the progress of individuals or organization. Before participating I would have to be thoroughly convinced that there is a rightful cause to protest against. Demonstrations are no plaything. Therefore, a person has to be willing to stay with the group until the cause for which we are fighting has been fully straightened out. And before I'd participate, I'd bear this in mind.

Florida high school students answered:

I would and have participated because this is what I believe in and if the issue warranted it, I would go out and show my feelings rather than sit passively and let someone else do it. Apathy never helped any cause.

*   *   *   *   *

I would not participate in a demonstration because I feel little help would be accomplished. I am against marches; I feel the country can do a good job without unorganized help.

When students were asked to discuss what is perhaps the classic dilemma of citizenship by answering the question "When, if ever, is a person justified in breaking the law?" they gave varied responses. In a Midwest suburb, students said:

I don't believe it is ever justifiable to disobey a law. A law is something which is put before people for them to abide by. If a law was meant for people to break then it wouldn't have been made in the first place.

I realize that the people who make laws may not always be right in making them, but as a unified body we should cooperate. If we don't, this is a small, but first step toward a separate and disconnected people. . . . It is not as if just one or two people made our laws, but they are people who represent us. They can't all be so wrong in making laws. They are careful in making them and I don't think there is anyone who could do a better job.

*   *   *   *   *

I think at times, when there is a very good reason, it is justifiable to break a law. But the person must be absolutely sure that he sincerely believes in his reason . . . I see no reason why a person should have to obey a law that was made with only the interests of a few in mind. In the history of our country there have been many unjust laws. If our ancestors had regarded these and gone along with the fact that a law is a law, and therefore must be obeyed, I don't believe our country would be as great as it is today.

Finally, students were asked to describe themselves 25 years hence as they would like their lives to be, to visualize, in other words, their own personal Utopias of the year 1990. Because an individual's personal goals may reflect significantly his image of society and his own place in it, this question could easily reflect his behavior as a citizen. Certain values and commitments are clearly suggested in these statements by high school seniors concerning the world they want for themselves 25 years from now.

Now that it's 1990, it's pretty easy for me to be happy. Although the U.S. is still the only real democracy in the world, we are able to live in peaceful coexistence with our Soviet and Chinese friends. The Vietnam crisis was settled in about 1970 with a conference. A number of summit meetings were held and debates at the U. N. and we now live in peaceful co-existence. How long this will last, I don't know. As for my family, my husband is a lawyer and my children are all in school. School is much different from when I was their age. Most of the teaching is done by TV. I don't particularly like this approach since a real live teacher is much easier to talk with. Math is extremely complicated, and so is chemistry and biology. English and foreign languages have changed little. Neither has history. I have a large amount of leisure time. I fill up this time by reading, sewing, and doing volunteer work. People are still the same though. With all this leisure, there is more griping, and I wonder whether all the pushbuttons are really worthwhile. I can't think of anything else science can invent, but I'm sure they'll come up with something. People seem to worship science.

*   *   *   *   *

Last night my oldest son asked me to tell him what made the present world so different from the world of my youth. First I told him about a program started when I was his age—the war on poverty. Over the last 20 years all forms of poverty have been almost completely destroyed. Of course, there are still people who are not as wealthy as others, but they are not poor. In my day the average income was much lower than it is today. Also, I told him that the cost of living was approximately one-fourth of what it used to be, because of improved and much cheaper methods of manufacturing. Also, I told him of the great diseases, such as cancer and tuberculosis, which now have cures and which occur only one chance out of a million. The major thing was that my teen years were during a period of world-wide tension, while he is able to live while the world is at complete peace; it has been since 1972, when all differences were solved, in Geneva, Switzerland, at perhaps, we hope, the last summit conference in history.

*   *   *   *   *

By 1990 I hope that the world political situation will be cleared up and all the nations will be at peace. By this time I will have been married for approximately 20 years and I will have four children, which will be two boys and two girls. I will have married Tom, the boy I'm going with now, and we will be living in St. Louis County in a two-story colonial house with a large yard and swimming pool. After many hard years of work, my husband finally will have worked his way up to vice-president of a growing corporation and we will be well-established in the financial world. Since all my children will be in grade school I will have time to do what I want during the day, such as being preoccupied with redecorating my home and being involved in my bridge club and church group.

*   *   *   *   *

It is the year 1990. My utopian world is realized. I am happily married to a successful business man and we have 2 children, 2 cars, and a four-bedroom ranch-style home in California. I myself have graduated from Purdue University or Iowa State University where I majored in home economics. I continue working (because I enjoy it) and I am writing for a national magazine in connection with home economics.

*   *   *   *   *

The world in 1990 will be much like the world now. There will be trouble spots but the forces of freedom will still be on top. As for myself, I would like to have a job that is never routine. Every day will present a new challenge. I will wear a tie and have an office with walnut on the walls and carpeting on the floor. I will live in a suite in a swanky hotel. The rooms will be small but decorated lavishly, with many electrical gadgets. I can see no wife but many girl friends in 1990. The cooking will be done by a male cook who will also do light housework. My car will be a foreign model like a Jaguar, something that costs about $24,000. I will be socially accepted and have somewhere to go on the weekends. But though I will have wealth, status, and social acceptance I will try not to let them take me over. That will be my life in 1990.

*   *   *   *   *

My family and I will have wonderful friends, perfect health, and enjoy a certain degree of social status. We will not be high society, however.

There will be peace in the world, with no wars, and small countries of today will be prosperous.

When 9th-grade students at West Leyden High School were asked in the course of a general survey "What do you wish for?", the three most frequent responses were good job, good education, and peace. The next four responses, in order of frequency, were money, health, happiness, and a good car. Some would say that this reflects a wholesome intermingling of altruistic and egocentric values, appropriate to 14-year-olds.

The reader will have to decide for himself whether these student opinions offer grounds for optimism that the civic education offered to youth, both in and out of school, is in fact producing knowledgeable, thoughtful, and committed citizens for a democratic society.

*We spend too much time
counting the pupils.*

Henry Scattergood, Headmaster
Germantown Friends School,
quoting the superintendent of
Scarsdale, New York, public schools

CHAPTER **7**

How Administration
Facilitates Civic Education

No one pretends that effective education—civic education or any other
kind—simply happens. If the climate is not right, even the best teacher
may fail. The teachers interviewed in this survey suggested a wide variety
of factors which they believe create a favorable teaching climate. Some
stated that the prime ingredient is community support. Others said that
the essential factor is a knowledgeable and devoted faculty; still others
believed that the best teaching climate results when the school administration maintains proper working conditions. Obviously, no single explanation is adequate. All of the suggested ingredients contribute to the
creation of an environment in which learning can flourish.

Although this report cannot examine thoroughly all the factors that
underlie effective civic education, it will mention some of the facilitating
conditions apparent during the project team's visits to the schools. Although team members were concerned primarily with the classroom and
the students rather than with central administration, attention was drawn

217

in a few schools to the front office and to the activities there that contributed to civic education.

CENTRAL ADMINISTRATION

When teachers were asked, "What makes this school tick? What makes possible the obviously superior program you offer?" the answer was often "an outstanding superintendent" or "a fine principal" or "a topflight department head." The project team pursued the inquiry, asking about specific administrative traits or practices that contributed most to the quality of education.

In schools where strong programs are in effect, teachers stated that their administrative officers are strong people, willing to work for realization of their own convictions and to examine with respect the convictions of others. These administrators encourage innovation and adopt policies which permit teachers to participate in summer workshops, curriculum reconstruction, or similar activities.

Administrative excellence, apparently, can often be judged by the level of faculty morale or by innovations adopted to improve the quality of instruction. There may even be a high positive correlation between these two measures, because the school in which morale is high is also the school which makes continuing effort to upgrade its curriculum.

The Intellectual Climate

"Learning is our business," said Superintendent Ivan Nicholas in Ladue, Missouri. "It is our job to be alert to new ways of stimulating it." Superintendent Nicholas and Ladue's curriculum director, Frank Morley, spend much of their time promoting within their faculty a spirit of discovery, alertness to change, and concern for improving habits of thinking and teaching. They recognize the great importance of scheduling so that enough time can be set aside to generate new ideas and then to digest and absorb them. They are committed to the view that, in this day of conspicuous change, teachers cannot cling to any one program for a long period of time and expect it to be adequate. This opinion lies behind an in-service program that will be described on pp. 226–28. Ladue teachers, apparently, have been infected by the insistence on intellectual alertness;

they were obviously more deeply involved in curriculum planning than many teachers and they were more willing to be self-critical.

In a city as vast as New York, administrative style assumes entirely different characteristics. Here, the personal influence of individuals at the central office or even at the district offices is greatly diffused, and ideas filter through the system to the teacher via committees, conferences, and publications. Curriculum bulletins are augmented by provocative aids constantly issued by various offices of this immense school system. *Bridges to Understanding*, published by the Human Relations Unit, and *Conducting School Civic Club Activities*, issued by the Bureau of Curriculum Research, are examples.

Another example is an eight-page publication titled *Strengthening Democracy*, issued four times each school year by the Division of Curriculum Development, which relates specifically to civic education. This thoroughly professional publication includes signed articles, editorials, and letters to the editor, which do not necessarily reflect the opinions of the Board of Education or Superintendent of Schools. One issue contained three major articles: "The Treatment of Minorities in Textbooks," by the coordinator of curriculum periodicals; "How the Curriculum Can Promote Integration," by the deputy superintendent; and "A Vote for Citizenship," by a social studies chairman. The last-named article pulled together in a single brief report dozens of methods for promoting civic education. Under the heading of "Efforts Directly Related to Elections," it listed:

Development of a series of lessons on elections

Preparation by teachers of special election information sheets

Distribution to students of election materials prepared by nonpartisan civic groups

Student organization of a Student Elections Council to plan election-day projects

School-wide straw votes on local, state, and Federal elections

Visits to local political clubs

Judicious use of tape recordings of speeches by candidates

Conducting assemblies featuring candidates for public office

Staging student mock political conventions

Publication in the school newspaper of interviews with local candidates

Student letters to parents urging them to register and vote

Post-mortem analyses of election results in social studies classes

Other suggestions were listed under the headings "Long Range Preparation for Intelligent Voting" and "Efforts Related to the Development of Good Citizenship Beyond Voting." Under the heading "Proposals for Citizenship-Training Activities Not Yet in Widespread Use," were listed:

Creation of a regular, annual, well-rounded program to give every Election Day, not only those of presidential years, the ceremony, dignity, and respect befitting the occasion.

Expansion of contacts between the school and political organizations in the community by establishing regular opportunities for students to serve as watchers at polls and at political headquarters.

Encouragement of programs in which foreign students visit or live with American students. This arrangement affords opportunities for young people to compare American conditions with those of other countries and to develop a deeper appreciation of the American way of life.

Occasional Polls of community attitudes on public issues, conducted by teams of students.

Provision for a teacher-coordinator or group of students to maintain a file of community service opportunities for young people and to oversee such activity.

More comprehensive treatment of some of the suggestions described in this article appear in two Board of Education publications, Developing Student Participation in School Government (*Curriculum Bulletin No. 12, 1960–61 series*) and Problems of Democracy (*Curriculum Bulletin No. 9, 1960–61 series*).

Although the central administrative officers of large school systems cannot exert the same kind of personal, face-to-face leadership that is possible in smaller systems, those who are convinced of the importance of civic education can, through the use of appropriate media, inspire increased attention to this area, as evidenced by the results in one of our largest cities.

**Creative Use Of
Federal Funds**

The Department of Special Projects is a dynamic, growing prong of the Detroit School System. Although many of the division's projects, begun under the leadership of former Assistant Superintendent Carl L. Marburger, are now supported by Federal funds, others were begun long before Federal funds were available. The department has a "catalytic function," to initiate new projects and then gradually bring them into regular established channels. An example is the Head Start Program, which started in the Department of Special Projects and now is conducted under the Department of Early Childhood Education. The Great Cities Program, now in operation in a number of schools, will be phased out as the program becomes mature enough to be handled by the regularly established organization of the schools. Another program, a work-training project begun in the Department of Special Projects, has already been placed in a regular established division and employs about 1,600 students in Detroit schools as gardeners' aides, clerical helpers, janitors' aides, and other maintenance workers. Some studies already made of the effectiveness of this work-training program at Eastern High School indicate that the dropout rate in that school has been cut in half and that student conduct has improved.

There is evidence that the communities in which the Department of Special Projects programs are most used are becoming more aware of their potential ability to change conditions. A dozen new programs use Federal funds, either through the Economic Opportunity Act or the Elementary and Secondary Education Act. The Detroit school system encourages the community and teachers to participate in initiating proposals for Federal funds.

It is apparent that the administrative staff of the Detroit schools is doing far more than passively administering a program. Instead, by constantly initiating activities to strengthen citizenship education, this school system has assumed an active, committed role in giving Detroit students the benefit of new Federal resources.

**Supporting
Academic Freedom**

An important factor in teachers' morale is administrative support of their freedom to teach topics appropriate to the age and grade level to which they are assigned. The attitude of the administration when a teacher is attacked because he has dealt with a "closed area" makes all the difference between high and low morale, not only for the teacher directly concerned but for the entire faculty as well. In some districts, principals and superintendents make special efforts to support teachers who deal with controversial issues, because they are convinced that teaching and learning should be concerned with live, debatable issues, including those which are delicate or controversial.

A sampling of local administrative pronouncements reveals a variety of emphases. In Colorado, the statewide policy strongly supports free exchange of ideas and a diversity of political and social thought:

Each pupil has the right and need, under competent guidance and instruction, to study issues appropriate to his interest, experience, and ability. He must have access to relevant information, and he has the obligation to examine carefully all sides of an issue. He has the right to form and express his own point of view and opinions without jeopardizing his position in the classroom or in the school.

Each teacher has the right and the obligation to teach about controversial issues. It is his responsibility to select issues for study and discussion which contribute to the attainment of course objectives, and to make available to students materials concerning the various aspects of the issues. He also has the obligation to be as objective as possible and to present fairly the several sides of an issue. Although he has the right to express his own viewpoint and opinions, he does not have the right to indoctrinate students to his views.

Not all official pronouncements on the subject of controversy are so unqualifiedly in support of freedom of inquiry. In some communities, the school administration has found it appropriate to qualify this freedom when communism is under discussion. The policy statement of one California system, for example, removes communism from the area of controversy by declaring it noncontroversial:

We believe in teaching about communism in our educational system, but only with a moral directive, in the same way that a medical student is taught about cancer, that it is evil, that tuberculosis is evil, and education about them is directed to their elimination and defeat. We believe that there is a great moral dynamic that reveals communism as a rationale of murder and lying and the destruction of freedom. It is totally immoral, and mental and emotional barriers against it should be erected in the minds of the young. Communism is not controversial in America. We do not believe in it.

In-Service Education
An increasingly important contribution of the central administration to the improvement of civic education is the provision made for helping teachers to improve the quality of their instruction. Such provision includes at least three interrelated areas of so-called in-service education: (1) improvement of course content by selection of better materials and organization of better courses; (2) improvement of teacher competence through learning more about the subject and how to teach it; and (3) the enlargement of the teacher as a citizen through wider or deeper participation in significant experiences outside of schools and libraries.

Many institutes, seminars, study groups, forums, and workshops are available to teachers. Several special in-service programs have already been mentioned, including (in Chapter 6) a program in Portland, Oregon, that prepares teachers for more effective teaching of the Bill of Rights by using case study materials prepared by the Oregon Bar Association.

The Passaic County Workshop in Economic Education is a program co-sponsored by the school and another agency (in this instance the New Jersey Council on Economic Education) and financially supported by a private bank. This workshop has as its theme the improvement of economic education, and it focuses attention on the functions, problems, and operation of the American economic system. Sixteen weekly evening sessions deal with topics such as Price Theory, Monetary Policy, America in the World Economy, and Comparative Economic Systems. Three semester hours of academic credit are granted and the $15 workshop fee is rebated for teachers.

The Mark Community School in Flint, Michigan, maintains an in-service training coordinator. One of his responsibilities is to orient new teachers during a 10-day training period, with emphasis on a community concept and mental health approach. The coordinator is also responsible for the continuing program, in which 52 interns and 80 other members of the school staff attend monthly lectures and colloquies throughout the year to strengthen their mastery of the school-community idea. This unique program is financed by a private foundation. The interns receive a stipend of $5,000 plus expenses if they are candidates for a master's degree, $8,000 if doctoral candidates. The in-service program, planned by the Flint staff, is accepted for credit by seven Michigan universities.

The in-service program at Darien, Connecticut, makes extensive use of television and some use of the electric voice-writer. Teachers gather around a television set and listen to the lecture, which may originate anywhere. They will see on the television screen a running, visual explanation of the lecture as the speaker writes explanations on transparent tape. This is comparable to the way students in a classroom simultaneously listen to the teacher and watch what he writes on the board. A mathematics group in Darien, for example, listened to Professor Patrick Suppes of Stanford University, a pioneer in the field of modern mathematics. The cost of transmission was $35 for this transcontinental lecture.

Many schools have conducted summer or winter workshops to prepare teachers for more effective school integration or to improve interpersonal relations. Prince George's County, Maryland, is among the many districts that report that school integration was highly successful in large part because of the workshop experience provided for all teachers during the summer of 1965.

Similarly, the Richmond, Virginia, schools have operated an ambitious program "to assist staff members in broadening their self-concepts in relation to co-workers and various subcultures in the total milieu in which they teach." Although the rationale for the program came from problems of desegregation and although it is funded through the Civil Rights Act, all children are expected to benefit. One of the six areas of work, for example, is speech improvement. The stated objectives are "to study the speech pattern of children in the Richmond area and to develop methods and materials for assisting children and youth in a sound program of speech development." Robert Anderson, assistant superintendent of instruction, pointed out that many groups of children in the Richmond area, including some Negro children from the lower socio-economic group, have speech difficulties. Even in the upper economic classes, speech problems occur.

In New York City, the Human Relations Unit develops programs for teachers to help them become better acquainted with the problems and the characteristics of minorities. One television workshop on "The Negro in America" was held once a week so that teachers could view a half-hour telecast and then participate in an hour-and-a-half discussion of the program material and their reading on the same subject. The assistant director of the program, Albert Brownson, reported that the workshop created a high level of involvement and controversy. Teachers in New York City, reflecting a variety of backgrounds, are not in accord on what should be done about race problems or what is the proper role of the school in this area. Mr. Brownson believes the workshop has succeeded in creating a dialogue that can lead to self-examination.

The Human Relations Unit taped a similar program entitled "American Minorities, Ethnic and Racial." It also conducted seminars for supervisors, assistant principals, and high school department chairmen to promote discussion of integration, discrimination, and other current issues. A primary concern of the latter project was to raise the aspiration level of youngsters from minority groups. The rationale for spending a great deal of time with the assistant principals, supervisors, and department chairmen was that through these key people there is often greater possibility for influencing school programs and policies and the attitudes of individual teachers.

School principals in New York City are responsible for distributing materials from the Human Relations Unit to teachers as they see fit. Principals are also encouraged to spend up to $200 for a professional library containing books useful to teachers in developing inter-group education programs. During 1965, the Human Relations Unit began publication of an eight-page bulletin (mentioned earlier in this chapter), for distribution four times a year to each of New York's 55,000 teachers. A member of the Human Relations Unit also attends all the important meetings of the curriculum council to assure that curriculum content and material will consider the needs of the disadvantaged population in New York City.

The school system in Ithaca, New York, encourages teacher participation in the community's Public Affairs Forum by allowing one credit toward salary increment requirements for attendance at any five of the seven scheduled programs. This series presents lectures and panel discussions on a variety of topics. Some recent ones were Communists and the Law, How It Feels to Be a Member of a Minority Group, Which Way Vietnam?, The Churches and Social Action, The Ecumenical Movement, and What Next for the Conservative Movement? This plan of encouraging teacher participation in general community programs offers certain advantages not shared by the more usual scheme of setting up special programs limited to teachers.

In-service education through the cooperation of an outside group is also provided by the programs co-sponsored by the Robert A. Taft Institute of Government. The Louisville and Jefferson County schools in Kentucky staged a summer institute in government, and the Detroit schools offered teachers a political education seminar during the school year. The focus of both programs was the practical realities of politics and government, with public officials delivering most of the lectures and leading the discussion.

The summer institute in Kentucky was a five-week experience for 25 social studies teachers, who received a $50-a-week stipend, three hours of academic credit, and a large file of suitable teaching materials about local government. The three areas given major attention by the seminar were Planning and Zoning, Urban Renewal, and Public Welfare.

The Detroit program, a series of all-day Saturday meetings, featured topics such as An Analysis of the Recent Election, Operation of Political Parties, Teachers in Politics, Election Laws and Procedures, and News Media and Politics. A before-and-after questionnaire revealed that certain attitudes shifted by 10 percent or more during the seminar:

More participants agreed that politics is a safeguard against anarchy.

Participants were less critical of lobbyists.

Many more agreed that politics contributes significantly to the transformation of the unorganized mass of people into civilized society.

Some felt more strongly that the quality of politicians is dependent on the quality of the voters.

Somewhat more agreed that the function of the Supreme Court is to reconcile the past and the present, continuity and change, and order and liberty.

Fewer agreed that independent voting is a healthy trend.

Many believed less strongly that split-ticket voting is important for good government.

Some felt more strongly that the differences within parties are greater than the average differences between parties.

At Ladue, Missouri, the administration has embarked on a carefully planned program to help the faculty become more receptive to new ideas so that students, in turn, will also be so. The master plan for accomplishment of this objective includes precise schemes for evaluation of many small plans. Upgrading of staff is evaluated in terms of behavioral change. The best way to upgrade staff, believes Superintendent Ivan Nicholas, is to involve teachers in local workshops and local planning, possibly with the assistance of outside consultants. In recent workshops, aimed at teaching more flexible patterns, teachers were asked to write statements of their goals for their pupils and then to write tests of pupil behavior which could indicate whether their goals had been achieved. Some resistance was evident, especially among older teachers, secure in their present teaching patterns, and the first job was to get the teachers personally involved in identifying the problems. Three results were expected of the workshops: (1) upgraded subject content, (2) better technology, and (3) use of a wider variety of teaching techniques. Teachers were asked to think about their goals in terms of the kind of graduate the school should produce.

The Ladue program is more than just another in-service workshop. It is a carefully planned approach to a long-range, developmental program, based on a thorough understanding of strategies for change. An excerpt from the official announcement of the 1965 workshop helps make this clear:

As in the past, we will continue to offer to selected staff special 1-day to 14-day workshops (under university consultants) in various disciplines both during the year and in the summer as an integral part of curriculum improvement, e.g., in elementary modern math and science, linguistics, economics, political science, and geography.

As a part of and follow-up of a statement of projected 20-year goals for our school district formulated by a summer Task Force of five staff members and many outside consultants, we offered two summer workshops for almost a third of our staff.

During this fall, and continuing through the rest of the year, we are pursuing an in-service study which will ultimately involve the total staff. There are three phases to this study:

Phase I. All participants will read the programed text, Preparing Objectives for Programed Instruction by Mager, Fearson Publishers, and write one sample objective in behavioral terms and a criterion test for checking out the extent the objective is achieved by the learners. . . .

Phase II. All participants are asked to write a series of objectives which treat a given portion of content at two or more levels of cognition as described by Bloom. A critique of these written objectives is then held to increase participants' understandings of the cognitive skills which can and should be dealt with in the instructional process.

Phase III. All participants shall engage in a 3-hour ETS workshop on how to construct classroom tests. Consultative help would be provided by Educational Testing Service. . . .

The purpose of this in-service effort is to improve each staff member's skill in specifying objectives, learning activities, and criterion tests in such a way as to make the daily educational effort in Ladue more efficient and worthwhile. Each group spends as much time and effort as necessary to accomplish one phase before moving on to the next. The sequence in which the phases are treated is also varied among groups.

Frank Morley, the curriculum director, believes that most teachers accommodate to change and accept it. Those who do not are likely to leave the district because they feel uncomfortable in the midst of change. "If they don't, you work around them," says Morley. The spirit of discovery, awareness of change, and willingness to examine one's own teaching are reflections of the new climate in education, which has been stimulated by the Federally financed summer institutes for teachers.

Strong local programs of in-service training such as this, in which teachers can work with experts to revise their own curriculum and improve their own teaching, may have incalculable effect on the quality of civic education. In a number of cases, these efforts are proving more useful than the more commonly used system of requiring teachers to enroll periodically for additional university courses. Administrators who help to make the needed learning available and attractive are making an important contribution to civic education.

BUILDING ADMINISTRATION—THE PRINCIPAL

High schools frequently assume distinct "personalities," reflecting the nature of the community, the tradition of the school, the composition of the faculty, and, to an indeterminate degree, the personality of the principal. In a number of schools, teachers unhesitatingly attribute to their principal the source of strength or vitality of a program.

At Yorktown High School in Arlington, Virginia, a spirit concerned with search for more effective curricular organization is evident, and teachers declare that the main reason for this atmosphere is the administrative style of the principal, Ralph Kier. One teacher said of Kier, "He has a great deal of power to make teacher selection and he uses his power wisely. He wants teachers who have strong academic backgrounds and who are in a sense intellectuals. He is also interested that they have broader goals than merely teaching their subjects. He wants them to be concerned about instructing students of all ability levels."

Kier gives broad freedom to individual teachers and departments. He treats teachers as professional people and has subtle ways to develop professionalism. Although he "leaves teachers alone, he is vitally interested in what is going on, and he shows this interest by continually circulating articles pertaining to the subject matter of a particular teacher or a particular department to be read and passed on." Kier also actively assists in evaluation of programs. The department chairman reports that "he has been in the social studies office several times in the past few years to help in a serious evaluation of what we were doing."

If a teacher makes a request that is reasonable, financially feasible, and within Kier's administrative domain, he can feel confident of his principal's support. If the request is rejected, Kier will explain the reasons and the teacher can feel assured that Kier will maintain an open mind concerning new conditions that might change the original decision.

Innovations come about at Yorktown High School as the result of much discussion, building on previous projects, and continuous planning; but it is likely that the leadership of the principal is as important as any other single factor.

Principal Lester DeMent at Rim-of-the-World Junior-Senior High School in Lake Arrowhead, California, spends many hours in the classroom or with teachers. More than half of his time is in curriculum development and improvement of instruction, according to his superintendent, Ben Wilkin. DeMent, who has been principal of the school since 1954, has some definite ideas about curriculum development. He stated:

We start with what the teacher believes in. We look at all of the textbooks that are available in the field which may support the goals that the teacher decides upon. And we might throw them all out. We select materials that are most appropriate . . . then we continually check back to see whether what we have developed is working toward accomplishment of the goals.

DeMent gets solid support from Superintendent Wilkin and the school board when he and his teachers begin to reorganize a course and develop a new outline. Sometimes his teachers are given released time to prepare curriculum materials and outlines, and at other times they are employed during the summer to develop a course. In 1964, for example, Roger Boedecker was employed throughout the summer to develop an elective course in social studies. Until this time, no social studies elective had been offered. The result of Boedecker's summer work was a course of study for a seminar in international economic problems with emphasis on the underdeveloped nations.

The principal also schedules experts in various fields to come to Rim-of-the-World to conduct in-service sessions. DeMent believes, "It is our responsibility to expose youngsters to all points of view because many points of view exist in our society." He is aware of the pressures that are sometimes brought to bear upon a school from a community, but his students are able to study and discuss sexual topics, venereal diseases, communism, and controversial and conflicting views of all kinds in politics and economics. Members of the community who want to check on what is being taught are invited to visit classes at any time.

At the time of the project team's visit DeMent was interested in finding out more about modular scheduling. Throughout the previous year, his teachers had been working on how modular scheduling might be introduced at Rim-of-the-World Junior-Senior High School. He told the project team that he is perhaps more ready for this form of scheduling than are his teachers: "I am a political conservative," he said, "but an educational liberal. My teachers are political liberals and educational conservatives."

In the main lobby of the McCluer High School at Florissant, Missouri, is a handsome bulletin board that came to the school through an unusual contact that grew between the principal and a group of students. In the lower right-hand corner of the display area is an inconspicuous plaque noting that the bulletin board was the gift of the Prospectors and naming the eight members of this group. An explanation of the Prospectors and their gift goes far to explain the administrative style of M. A. Ludwig, the principal, and his three assistants.

A group of eight students constituted a potential gang in the school. They had known each other in the YMCA, where their families had family memberships; but the YMCA memberships had not offered enough activity, and the boys were on the verge of becoming troublesome. The administration made subtle appeals to the boys, one or two at a time, to interest them in positive activity and to suggest positive values. One was drawn into active work with the election committee of the student council, one was elected a junior representative. The school bent rules to find responsibilities for these mavericks. During the spring of their senior year, the administrators suspected that the boys were planning a serious final prank, so they encouraged them to become involved instead in a constructive job for the school. The boys organized a Saturday car wash and raised $200 to provide the bulletin board that is in the main lobby of the school.

Fred B. Dixon, principal at the John Marshall High School in Richmond, Virginia, exercises considerable influence on the tone of the school, in part by many communications to the faculty and to the students—by memo, conference, and printed pamphlet. The following memo to the Administrative Council is an example of the way Mr. Dixon passes ideas along to others. It illustrates one aspect of his leadership style in his relations with the John Marshall faculty:

One of the interesting articles I read during the holidays was "Children Under Pressure" by Dr. Robert A. McGuigan, director of school health services for Evanston, Illinois, and an associate in pediatrics at the Northwestern University Medical School.

This article was in the Rotarian for January 1965. Miss Dearheart has a copy in the library. Would you care to react to anything Dr. McGuigan pointed out? The following quotation indicates his concern:

> Pressure is the great enemy of American civilization. It is especially the enemy of the child, who more and more is expected to adjust himself to adults. It is applied by the colleges to the high schools and by them to the junior high schools and the elementary schools. Pressures are applied by parents, who themselves are overpressured in our society. From every angle the child becomes less and less able to experience a normal childhood. . . .

> We do so much for our children, we try to do so much more, and we probably do far too much. Let them be well educated, but let them be children. There is no such hurry as we have been told—and there is far more reaction to the stresses of our current program than people realize.

At New Albany High School, where faculty morale appeared to be conspicuously high, teachers were asked about the factors they thought contributed most to this situation. The first response was revealing:

> We are never forced into doing anything. Our principal, Delbert Brown, gives us complete freedom and complete support. Second, the administration is interested in new teachers. New teachers are invited to a picnic. A retired teacher in the community gives them orientation talks about local history. They are taken on a tour of the city, and they are entertained at dinner by the Chamber of Commerce, so they get to know the community and feel that they are a part of the community. The annual business day is alternated with an annual school day, a reciprocal program of teachers visiting businessmen and business leaders visiting the school. Third, a careful selection of teachers keeps quality high and this, of course, keeps morale high. And fourth, communication across department lines is strong. The English teachers and the history teachers work closely together, not only with each other but with other

teachers throughout the school. The acquisition and retention of a good faculty here is based on salaries and freedom.

It is possible that some of the feeling of close communication between teachers and principal in this school exists because the school does not have department heads. This unusual situation arises from unusual local conditions. Although it is not recommended as a promising practice, it is an arrangement that is used by this principal and this curriculum director to improve communications. Delbert Brown, principal, feels that the value of encouraging the spontaneous leadership needed for each project in a department is far more important than the advantages of a stated, established, and unchanging leadership. He is also happy to have teachers bring their queries, hopes, and aspirations directly to him, without having them channeled and diluted through a department chairman. Curriculum coordinator Robert Holmes adds the observation that the absence of department heads means much less paperwork.

In other schools, a particular combination of persons who constitute the administrative council or faculty cabinet may provide the key to a smoothly working team. In the Monmouth High School in New Jersey, for example, the cabinet consists of the superintendent, principal, vice-principal, all department heads, the nurse, librarian, president of the teachers association, and the secretary of the school board. This group meets weekly to establish school policy. The president of the Student Council is also invited to attend part of the meeting.

A SCHOOL-WIDE CONCERN FOR CIVIC EDUCATION

At the Fairmont Heights High School in Prince George's County, Maryland, students and teachers alike reflect a unique spirit of personal aspiration and respect for others. In this upward-bound but largely low-income community, the principal has sparked the imagination of teachers and students and has created a contagious aspiration for a better life. The visitor is likely to become aware of this enthusiasm as soon as he enters the school.

Operation Awareness at Fairmont Heights High School is not a program in the usual sense of the word. It is a slogan, or a reminder phrase,

Tree planting at Fairmont Heights High School, Maryland.

to indicate the tone or thrust of the whole school program. It is a continuing signal to faculty and students alike to be alive to the opportunities around them. Operation Awareness, for the faculty, is a constant reminder of the school's job to provide experiences that will remedy the deficiencies of educational and cultural deprivation and strengthen personal dignity and worth. The aim of Operation Awareness is to transform deprivation and lack of confidence into a rewarding cycle of rich experiences and growing confidence and ambition.

An official school statement identifies Operation Awareness in these terms:

"Operation Awareness" is an attempt to get youngsters to move beyond the superficial and self-defeating activities found in so many of the local communities. Our goal will be to encourage these youngsters, in

terms of their maturity, to explore many facets of American life. This will include significant civic, social, governmental, scientific, technical, cultural and recreational experiences in the metropolitan area, as well as creatively structured co-curricular activities in the immediate school setting. More specifically the purposes of "Operation Awareness" are:

To make goals of the school more meaningful for students.

To aid students in developing the attitudes, skills, and powers for discovery.

To aid students in developing a creative sensitivity to their world.

To aid students in developing a wholesome and fulfilling self-concept.

These goals are accomplished through a series of school-wide activities fostering awareness of opportunities. Just before the Christmas holidays, Principal G. James Gholson circulates a newsletter listing local events, television programs, cinemas, and drama to encourage students to spend an enriching holiday period. The events listed also include municipal pageants, art exhibits, and special displays.

During Education Week, a special assembly hears graduates of the school report their experiences since leaving Fairmont Heights. In 1964, for example, the speakers included a teacher, a college senior, a cartoonist with the Department of Agriculture, a legal secretary at the Agency for International Development (AID), a nurse, another teacher, a secretary with the Department of State, an architect, a student of social work, and a student in the fine arts. Recent graduates have a special appeal to students and, consequently, a special ability to influence them.

A community-school dialogue along the lines of a forum has been established for the dual purpose of raising the cultural aspirations of the community and explaining the purposes of the school to the community. This program was inaugurated in October 1965, at a meeting attended by 83 parents, teachers, and students, at which "Problems Facing the Contemporary Family" was selected as the major topic for the year.

All teachers are drawn into Operation Awareness, partly by assignment to committees, partly by being given hints and reminders of ways to spark their own activities. Some of these hints come in general lists distributed from the principal's office, while others take the form of advice offered in personal conferences.

The spirit of Operation Awareness permeates the school and does not cease with graduation. A letter from Mrs. Charlotte Denison, guidance counsellor to graduating seniors, says, "I am proud that I had an opportunity to teach you. Maybe I helped to add something to your skill. Now that you are graduating I want to congratulate you and wish you success in all of your future activities."

Another letter says:

The Fairmont Heights family feels proud of you; we hope that you will make the family happy by upholding the ideals and values which were ever before you. Remember to think and you will experience less difficulty in facing the problems of life. . . . If we can be of any help to you, always feel free to contact the school. There will be someone here who will try to help you.

THE ROLE OF THE SOCIAL STUDIES DEPARTMENT

Department chairmen perform a valuable function in creating the atmosphere that facilitates creative teaching. By their example, leadership, and specific assistance and advice, they can contribute to the improvement of instruction.

Some department chairmen provide large amounts of teaching materials in the department office, to meet specific instructional needs, and to inspire teachers to broaden their own awareness of available materials. David Turner, department chairman at Yorktown High School, has a department collection of approximately 4,000 volumes, including many classroom sets of paperbacks; a vertical file of 45,000 bulletins and other fugitive materials; 200 classroom sets of mimeographed materials including historical documents and significant articles; and bound copies of all course outlines, tests, and mimeographed give-aways used by each teacher in the department. In addition he maintains a personal guidance file on every social studies student, including all the test scores and other data that can help in meeting individual needs in heterogeneous classes; an exhaustive publishers' file kept up to date each year; a topical file containing, for example, materials on communist and fascist propaganda and propaganda from other sources; and a simple but effective system of accounting for books signed out of the office. A shortwave radio was installed in 1965 to provide foreign broadcasts for taping. Impressive evidence of creative leadership and resources is apparent in this department office.

Joachim R. Schneider, department chairman at West Leyden, sees his role in a similar light. He lists his three chief functions as encouraging the use of new and current materials, keeping teachers up-to-date on the availability of new information and new materials, and visiting and encouraging new teachers. He considers it especially essential to use a variety of resources, because many students in this school are from homes where education is not given high value.

An important aspect of any social studies department is the overall philosophy and tone, whether or not the source is the department chairman. Often the teachers in the social studies department are unable to identify specific sources of their spirit or their philosophy.

In some schools, a pooling of statements by the social studies' teachers results in a composite statement which all accept and which then has influence on the thinking and teaching of newcomers to the department. The statement of purpose at DeWitt Junior High School in Ithaca, New York, where John P. Bozzone is chairman of the social studies department, was described to the project team by teacher James Campbell:

Given the current situation of stress in the world today, it is of vital importance that a social studies course provide the student with an intellectual approach which will help him to sort through the varied sources of information and range of opinions in order to build an objective attitude toward the world. He should then be encouraged to begin to form his own point of view concerning problems both at home and abroad. The proper classroom environment is one which promotes in the student an appreciation of the importance of the search for truth, respect for all people, and a feeling of responsibility to help fulfill the ideals of his own democratic society.

The similarities and differences of official "philosophies of the teaching of the social studies" can be suggested by presenting, without comment, statements from a number of schools. Published statements of philosophy are more commonly found in large school districts than in those that have only one high school; such statements are likely to reflect the combined thinking of social studies teachers from a number of schools within a school system.

The New Albany, Indiana, High School offers this statement:

The social studies are those learnings held to be of importance in the education of students which are drawn from the various disciplines that comprise the social sciences.

These selected learnings (the social studies) are concerned with an understanding of man and society. And since neither man nor society can be understood apart from the physical environment of soil and sea and sky, the systematic study of man will include the study of the human habitat—the planet Earth and the universe of which it is a part. Thus the objects for study in the social studies are man, society and the Earth. . . .

The social studies curriculum herein recommended should provide ample opportunities for young people growing up today to gain the understanding, the appreciation of the values, and the skills which history, geography, political science, economics, anthropology, sociology, and psychology can help provide and without serious overlapping of content. The major portion of time is devoted to studying the history and development of American Civilization—and economics. At other places in the curriculum opportunities are presented for the student to learn of men and societies other than his own and to draw comparisons between the men and societies under study with his own.

The Ferry Pass Junior High School at Pensacola, Florida, asserts:

We believe that the social studies should help the child attain (1) a factual basis for understanding himself as an individual and as a member of society; (2) appreciation of the cultural achievements of man and of the significance of basic American beliefs and ideals; and (3) practice in the art of good citizenship, including opportunities for individual accomplishment and social cooperation and responsibility. . . .

We believe that social studies teachers should cooperate with their colleagues to teach and stimulate student interest in language arts, art, music, literature, comparative religions, and the sciences to bring children an enriched understanding, appreciation, and enjoyment of the world in which they live.

The course of study in Denver is preceded by a statement of point of view:

The most important goal of the social studies program is to develop informed citizens, dedicated to the preservation and improvement of the society which they have inherited. This involves learning to respect the rights of others, accepting the responsibilities commensurate with our rights and freedoms, developing the ability to use reason instead of force in problem-solving and decision-making, and learning those skills and understandings which will allow the citizen to meet ever-changing views, approaches, and events which occur in our society and in other parts of the world.

The subject matter of the social studies is drawn from history and the social sciences of geography, political science, economics, sociology, cultural anthropology, and psychology. It is from these disciplines that pupils derive the fundamental knowledge about man's geographic environment, the history of civilization, how man governs himself and is governed, the structure of society, the behavior of people, and how different societies meet their economic needs and wants.

The social studies program must foster in pupils the ability to fuse subject matter learnings, skills, attitudes, and values into comprehensive and useable understandings. Through the attainment of this purpose and these understandings, the goal of the social studies—to develop informed citizens dedicated to the preservation and improvement of the society which they have inherited—can be achieved.

The Plumas Unified District of Quincy, California, has issued this statement:

. . . We want each child and youth to be an active, participating citizen. To achieve this, each individual must (a) give allegiance to the ideals of democracy; (b) recognize and endeavor to help in the solution of social problems; (c) be aware of the importance of basic human needs; (d) recognize the interdependence of all people—in family, school, community, national and world relationship; and (e) possess and use knowledge, skills, and abilities to facilitate the process of democratic living.

The differences among schools' statements of their "philosophy of the teaching of the social studies" are apparent, but the likenesses are even more conspicuous. All reflect an intelligent concern for the effect that social studies instruction will have on the lives of students. They display awareness of the teacher's responsibility to contribute to civic education. Further, they indicate an interest in providing high-level scholarship, as well as concern for attitudes and civic action. In short, these social studies staffs have stated, each in its own terms, recognition that citizenship education is a composite of knowledge, analysis, and commitment.

CONCLUSION

At every level, administrators help to create the atmosphere in which civic education can succeed. Superintendents, principals, and department heads all play their roles. The importance of the classroom teacher as the key figure cannot be questioned, but the administration can also make a variety of contributions by creating the physical and social climate in which the teacher can operate successfully.

*I think one of the troubles
of the world has been the habit of
dogmatically believing something or the
other. . . . I think we ought always to
entertain our opinions with
some measure of doubt.*

Bertrand Russell

CHAPTER **8**

Curriculum Patterns and Teaching Arrangements

HUMANITIES AND RELATED COURSES

Humanities and other multidisciplinary courses serve civic education by providing students with a classroom setting in which the relationships within society are the dominant concern. These courses, which are usually offered as electives to especially capable seniors, lend themselves to cooperative teaching, seminars, and other departures from the traditional curriculum and teaching methods. Although the humanities course in some schools offers neither grades nor credit, it often stimulates perceptive and enthusiastic response from students.

Liberal Studies   At Mount Hermon School in Massachusetts, the summer Liberal Studies Program is regarded as the school's laboratory for new approaches in teaching. Each summer, students of high ability from public and private schools throughout the nation come to Mount Hermon School for 6-week advanced courses in humanities, social studies, mathematics, and other fields. Students live in the school in close contact with teachers, who insist on a high level of performance and who guide students inconspicuously toward realization of their abilities. No final grades are given and few courses are taken for credit. Students enjoy the experience of learning for its own sake.

John W. Clarke, director of this broad program of humanities, says, "The real benefits lie outside the normal track of information. . . . The student of high ability gets a much more accurate concept of his potential when he is challenged to think more deeply than he has before, and when he is asked to compete and communicate with those of equal or higher ability."

The project team visited a number of other schools offering excellent humanities courses. In Lebanon, Oregon, Ralph Wood teaches an advanced placement humanities course that makes use of the art museum and other facilities of the University of Washington. At Mountlake Terrace High School in Washington, Derris Schlieman's students in humanities perform college-level work and do an impressive amount of reading. The Phoenix West High School, in Arizona, uses team teaching to give students the benefit of its teachers' varying backgrounds. The four teachers give lectures: David Fuller, in art; Ralph Johnson, in literature and philosophy; Serge Huff, in music; and Eugene McMullan, in history.

The Thematic Approach At Three Schools

By developing the student's language skills and literary perception within a framework of exploration of values, English courses frequently make a direct contribution to the cultivation of civic competence. At Miami Beach High School in Florida, for example, the suggested themes are Man and the Sea; Man and Society; Man and the State; The American Abroad; and Men at Work. At Monmouth Regional High School in New Shrewsbury, New Jersey, the suggested themes are expressed differently, but here also, the purpose is to integrate the development of skills with an increased awareness of values.

At Community High School in Naperville, Illinois, the material of the social studies program is grouped around 18 concepts:

1. Conservation
2. World interdependence
3. Dignity and the worth of the individual
4. Intelligent living
5. Education to strengthen democracy
6. Obligations in a democratic society
7. Bolstering the family
8. Developing moral and spiritual values
9. Gaining justice through law
10. Wise use of scarce resources
11. Patriotism and loyalty
12. Peace through governments
13. Achieving constructive social change
14. Aesthetic living
15. Better livelihood through social studies
16. Attitude toward authority
17. Appreciating our heritage
18. Intellectual development

The individual teacher has the ultimate responsibility for selecting concepts and concept objectives relevant to the subject matter of each unit.

NEW ROLES FOR THE SCHOOL LIBRARY

Many schools have found that the values for civic competence developed in humanities, English, and social studies classes can be fortified by expanded roles for the school library.

A Social Studies Library Consultant

At Yorktown High school in Arlington County, Virginia, a social studies teacher serves as a consultant to students in the library during every period of the day. A special desk is provided in the library for the social studies consultant. The assignment rotates, using a different teacher for each period, in place of study-hall duty. The

Combination bookstore and library, Germantown Friends School.

teacher serves as a resource person and assists students in developing the study and research skills needed to work on independent projects.

Instructional Materials Centers

Some instructional materials centers are primarily an extension of the central book collection to include records and films. Some are vastly expanded study areas designed to provide space to accommodate students in independent study programs, while others simply substitute individual study carrels for study tables. Some are entire complexes of reference rooms, reading rooms, conference rooms, faculty offices, materials collections, and study carrels. Many instructional materials centers combine several of these functions.

The Instructional Materials Center at Lakeview High School in Decatur, Illinois, includes four reference rooms, three conference rooms, six small listening rooms, 150 separate study carrels, and a large and comfortable reading room. Adjacent to the IMC are the offices of faculty members, who are available for consultation.

With the approval of the student council and its sponsor, students are permitted to go to the IMC during their study-hall periods, and almost half of the students take advantage of this opportunity. As one student expressed it, "This independent study gives you a sense of freedom. In the regular study-hall, you just sit and study; you have few materials with which to work. At the IMC you can stretch and relax, and there are many materials available here, including records."

Throughout this center the project team observed an apparently relaxed but serious attitude, a tone of attention and interest that contrasted sharply with the aura of escape from learning sometimes seen in school libraries. Records and tape recordings were being used extensively by some students following independent interests and by others pursuing course work.

TELEVISION AND RADIO IN TEACHING

Radio, television, and motion pictures can dramatize lessons that the student cannot experience directly.

A School Radio Station
In New Albany, Indiana, radio station WNAS is owned by the city school system and directed by the school's audio-visual director, Jerry Weaver. Thirty-one seniors work at the station, which not only answers school needs, but also brings news reports and cultural programs to 10,000 listeners within a 40-mile radius.

WNAS subscribes to the United Press International teletype service on a 24-hour-per-day basis and uses the material in several ways. Social studies teachers in government and current events classes consult the wire service news regularly, and analysis of the stock market reports is a part of the school's economics program. Overnight news is condensed and a summary is placed in each teacher's mailbox in the morning. The school's public address system broadcasts any news story of particular significance during the day. Initially, radio was used for a geography course broadcast by a local station, to upgrade elementary school geography teaching. Now the course continues, broadcast by the school-owned station as one of its regular offerings. A senior student frequently travels by air around the country, gathering first-hand transcribed sounds and course material to use for the broadcasts.

A particularly interesting feature is an English class in which the 31 carefully-screened seniors use WNAS facilities to study broadcasting functions. In recent years, 40 percent of the students from the course have followed broadcasting careers after graduation. One member of the class has a twice-a-week news beat for which he checks important city offices, and interviews public officials such as the mayor, the superintendent of schools, and the director of the Chamber of Commerce.

The costs are remarkably low. Original cost of the radio equipment was about $15,000. Annual operating costs are $5,000, including $1,100 for the teletype service at half the commercial rate. Some of the expense is covered by the school system's budget, but much of it comes from student council funds. At the council's suggestion, candy-vending machines have been installed and net about $40 per week to supplement the station's income.

Television Teaching
During the past six years, New Albany High School has also subscribed to a television service to supplement its teaching. Edmund Goerlitz teaches all five sections in American history. Four are traditional classes. Students in the fifth class watch a telecast four days a week, followed by one day of class discussion, project reports, and tests. Goerlitz appreciates the advantages of the telecasts, which use a talented teacher who has a professional delivery and access to teaching aids not available in the classroom. On the other hand, he admits that television programs may impose rigidity on the class through overly rapid or inappropriate presentation.

A television program entitled "Government, Darien-Style" has been prepared and broadcast on the Darien, Connecticut, schools' own closed-circuit system by their instructional materials department, headed by J. Robert Parkinson. "Government, Darien-Style" is a series of 20-minute programs produced by Mrs. Wilnore Weck, a teacher who has been active in local political affairs for many years. For the series, Mrs. Weck recorded interviews with local government officials. "This way," she explained, "local officials are shown to every classroom that wishes to see them." By means of one interview, the information can be beamed to many classrooms and at many different times.

A second television series produced by the Darien schools spotlights events, places, and people in the news. A mobile unit, owned by the school system, moves from school to school to tape programs and occasionally goes into the community to record outstanding events for this series.

A third series of television programs for the Darien schools is called "Social Conscience of Youth." It broadcasts discussions of controversial issues such as demonstrations, and interviews with representatives of the Peace Corps and other agencies which have a strong appeal to youth.

The Instructional Materials Department in Darien has assembled a library of videotapes produced elsewhere for use by any teacher in the school system. It also issues a bulletin of broadcast schedules to alert teachers to programs, which deal with topics such as the Peace Corps, Martin Luther King, and changes in Southeast Asia.

A variation of the closed circuit television technique is employed at the De La Salle High School in New Orleans, where Alvin Murphy teaches several groups of American history students simultaneously with a live broadcast. Murphy and one class of 30 students use the studio, while another class of 60 students shares the lesson in the viewing room. Two-way oral communication operates between the two rooms at all times.

A city-wide television service in Kansas City, Missouri, prepares lesson sequences for many courses, complete with lesson plan, bibliography, and supplementary activities. The topics in the 9th-grade citizenship sequence include: law enforcement; the FBI; city planning; water supply; the city manager; the Armed Forces; police protection; the fire department; the Human Relations Commission; and programs on the Hebrew, Catholic, and Protestant faiths.

Many schools use commercial television programs designed for the general public, such as the National Driving Test, the National Health Test, and the National Citizenship Test. One reason for the effectiveness of television as a teaching tool is a quality described by Marshall McCluhan of the University of Toronto, who says, "The elementary and basic fact about the TV image is that it is a mosaic or mesh, continuously in a state of formation by 'the scanning finger.' Such a mosaic involves the viewer in a perpetual act of participation. . . . The TV image is not a shot or a view of anything so much as an experience."

The hazards and potential abuses of this electronic marvel are equally well-known to teachers. Many students like television classes because the television set eases their job. They find it easy and pleasant to sit, listen, and watch; they consider it a chore to go to the library (or even to the textbook) and learn material from the printed page. Secondly, few television classes go beyond the excellent presentations to problem-solving, critical thinking, or inquiry-directed learning. A third danger of television in the social studies curriculum is the impetus it gives to the predigested approach, often loaded with the danger of subtle indoctrination. This danger might be avoided by using the time gained to provide more and better discussion groups and independent study situations as supplements to the telecasts.

TEAM TEACHING

At Darien, Connecticut, a four-man team teaches a current social issues course. All four began by spending six weeks preparing a detailed plan of the course with specific allocations of time and resources. The team chose significant topics and challenging reading, including paperbacks, textbooks, and a great deal of mimeographed material.

The first unit in the current social issues course is "The Nature of Culture," in which students examine value systems of various countries and societies, including our own, and begin to understand cultural change. This unit is largely lecture and seminar instruction. It also requires students to write a paper on "Darien as a Subculture," in which they look at their home town through the eyes of an anthropologist. The second unit involves critical thinking, especially as it is related to the use of mass media. Here, the major activity is an analysis of various magazines. In the unit on "Communism in Practice," much of the work is presented through carefully planned panel discussions.

The four imaginative, articulate teachers of this course enjoy good rapport with their students and are enthusiastic about certain features of team teaching, cooperative planning and cooperative evaluation in particular. They agree upon common procedures, but each instructor has latitude in developing topics for which he is responsible.

Large group sessions are held to a minimum. Most are used for introductory lectures and outside speakers. Students move frequently from one instructor to the next, returning to each of the instructors several times during the year. Students seem to like this change of instructors and the arrangement helps teachers to evaluate the work of the students more accurately. When the teachers were asked about the advantages of team teaching they made these points:

With several people working together the course is much better organized. Team teaching provides opportunity for a cooperative way of working and a chance for keeping our materials up-to-date, and prods us into using more up-to-date materials. Team teaching also provides an opportunity for a better evaluation of students because there is more than one adult involved in this evaluation. The methods we have used in team teaching include teacher-led discussion, outside speakers, some role playing, court sessions, and panel discussions.

All seniors at Glastonbury High School, in Connecticut, take a current social issues course under the direction of Miss Betty Jane Ladd. Sometimes the class meets as a total group; sometimes it meets in two sections; more often it meets in groups of 12 students each. Three or more dis-

Team teaching at Mountlake Terrace High School includes large-group instruction.

cussion meetings may precede a large group lecture, or this pattern may be reversed, or large group sessions may meet for three or four days in succession.

An unusually wide variety of speakers has addressed the Glastonbury students. Several years ago a group of Russians, including a member of the Praesidium of the USSR, came to the school; in 1964, a representative from the Black Muslims spoke. Students may be excused from their second-hour class twice each semester to continue discussions with noted speakers who appear before large group sessions.

The team teachers carefully organize the 12-member discussion groups, to achieve an equal distribution of boys and girls and to include a balance of liberals and conservatives. They also take into account personality characteristics and any other conditions that might help a student to succeed more readily in one group than in another.

Two student leaders are selected from each group to meet periodically with the teaching team as "an extension team." Each teacher is responsible for four groups and is the base teacher, guidance source, and resource person for students in these groups. He must also make the final evaluation of the work of the students in his groups. Teachers shift groups at the end of each grading period, so that the students have an opportunity to work with each of the teachers during the year. At the end of the first semester, students are entirely regrouped.

The content of the Glastonbury CSI course and the organization used contribute in a very substantial way to civic education goals. Students have a chance to hear varied views on any relevant issue; there are no closed areas.

Cooperative Teaching   Local traditions, available space and resources, and differences in teacher personalities and competencies dictate wide variations in team teaching plans. At McCluer High School, in Florissant, Missouri, the term "cooperative teaching" is used. Teachers say of their innovation:

The team was organized because we saw a need to review the course. When we asked for volunteers to go into this idea of cooperative planning and teaching, some teachers disagreed with the whole thing. We four agreed and went ahead.

We didn't want to organize so that each week would be the same; we have team lectures when team lectures suit our purpose.

After we finish our team lecture on the Monroe Doctrine and something on John Marshall, we will get into a section on culture and we will have another music session, a hootenanny. Miss Ratcliff is in charge of that; she knows more music than we do.

The most important thing is that we get together and plan, and we are beginning to agree on concepts. I'm sure we are teaching more ideas than we did when we taught separately. And research! I never worked so hard in my life.

It has exposed the students to a new kind of history, and I think this has stimulated them as much as it has stimulated us. We all agree that learning ought to be fun. That's where the hootenanny fits in.

We sit down regularly to plan together and we watch for the concepts we are developing instead of just stumbling through a lot of unrelated facts. By being constantly together as a team, we are more aware of this than if we simply met together for an hour or so in a planning session and then went into our separate classrooms to do what we wanted.

The students not only have the advantage of better-prepared lectures because we have more free time to prepare them; they also receive a great deal more individual attention. We have many opportunities to take students aside from the large group and work with them over missed work, tough assignments, or some unique research. And the students sense our feeling of working together and reflect it by being more cooperative themselves.

FLEXIBLE SCHEDULING

At Ladue, Missouri, an English teacher, a biology teacher, and a social studies teacher constitute another type of team. They do not plan integrated instruction, but simply agree on efficient allocations of class time among their three classes, because they share the same group of 60 students during the first three periods of every day. Traditionally, each teacher in turn would have three classes of 20 students each. In the Ladue plan, the teaching team meets weekly to arrange the time distribution for the following week.

In the American problems course at Marshall High School in Portland, Oregon, approximately 400 students meet twice weekly in groups of 200 and twice in small groups of 15. The large group meetings last 40 minutes; the small-group meetings, 60 minutes. Four teachers are assigned to this course. The schedule is termed flexible, but it is actually set for the year; it allows for a great deal of independent study. Many students are unassigned to any class for as much as one-third of the school day. They may go to resource centers, to the library, to the cafeteria, to a study-hall, or to several other rooms that have been opened to accommodate unassigned students.

INDEPENDENT STUDY

At Norwalk, Connecticut, high-ability students who have the recommendation of their English teacher can enroll in an independent study program. These students meet three times a week in the library and twice weekly in the classroom. During the classroom periods, students report to the group on their research. Students select their own topics and the teacher discusses the topics with the student and with the entire group. Miss Marilyn Spence, the teacher, says, "We help to sharpen the question, to make it more precise, to help the student word the question in such a way that a definitive answer becomes possible."

An independent study program is now in its third year at the Mount Hermon Academy. Here, if a student wants to do research on a particular topic, he selects a faculty sponsor to help him formulate his project. If the topic is approved by a faculty committee, the student is released from required athletics to pursue his independent study.

At Monmouth Regional High School, New Shrewsbury, New Jersey, the independent study program is operated by the English department, even though some of the study projects are in other areas. If a student applies for admission to this program and if he submits an acceptable topic and secures the recommendation of his English teacher, he is admitted to independent study for a five-week period, during which he is excused from his English class and works instead on his project. This program is currently limited to 30 students, and no student is allowed more than two five-week enrollments. One student prepared an analysis of the dispute involving Professor Genovese, a Rutgers University faculty member who publicly stated his beliefs concerning the Vietnam struggle. Another student worked on a community survey of attitudes toward censorship; a third, on the use of language as a propaganda tool to mislead the consumer. In speaking of the value of this program, Mr. McLaughlin, director of the program, said:

Independent study offers a student opportunity for in-depth examination of a problem he has chosen. He organizes and directs his project and he is able to test his ability to use his time and talent. Emphasis is shifted away from teacher-directed activity and focused upon individual inquiry and creativity.

A research paper, scenario, tape recording, combination paper and oral report, essay, or an oral examination are some of the possibilities submitted for evaluation. Although the primary means of evaluating a student's work is the paper, tape, or oral exam completed at the close of the five-week period, some weight is given to the student's ability to work independently during the five weeks.

LEARNING THROUGH SIMULATION

Of the innovations in education, one of the most promising and least understood is simulation. Like team teaching and independent study, simulation is something different in almost every school where it is used.

Simulation is basically role-playing. In the classroom, it can be a simple exercise, such as "Pretend you are a Southern slave owner; stand up and tell us how you feel about the Fugitive Slave Law." It can be a more complex game, played by every student in the class according to precise rules and lasting for one period or several weeks.

Standardized simulation games have been used as pilot programs in a number of schools to test this way of learning. Several games have been developed and tested. A career game gives students experience in making decisions about education, jobs, and family life. Democracy games show the processes by which differences between members or groups in a democratic society are resolved. One game, on legislative procedure, is played by five to 13 persons acting as legislators. By placing the student in the role of a legislator trying to get reelected, this game seeks to show the dependence of a legislator's reelection upon his ability to satisfy the desires of his constituents.

Simulation games are usually concerned with interaction among Congressmen, nations, businesses, or whatever units are central to that particular game. Students strive to win the nomination, the election, the war, or whatever is at stake. The game appeals to the students' love of competition, contest, and problem solving. Every teacher the project team consulted who had used simulation reported very high levels of student enthusiasm.

Sister Constantine at Trinity High School in Bloomington, Illinois, reported, "This is a wild experience. I almost lose my head. It is also an exceptionally valuable experience."

One teacher who makes full use of games is Stanley Schainker of Horton Watkins High School in Ladue, Missouri. For his teaching of a course in American principles, he uses three different types of games. His Type-1 games are used primarily for review purposes and are usually patterned after popular games that appear on television shows, such as Password, Match Game, and To Tell the Truth. Type-2 games provide role-playing situations and a stimulus for creative work.

Type-3 games are the true simulation games, of which Schainker uses six. One deals with a political party nominating convention; another with a citizens action meeting. One is a Congressional game, with legislators trying to pass bills consistent with their assigned information about constituents, political philosophy, and the cooperation they can obtain from fellow legislators.

Perhaps the most popular as well as the most dramatic of the simulation games is "Decision," which was developed by Cleo Cherryholmes of Northwestern University. This game was played in at least four of the schools visited by the project team.

In "Decision," students take active part in the affairs of a simplified model of the world of nations. Naturally, to reduce world affairs to fit inside a classroom and to shrink a year of complex international relations into one hour requires a great deal of simplification, but many of the essential principles can be retained.

Each of the five nations involved in the world of "Decision" has a given description, including certain fixed features. Full descriptions of these features, which vary from nation to nation, are given to all who participate. The nations are not evenly matched, but this has no effect on the game, because each nation is competing against itself and its own history and resources rather than against the other nations. No nation is without advantages and no nation is without some problems. The objective is to make the most of the resources and to find the best approaches to the problems, while coping with the pressures of a world of other nations with their own ambitions and problems.

Each nation is composed of nine students, of which four start as government officials and five as citizens. The highest authority in each nation is the Chief of State. He may discharge any of his cabinet at any time and fill the vacancy with any other official or citizen. Every decision involves the entire government to some extent and a balancing of the concerns of the various officials; the weighing of these factors and needs is the heart of the simulation. Decisions are made with interests of citizens in mind, because citizens have considerable power as leading representatives of the various interest groups of the nation. They watch the officials and their decisions with care and interest, and work out their own ideas on national policies. Final decisions for each year are recorded in the Economic Plan.

The simulation continues for 10 class periods; class simulation sessions, each representing a year, alternate with planning sessions. At the beginning of the simulation year, each government files with the judges a carbon copy of its economic plan, including a full section on the budget. At the close of each year, the government files with the judges the original copy of the economic plan, completed to show all economic transactions and decisions during the year.

Government officials conferring together must decide what standards of living and what standards of education they will consider acceptable for their nation and then devise their strategy for attaining their goals, within the framework of wealth and population assigned to the nation. They make the best use they can of research and development facilities, deficit financing, international trade, and, if necessary, their armed forces. The armed forces may be increased or decreased by the government or maintained at their initial level.

Conflicts in "Decision" can be limited or nuclear, but all conflicts require support by a functioning government and at least one citizen. If the Chief of State has this support, the war proceeds. If the attack is nuclear, no defense is possible. The attacked nation can retaliate however. The damage done by a nuclear attack depends on the targets selected by the attacker. When war is limited to conventional forces, it is directed against an entire nation rather than specific targets. The attacked nation may negotiate terms for peace, or it can respond to the attack by meeting conventional forces with conventional forces. After each battle, the attacking nation signifies whether it wishes to continue the war or drop the attack. If the decision is to continue, the defending nation chooses whether to respond again or to sue for peace. Other nations, singly or in alliance, may threaten some action against an attacking nation which might cause it to drop an attack. When a limited war stops, reparations are arranged as part of the peace treaty and shown on an international agreement form.

If a war continues until one nation's conventional forces are completely destroyed, the nation with remaining forces may dictate the peace treaty if it is prepared to station 100 conventional forces in the conquered nation for each 50,000,000 people in that nation. For each year of occupation, all the normal maintenance costs on the budget are doubled. Occupation forces are not available for national defense at home. If a conquering nation is not willing to occupy a conquered nation on these terms, the treaty must be negotiated and not be simply dictated.

Games as sophisticated as "Decision" require complex ground rules. They also require a considerable amount of class time just to familiarize students with the rules before any particiaption is possible.

Locally Constructed Simulation Games

Considerable time is needed to construct a simulation game. Yet, some experts, including Cherryholmes, believe that locally constructed simulation games are likely to be more successful. At Maine Township, East, students in Gil Mickina's class simulated a House of Representatives session and considered several pieces of proposed legislation:

Should the voting age be lowered to 18?
Should the Civil Rights Act be expanded?
Should a national censorship board be established?
Should defense spending be increased to support the Vietnam war effort?

Two minutes were allowed for making political deals, trading votes on any issues, or campaigning for votes. Then the Congress was called to order by the teacher, who acted as chairman. A motion was made to call up the issue of national censorship. A motion to table it was defeated, and the legislature was given one and a half minutes to bargain on this particular issue. The issue was defeated by a vote taken by a show of hands. Each student gained or lost points according to the directions on his tally card.

The chairman then called up the bill to provide for lowering the voting age to 18. This was followed by two minutes of bargaining and discussion before voting. This bill was passed, and the points were added to or subtracted from students' previous scores.

A third bill called for extending the Civil Rights Act. Again, debate and two minutes of bargaining preceded voting. This proposal was defeated. A bill on increased defense spending was also defeated. At the end of the class period the student with the most points won the game.

Miss Eleanor Baldwin, at Maine Township, West, Illinois, has used a similar kind of simulation dealing with single legislative issues, including a Medicare bill in one class, and a civil rights bill in another. Three or four class periods were given to the bill, for hearings, debate, informal bargaining, and voting. The simulation was realistic, with some students serving as committee members and others as lobbyists. There was filibustering, discussion, and questioning; the party whips checked on the number of votes they might be able to get for or against the bill. Finally, on the fourth day the bill was brought to a vote.

The value of simulation is in teaching students to deal with ideas and with people. Students learn that compromise or negotiation need not be a cynical and underhanded business, but is often an inescapable necessity when a large group deals with multiple issues. Like other teaching devices, simulation has limitations. Although it helps immensely to demonstrate the process of handling issues, in the forms observed by the project team, too little attention was given to the merits of the issues themselves.

STUDENT LEADERSHIP CONFERENCES

Student leadership conferences are increasing in popularity and are receiving widespread acclaim for their contributions to civic education.

Conferences are local, state, regional, and in a few cases national, and may last a day or two or several weeks. They may be organized and financed by the school or by a non-school agency. Typically, they enroll student leaders, particularly officers of student government organizations. At the state level, they include gatherings such as the Governor's Youth Conference, Girls' State, Boys' State, and the Student Council Convention, each of which operates in all 50 states. In addition, the Student Council Association operates many summer workshops and the National Honor Society stages conventions in about half the states of the nation.

Student leadership conferences have as a major objective the goal of making students so familiar with group procedures that they can operate confidently and comfortably in a realistic situation as student body leaders. The conference emphasis may be parliamentary procedure, legislative process, or interpersonal relations. Usually it is a combination of all three and may include other concerns. The 72 summer workshops held during the summer of 1965 by state associations of student councils were geared to helping students assume responsibility for leading group action. The participants were concerned with how they could help solve some of today's problems—maintaining good community relations, developing community service programs, and helping people of various backgrounds to get along with each other. Throughout the nation, teachers and students found the workshops and conferences valuable.

Many large school districts operate leadership conferences to which representatives from all high schools in the system are invited. In one such conference, six student leaders from the Ingraham High School in Seattle joined 160 others from the Seattle area for a one-week camp experience. As in most such experiences, the delegates were juniors who presumably would be in a position to provide the school's leadership during the coming year.

The New York City schools rent a 500-acre New Jersey farm for a variety of camping and conference experiences, and the DeWitt Clinton High School makes good use of this facility for a series of week-end conferences. A letter to parents of DeWitt Clinton students describes the purposes of the week-end:

Our school is interested in your son and in helping him develop every facet of his personality to the utmost. As part of this program we are holding a leadership week-end at Hudson Guild Farm. We are arranging a program of discussion, social, athletic, and work activities. Your boy will have the chance to meet prominent alumni, members of the faculty, and his own schoolmates in an informal setting.

The week-end is financed by the Alumni Aid Fund, which defrays the cost of approximately $15 per boy. Parents are given this invitation, "If you feel that this is a worthy project, you may send the DeWitt Clinton Alumni Fund whatever contribution you feel you can afford. Your contribution will help a less fortunate student in the future."

Many of the worthwhile organizations that now exist at DeWitt Clinton were organized during one of the week-ends at this camp. Unfortunately, there are not enough accommodations for all students who want to go. At one time there were 800 applicants and space for only 35. James Stein, the director of activities, pointed out that the only thing that causes a boy to be screened out is unreliability. "We have to be able to count on him." Sometimes the program for a given camp is made before a week-end begins. At other times, the week-end is unstructured. The camp week-end provides a time when students can be oriented to their new school situation. They can talk about questions related to leadership, and can discuss problems.

The Mississippi Youth Congress is sponsored by the Mississippi Speech Association. During the first 16 years of its operation, the Mississippi Youth Congress enrolled 2,423 student delegates from 79 high schools and 19 colleges, and during these 16 years the Congress debated 1,061 bills and passed 124 of them. High school students serve in the House of Representatives of the Mississippi Youth Congress; college and junior college students make up the Senate. Each school may send up to 5 delegates. Youth conferences can be an excellent introduction to adult processes in citizenship. Although only a small fraction of the total student body of any school ever has the opportunity to attend a state leadership conference, the number is increasing and many more students are attending local conferences.

CONCLUSION

The ferment in the public schools extends in many directions. Some of the innovations are directly aimed at the social studies area; others are more general. Interdisciplinary courses and other curriculum changes, more extensive library services, use of television and other media, team teaching, flexible scheduling, independent study, simulation techniques, and student leadership conferences are only some of the educational patterns and processes now in use in many schools. They contribute much to the preparation of students for effective roles as citizens, especially by making education more meaningful and by enlarging the opportunities for active and realistic participation.

The night is beautiful
so the faces of my people.
The stars are beautiful
So the eyes of my people
Beautiful also is the sun.
Beautiful also
are the souls of my people.

Langston Hughes

CHAPTER **9**

Meeting Special Problems

THE COMMUNITY INFLUENCES CIVIC EDUCATION

Many city school systems have recently recognized their responsibility to provide appropriate educational experiences for students identified as culturally deprived, underprivileged, disadvantaged, or as children with limited backgrounds. Frequently, academic retardation is complicated by the economic deprivation and the racial issues with which it is often associated.

Meeting The Needs Of The Culturally Deprived

Central High School, Kansas City, Missouri, has adapted its program to improve the civic education potential for the rapidly changing inner-city population it serves. The school has 2,700 students in a building designed to accommodate 1,800. At one time, approximately 60 percent of the students were Negro and 40 percent were white. Three years later, almost all of the school's students were Negroes.

James F. Boyd, the principal, helped his faculty keep all students working to the maximum of their abilities. He encouraged each faculty member to look for abilities within each youngster rather than to think in terms of a group of children or of group scores. One of the first objectives Boyd and his staff set for themselves was a systematic study of the student body then enrolled at Central. They charted scores obtained on the Otis and Terman Intelligence Tests and the Stanford Achievement Test and found that their students were far below the norms in reading and spelling. The findings of the initial survey were presented to all departments, and teachers were encouraged to suggest ideas for solving the problems identified. Because reading was one of the most chronic problems, a remedial reading program was established at the outset. English teachers brought their students to the Reading Laboratory for 23 days of intensive instruction. Tests before and after the 23-day period showed gains in reading ability ranging from eight months to one year. The reading program has been developed from a remedial to a developmental program, using the SRA Reading Laboratory materials supplemented with reading pacers, controlled readers, and shadow scopes.

Another aspect of the program to raise levels of aspiration of students in the Central student body is an 8-week humanities course offered during the summer for those who have just finished their sophomore or junior year. The readings include selections from *Patterns of Culture*, *Oedipus Rex*, *Antigone*, *Gulliver's Travels*, *The Aims of Education*, *The Prince*, *Franklin's Autobiography*, *Religion and the Rise of Capitalism*, *The Federalist Papers*, and *The Bridge of San Luis Rey*. In addition, students receive instruction in music and art, culminating in group research on music and art history, and attend plays and art galleries. Student response has been excellent. Many students want to take the humanities course a second time.

Central High School is planning to conduct four-week summer sessions with emphasis for pre-9th-graders on study skills in reading, vocabulary, and spelling; for pre-10th graders the focus will be on attitudes, attacking defeatist attitudes in particular; and for pre-11th graders, the sessions will include laboratory experiences in reading, writing, and citizenship.

Another program described by Boyd is the courtesy-competency campaign launched a few years ago when prominent alumni of Central (including Robert Powell, Casey Stengel, Gladys Swarthout, and Walt Disney) were asked to send to the school telegrams mentioning the courtesy-competency campaign. Telegrams were read at a student assembly, and badges were presented to honor students and to students who had shown unusual courtesy. The students were surprised and pleased that prominent people would take time to send a telegram to show their interest in competence at Central High School.

Concentrated in Detroit and other large cities across the nation are countless families whose children are severely hampered in their schooling by a complex of community, home, and school conditions. Changes in the population of the inner cores of most large cities have created localities in which the majority of children have extraordinary needs that the public schools are not prepared to meet. These children with limited backgrounds comprise one-third of the 3.2 million children now enrolled in America's 14 largest school systems. To meet the educational needs of these children, several cities participate in the Great Cities Improvement Project of cooperative effort to implement, study, and evaluate the many facets of an appropriate total educational program.

Detroit, as part of the Great Cities Improvement Project, has inaugurated improvement projects involving 27 schools, 1,250 school staff members, and 32,250 students.

In Detroit, the effects of the four-pronged Great Cities Improvement Project are evident. Parent and community involvement in school activities has increased measurably, with mutual support evidenced where hostility existed before. Parents have been urged to join the school in the total process of teaching and learning. The parents themselves have learned some of the skills they have lacked, and many have developed some idea of how important they are to their child's success in school. "Short-term" forecasts for the Great Cities Improvement Project in Detroit are for larger numbers of children and youth to leave project schools with increased academic and social competence, to stay in school longer, and to have a greater capacity for financially and politically independent citizenship.

A parallel program to bring additional educational opportunities to disadvantaged youth in Detroit is the Extended School Program, which brings special services to 20 schools in areas identified as deprived. Prominent among the special services established are remedial help for students, extended use of the school library, and adult education activities. The additional effort exerted as part of the Great Cities Improvement Project was financed at first by private foundation funds, but recently it has been assumed as part of the regular expenditures from the general school funds. Much of the vitality and imagination of programs now financed by the school system for services in individual schools is the result of the stimulus the Great Cities Improvement Project gave to the Detroit schools.

Spain Junior High School is a new school located in the middle of the target area for Detroit's primary anti-poverty program. Many of the slum dwellings which formerly surrounded the school site have now been razed. Eventually, the area will be developed into a vast medical center for Wayne State University, but today students still come from an area which reportedly has more persons with incomes of less than $1,000, more dilapidated houses, and higher divorce and crime rates than almost any other area in Detroit.

In 1962, Spain Junior High School initiated courses in German, French and Spanish, on the assumption that youngsters would learn to express themselves better in their own language if they could practice a foreign one. Miss Julia Wilde, the former principal, explained:

The staff at Northeastern High School tells us that students from Spain use the English language better and express themselves more fluently than children who come from other junior high schools. We believe that our stress on foreign language has a great deal to do with this.

The principal objectives of the course are the following: (1) to give every student a chance to learn a foreign language in which he can talk precisely because he has no bad models to copy; (2) to improve the self-image of the student and enhance his concept; and (3) to help students with definite speech problems.

Another program at Spain Junior High School is the "image program" for improving the self-concept of students. It involves a series of assembly programs featuring speeches by prominent and successful Negroes. Speakers have included pediatricians, firemen, a psychiatrist, and other professional and skilled workers. The program is based on the premise that there is a connection between what a student thinks he can accomplish and what he aspires to be. In order to dramatize the contribution of these speakers, each one supplies a photograph which is suitably framed and hung on the wall of the library as a constant reminder that with enough will and work and brainpower every student can accomplish a great deal.

A third program at Spain Junior High, designed to raise the level of aspiration of 20 top students in the 9th grade, is an after-school humanities seminar which meets three times a week from November to April. Mrs. Johnson, the sponsor, believes that the seminar stimulates the student to a self-knowledge that enables him to aspire to things higher than he anticipated. Among the readings have been *Hamlet, Romeo and Juliet, Oliver Twist, The Odyssey,* and *The Apology.* The interest of students in the books covered in class does not end with the class period. Last spring Mrs. Johnson took the entire group to see a performance of *Romeo and Juliet* at Wayne State University, and many students not enrolled in the humanities course also attended. After the group had studied some of Shakespeare's plays, one of the best-sellers at the school bookstore was *King Lear,* a play not included in the course. Mrs. Johnson takes her students on all-day field trips to Detroit's cultural center, which includes an art museum, historical museum, and library. Even though many of her students live near the center and have passed it often, she finds that most are not aware that so much is available to enjoy just a few blocks from home.

To facilitate the job of providing adequately for all students regardless of economic and racial backgrounds, Detroit's regional organization is built around groupings of schools which include diverse socio-economic areas rather than the usual pattern of contiguous geographical areas. Field executives in the Detroit school system, positions similar to assistant superintendents, are in charge of non-contiguous regions. These are deliberately arranged so that they represent a model of the entire city system, from the highest to the lowest socio-economic level. Field executives are thus able to plan the cooperative experiences within their area without breaking down neighborhood patterns. Integration in school activities becomes a reality through enrollment in region band, orchestra, student council, and similar activities.

Detroit's Division of School Relations and Special Services, under the direction of an assistant superintendent, is responsible for helping the schools to recognize and adapt to community needs.

One responsibility of this division is arranging for community use of school buildings. The school system assists block clubs and other community groups by finding rooms for meetings in neighborhood schools.

Schools and communities also work together in planning new school buildings and additions to existing buildings. Community committees, with 12 to 15 members selected by school principals and PTA officers, give neighborhood leaders an opportunity to work with architects and school personnel in developing building plans.

The Division of School Relations and Special Services also sponsors Human Relations Clubs, organized as a result of the NAACP request for junior NAACP chapters. A booklet of guidelines for human relations clubs was developed by a committee of school personnel and NAACP representatives. It includes a list, prepared by the NAACP, of speakers available in the community for talks on careers in human relations. Eighteen of the 22 high schools in this city now have human relations clubs. The Detroit NAACP has offered a trophy to the outstanding human relations club for the year. It is clear that the schools and the NAACP share interest in an important common value, improved human relations.

A third responsibility of the Division of School Relations and Special Services is to monitor texts and other instructional materials to ensure an appropriate interrelation between races and nationalities and to avoid derogatory remarks or emphasis in school materials. This role is particularly important in the Detroit area, which has large Slavic, Mediterranean, and Negro population groups. The effort has not been without difficulties. At times, textbook publishers have removed passages or illustrations offensive to one group only to substitute others that other minority groups found distasteful. At other times, groups have perhaps misinterpreted the materials of these publishers, seeing derogatory references in unexpected places. The Detroit Division of School Relations and Special Services acknowledges the difficulties, and it appears to be opening new avenues of communication to meet them. It hopes that, with time, mutual understanding will develop.

**Taking Part In
The Extension
Of Civil Rights**

In the R. B. Hudson High School, in Selma, Alabama, faculty and students appreciate the importance of education and the effort necessary to raise the educational level of the Negro. The principal, William J. Yelder, is dedicated to the civil rights movement, and his enthusiasm is shared by faculty and students alike. The day before the project team's visit, Yelder had met with 700 persons in the school to plan a march. He has participated in a number of demonstrations but will not permit them to interfere with school. "We tell our students through their teachers that freedom costs something," says Yelder. "You must respect the rights of others. Freedom and responsibility go together."

A student who moved to Selma from Detroit was one of many students the project team interviewed who showed awareness of the relationship between freedom and responsibility. The boy admitted that the level of instruction is better in Detroit and that the stimulation, the incentive to learn, and the freer interracial associations in the North are real advantages. This student, however, recognizes the importance of the civil rights movement and wants to stay in Selma and try to make conditions better. Going north, he says, is comparable to a general leaving his army.

After the extended civil rights demonstration in Selma in January, 1965, which resulted in the loss of about 10 days of school, the slow learners tended to drop out, but the eager ones came back to school with a new enthusiasm for learning and a new purpose in life. The faculty at R. B. Hudson believes that students gained a sense of responsibility by participating in the Selma demonstration. The dedication students feel for the civil rights movement adds a powerful motivation to do well in their school work, according to the principal and teachers at R. B. Hudson.

The attitude of some students is suggested by their responses to four written questions:

	Yes	No
Does a march or demonstration do any good?	59	1
Does a good citizen participate in a march or demonstration?	58	2

In the event of a conflict between the local and a Federal law, would you obey the local police?	13	47
Have you personally taken part in a march or demonstration?	54	6

One of the classes the project team observed in this school was the cosmetology class begun in 1965 and taught by Mrs. Mark K. Cage. The poise and good grooming of the girls in this class are impressive when one recognizes that almost all of these girls came from extremely poor homes. Most expect to earn a living in some phase of beauty-shop operation, but Mrs. Cage stresses many values in addition to preparation for a vocation. She believes that learning to groom properly will add to a girl's self assurance.

One of the most enjoyable experiences during the project team's visits to schools was listening to the R. B. Hudson High School choir. This choir, under the direction of Perry Louis Anderson, received nationwide publicity during the summer of 1965. When the choir sang at the memorial service for Reverend James Reeb, who was killed in Selma, clergymen from throughout the country who attended the service were so impressed that they arranged with the National Council of Churches and other groups to sponsor a two-month tour. The first trip took the students to Rockville, Maryland, and to the New York World's Fair. After returning to Selma for a day, they left again for an extended stay in California.

Seven members of the choir talked about the tour and what it had done for them. One boy said, "It gave us the feeling that there are people who care about us as human beings. Living as we do, we have had the impression at times that we are unknown, that we don't matter." A girl reported that the most worthwhile experience for her was being a guest in white homes. The girl suggested that even though she had known that there were places where she might stay safely in a white home, she could not believe it until it actually happened. A boy reported, "We got acquainted with those Northern Liberals that our newspapers talk against. We found that many of them did practice what they preach." Another boy said, "I didn't know before what it was like to feel free, really free." These students exhibited a great deal of understanding. They said that many white people who were sympathetic to

their aspirations were afraid to speak out, because they were afraid their children would be harmed.

Many choir members kept contact with the whites they met during the tour, some of whom have sponsored scholarships for R. B. Hudson students. The accompanist, Quentin Laine, is now at the University of Alabama, taking organ lessons paid for by someone he met while on tour. He said, "This tour has opened a lot of doors for some of us."

GROUP PROGRAMS FOR STUDENTS WHO NEED ADDITIONAL HELP

In addition to the schools whose programs reflect concern for the needs of a dominant disadvantaged group, many other schools, free of the special problems of the severely underprivileged communities, are nevertheless conscious of the less able students in their ranks. The project team observed several special education programs in schools in Connecticut, Michigan, California, Ohio, and other states.

**Instruction For
Special Students**

In the "Norwalk Plan," at Brien Mc-Mahon High School in Norwalk, Connecticut, a team of four certified special education teachers and a full-time teacher's aide work with students between the ages of 13 and 21. This plan integrates special students into the regular school program as much as possible. Student instruction is divided as follows:

With Special Education Teachers	*With Regular Class Teachers*
1. *Language Arts*	1. *Music*
2. *Social Studies*	2. *Physical Education*
3. *Vocational Information*	3. *Crafts*
4. *Mathematics*	4. *Home Economics*
5. *Science*	5. *Industrial Arts*
6. *Driver Training*	6. *Clubs*
7. *Typing*	
8. *Group Guidance*	

The Norwalk Plan statement continues:

In some cases a retarded child may be placed in a regular class program on a part-time basis and, if successful, a full time program will develop. There have been several successful results of such placements. Constant evaluation of the child's progress is being made with the help of interested school personnel and the head of the department.

Important in the Norwalk Plan is the work-study program. Special students work as stock boys, repairmen, operators of looms, cable weavers, workers in the plastics and hat industries, bookbinders, dishwashers, salad girls, and custodians. Continuous guidance is provided, with an occupational stress in all subjects. Course material is adapted to the needs and abilities of the group, consistent with the general educational objectives. Special students are required to meet the following standards leading to graduation certification: (a) good social development; (b) good work training; (c) regular attendance; (d) maximum academic achievement. Special students graduate with a diploma and participate in all graduation activities.

Twenty-one students have now graduated from Brien McMahon School under the Special Education Program. Team teaching has undoubtedly contributed to the success of this program that prepares handicapped students for personally successful and financially independent living. All graduates are employed and there are few dropouts. Frederick Choromanski, the team leader, believes that these young people are very much aware of their responsibilities as citizens.

Glastonbury High School, also in Connecticut, offers a course in the humanities to seniors of limited academic ability who have definite reading problems. The course is taught by Mrs. Wilmer Kelley Speed, whose undergraduate major was Greek literature. Mrs. Speed has experienced considerable success with these children because they realize that she believes in them. She helps them to relate the world of reality and the world of imagination. The course is designed to help the student to acquire a realistic concept of man's work, leisure, concern for others, hopes and role in life.

A part of Mrs. Speed's success may be attributed to her refusal to talk down to students. Solid literary materials are selected and used. Books read by these slow students include *To Kill a Mockingbird, Julius Caesar, Emperor Jones, All Quiet on the Western Front,* and *Lord of the Flies.* Many quality films are included in the course, and students often read plays aloud. "A play is to be played," says Mrs. Speed, "and that's what they do with it."

Although Mrs. Speed is greatly interested in the effect the humanities course has upon the values her students accept and admire, she does not neglect the study of form. She wants students to recognize good literature and good art. She believes that what is literary and what is truth cannot be separated for purposes of teaching. Through teaching about the persistent problems of man and raising significant questions about ideas and values, she hopes her students of lower ability will develop self-awareness and confidence.

A Personalized Curriculum   Efforts in Flint, Michigan, to provide additional help for students who need it have taken the form of a Personalized Curriculum Program. PCP is an arrangement for identifying under-achievers, on the assumption that under-achieving is a primary signal for a potential dropout. The under-achiever, says Chuck Whitely, an advisor in Flint's PCP, is losing contact with the school program. He isn't caring, he isn't performing, and he often moves from non-performance to estrangement, alienation, and eventual delinquency.

The PCP involves 560 students from the senior high school and 240 from the junior high school. These under-achievers are placed in classes of not more than 15 students per teacher. The three features of the program are small classes, special additional academic counseling, and special job counseling. In the regular school program there is a counselor for every 400 students; in the PCP there is an academic as well as a job counselor for every 120 students. It is hoped that PCP will develop principles of counseling that will be applicable to all students. Of the students identified as potential dropouts, 81 percent are being retained in school. The total dropout rate between grades 9 and 12 has been reduced from 30 to 27 percent in the two years the PCP has been in operation.

Another feature of the PCP is the use of two-hour time blocks in the sophomore year. The humanities block includes social studies and English content; the science block provides science and mathematics content. Here, the purpose is to provide closer teacher-pupil relationship and to increase the contact time between the block teacher and his students. Eight teachers in this school are in the PCP and each of them has one PCP class in addition to classes of regular students. Because many PCP students have reading problems at the base of their under-achieving there is much emphasis on reading for PCP students. Teachers provide appropriate reading materials for each student, depending upon his problem. Individualized instruction in PCP classes means multiple text adoptions, and many supplementary instructional materials must be used. All classes are oriented to the world of work. Most PCPs are enrolled in a weekly paid work program. They work 20 hours per week, supervised by both the employer and the school, and receive academic credit while gaining work experience. Some students work in the Community Hospital, gasoline stations, or supermarkets; others have jobs as waitresses, clerks, sales workers, carpenters, or helpers in the school.

In general, PCPs tend to be outside the mainstream of student life. For financial as well as social and psychological reasons, they participate less in athletics, clubs, social life, and in the total out-of-class program. The PCP has three recognized goals: (1) to help under-achieving students attain their academic potentials, so that they can be transferred to the regular program; (2) to involve these students in the mainstream of student body life; and (3) to help them feel a responsibility to the whole group and to develop their citizenship awareness.

Vocational Training

The Detroit school system cooperates with the Michigan Employment Security Commission to operate a Skills Center currently serving 700 adults and 700 youths certified as unemployable without special training and schooling. A Special Youth Program was begun at the end of 1964, under the Manpower Development and Training Act, as part of the Skills Center Program. To be eligible for the Special Youth Program the individual must be out of work, out of school, and unable to find or hold a suitable job without additional training. Students who have been out of school for a year or more may be eligible for a $20 a week subsistence allowance. Many of these youths have been rejected for military service, and most have a language problem, a social adjustment difficulty, or an emotional problem that interferes with employment.

The center attempts by concentrated individual guidance, personalized academic programs, and practical vocational training, to help these youths and rehabilitate them for productive work and creative lives. Six occupational areas are now taught at the Skills Center: service trades; metal trades; auto trades; commercial trades; clerical trades; and retail sales. Small groups of students meet with counselor aides in the Planning Center to discuss topics such as personal hygiene and grooming, how to apply for a job, and personal problems of adjustment. When the individual student is judged employable, usually after 52 weeks of training, he is referred to the Michigan Employment Security Commission for placement.

The appeal of this program is evidenced by the 4,000 applicants for 1,500 places and by the enthusiasm of faculty and students alike. Its success also can be measured by the testimony of students and by the large number who complete the course and are satisfactorily placed in appropriate jobs.

Americanization Programs

Another kind of handcapped student is the youngster whose native language is not English, but who must compete with boys and girls who have always used English. In California, Oakland Technical High School enrolls more than 200 students from other national backgrounds whose mastery of English is so limited that they require special instruction. These students—Chinese, Japanese, Mexican, Italian, and as many as 40 other nationalities—attend classes of not more than 35 students in the International Department, which is staffed with 7 teachers. Some of these students have come to the United States as permanent immigrants, others as temporary visitors on student visas. Both groups must master the English language and the rudiments of American citizenship.

Mrs. Ruth Wilcox, head of the International Department, is as concerned with the civic education aspect of her department as with the language role. She encourages teachers to aid international students in understanding the responsibilities of citizens of the United States as well as to help them overcome their language barrier.

When international students enter Oakland Tech they are placed in a special program. The first year emphasizes vocabulary and the basics of English. After the student has become relatively familiar with the English language he enters regular classes. The faculty is unanimous in its decision not to force international students to speak English outside the classroom and never to disparage the ancestry, traditions, or heritage of anyone.

Mrs. Wilcox also believes that warm acceptance throughout the school is the key to the rapid progress of international students at Tech. Morale is enhanced for international students by their membership in the Orientation Club, which provides social occasions and a congenial group for sightseeing and visiting.

When these students become seniors, Mrs. Wilcox takes them—the boys in one group, and the girls in another—to visit Laney Trade School (a Junior College in Oakland). This school has practical courses in shoe repairing, cooking, plumbing, mechanics, and beautician work, along with other trades. The staff members at Laney explain their offerings to the Oakland Technical High School students in the international department, encouraging them to continue their education and learn a trade. Three-fourths of the students do go on—some to Laney and others to Merritt Junior College, which offers business and academic courses. Others get married, find jobs, or enter private schools.

In Cleveland, Ohio, 20 of the 24 boys and girls in an Americanization class the project team observed at Lincoln High School had arrived in the United States within the past three months. Normally, students remain in the special class for one semester, although they may remain as long as two semesters.

The teacher, Miss Day, who is free to give students anything she thinks they need as orientation to the school and the nation, uses music extensively in getting her students started with English. She visits almost every home, and makes a telephone contact with each family once a month, usually through an English-speaking neighbor. She prefers oral contact to writing, because for most immigrants writing represents bureaucracy and elicits suspicion.

Emphasis is given to English language and vocabulary building as well as to the basic concepts of tolerance and responsibility. A typical day begins with an exercise in new words, the Pledge of Allegiance, and some songs. Then students study geography, history, and vocabulary. The day ends with stories, more poems and songs, and a discussion of the day's progress.

FACILITATIVE PROVISIONS FOR ALL STUDENTS

In addition to programs for students in some way deficient or deprived, there are many facilitative plans to benefit all students, able and limited alike. Included are programs of grouping and guidance and other arrangements.

Grouping

The Yorktown High School Social Studies Department in Arlington, Virginia, once followed a grouping policy of advanced placement classes for gifted students and special classes for slow learners. After consulting with the Guidance Department, the Social Studies Department called for a reevaluation, saying, "It seems to us that in the past the grouping policies that we have followed have resulted in protecting the teacher's interests and needs rather than coming to grips with the best interests of our student body." It had been assumed that highly competitive and competent students would find it easier to maintain their competitiveness and to become better scholars. The Yorktown Social Studies Department found that the reverse was true. Although competitiveness was extremely fierce in attempting to gain admission to an advanced placement program, students felt they had "arrived" once they had been admitted. This led to a smug attitude of intellectual superiority. Many of the faculty believe that this policy placed the gifted student in an unhealthy relationship to the total school environment, and that it had an adverse effect upon students who were assigned to modified or special classes. "These young people, grouped because of their difficulty in mastering academic subjects due to limitations in native intelligence or emotional disturbances, quickly recognized the nature of their class and tended to feel they were the scum of the school. In a sense they were right."

The social studies department felt that it needed to find a new arrangement that would "bring faith and actuality together," and would meet the abilities and needs of students as individuals. It recognized that heterogeneous grouping would require more intensive pre-planning and more flexibility on the part of the teachers, but it was convinced that it would result in more effective teaching.

Yorktown's social studies department evolved four approaches which are expected to provide effectively for individual differences. First, a team of two teachers is assigned to a group of 50 to 70 students. This practice makes it possible to group and regroup students according to ability, interest, background, and achievement. Secondly, a social studies teacher is assigned to the library each period of the day to help social studies students who come to the library for independent study. Thirdly, personal data on each student are readily available on cumulative record cards in the social studies office. These personal data files are used every day by social studies teachers, who examine the records of pupils to help them determine what they might expect of individual students and how they as teachers might motivate students to do their best work. Finally, instructional materials are available in the social studies office to supplement the library facilities. The 4,000 volumes in the office meet the academic needs of almost all students. More than 200 mimeographed handouts are catalogued and ready for any teacher who wants them.

The social studies department intends to have every teacher trained in group dynamics techniques. Assistant Principal Leon F. Williams, who is responsible for curriculum development in social studies, is highly competent in this field. Also, the English department Chairman, John D. Benzich, has prepared a study guide to help teachers become familiar with the essential characteristics of group dynamics.

Scholarships

An outstanding program for salvaging intellectual talent that might otherwise be lost is the Special Scholarship Program in Kansas City. It is unique in that it begins in the 9th grade and continues through college. Grants totalling $480,000 have been authorized by the Kansas City Association of Trusts and foundations and its member trusts to support scholarships for students of ability and promise who come from limited financial and cultural circumstances. One of the member trusts has specifically asked to assist promising Negro students. Forty percent of the scholarship recipients are Negro, the same percentage as that of Negro students in the total school-age population of Kansas City.

The scholarship program begins in the 9th grade by identifying potential scholarship recipients. These students have average or above-average ability, but their families are so poor that these youngsters may need encouragement and assistance even to stay in high school and to develop expectations of going to college. Scholarship recipients must pursue the undergraduate degree program of any accredited college. The grant provides for all necessary expenses, sometimes including money for clothing and incidentals as well as for tuition and living expenses. Many of the recipients are so poor that they request that clothes be given to them at school rather than at home. As one boy explained, "My mother would give the clothes to one of my younger brothers."

The Kansas City scholarship program is not limited to exceptionally gifted students, although many winners do have unusual ability. The Stanford-Binet Test Scores of the 1965 recipients ranged from 89 to 158. Mrs. Anne Johnson, Scholarship Coordinator, reported that the boy with a score of 89 would undoubtedly need five years to finish college, because he would not excel in a highly academic program. But she added that he can succeed if he chooses his college and courses carefully.

During the high school years, Mrs. Johnson and the regular counselors work with the students in the program and with their parents. They tell the students that they are eligible for scholarship aid and will receive a scholarship if they maintain their grades at the level of which they are capable. The student's knowledge that a college education is within his grasp acts as a powerful counteracting influence to personal or family conditions that might lead to discouragement and low achievement.

In order to give scholarship recipients added preparation for college, the program requires all winners to participate in a college readiness class during the summer following high school graduation. The bulletin describing the college readiness program during the summer of 1965 began with this paragraph:

It has often been said that the first semester at college demands a radical adjustment on the part of entering freshmen. It may be reasoned that the problem of adjusting for recipients of special scholarships would be greater because of past experiences and opportunities which have tended to inhibit their development, so the college readiness course is organized from these particular units of work: (1) English grammar and punctuation; (2) spelling and vocabulary improvement; (3) writing skills; (4) reading improvement and reading comprehension; (5) library usage; (6) study techniques; (7) career development; (8) college adjustment; and (9) actual college campus experience.

The concern of project personnel does not end when the student enters college. Early in the freshman year Mrs. Johnson writes each a student a "home sickness letter." She writes:

You know it's strange to think that this is about the time when every freshman experiences a feeling of frustration, a sense of pressure. This is often brought on by the uncertainty that settles over most freshmen as soon as they get into the real business of college life—the overwhelming assignments and the feeling that they will never get done and the newness of teaching procedures and methods, or mid-semester examinations coming up. I am most anxious that you make the most of every opportunity so that you can fulfill your dreams and expectations. You may write to me whenever you feel the urge and have an extra second.

Mrs. Johnson works very closely with Deans of Students at the universities and colleges chosen by the students, to keep informed of their social problems as well as their academic problems, because the two are frequently intertwined. She visits most of the colleges twice a year, and she arranges for students at distant colleges to come to her office during the Christmas holidays.

At the time of the project team's visit, 302 people were in the program, including those in college. Between 275 and 300 students apply each year and about half of these are accepted, although not all of them enter college. Some get married; some join the army; some enter hospital training or other training which takes less than a four-year college degree course. Students who marry are not dropped from the scholarship program, nor do they automatically receive increased allowances. Many students supplement their scholarship aid by participating in a college work-study program, under the Economic Opportunity Act.

The experience of the first three years has convinced Kansas City educators that the program not only is a great success but provides an example of how the Federal government could handle scholarship aid for needy students. An article in the *Kansas City Star* for September 19, 1965, quotes Mrs. Johnson as saying that although it is essential to provide needy students with the money to reach college it is equally important to keep them there.

Nationwide, one-third of the young men and women who enter college drop out at the end of the freshman year; half never graduate. Mrs. Johnson points out that the Kansas City scholarship winners take frustrations of economic, social, and cultural deprivation to college with them. Furthermore, although some are extremely bright or talented, most scholarship winners are average students who show some promise of succeeding in college. Yet, despite their disadvantages, 80 percent of the first class were still in college at the end of the freshman year and 50 percent at the end of the second year. The record has been even better in subsequent years. In 1965, a phenomenal 92 percent of the freshmen survived the first year. Of those who entered in the first three classes, 73 percent were still attending college at the end of the spring term in 1965.

In Altamont, Kansas, Richard Howell, chairman of Labette County High School's social studies department, frequently recommends students for scholarships, but he insists that the student do as much of the work and investigation as possible. For example, Howell put one student in contact with a Kansas City firm known to be sympathetic to capable but needy students. The executives of this firm were so impressed by her initiative in coming to Kansas City to negotiate personally for scholarship aid that they agreed to finance her next two years in college and offered her a summer position in their office.

Howell operates in the same way to help boys who express an interest in attending the Army, Navy, and Air Force academies. He sends the students to see precinct party leaders to become acquainted with political procedures at the local level and to plan an interview with the Congressman who controls the appointment to West Point, Annapolis, or Colorado Springs. The social studies chairman repeated, "I like to put kids into situations like that and see what they come up with. Of course, I will rescue them if they need help."

**Using Students
As Resources**
Durfee Junior High School and Central High School in Detroit are trying out programs in which selected older students are paired with younger students who need help in their classwork. This plan, reminiscent of the British Lancastrian scheme, was developed by Peggy Lippitt and was first tested in two elementary schools and in a summer day camp. Although an extension of this plan could aid learning by providing the teacher with a number of helpers, its main purpose is the psychological gain to both the older and younger student in each pair.

Each "receiving teacher" chooses two or three students in her class who can profit from individual attention. She and a "sending teacher" select older students capable of providing the kind of help deemed appropriate. The older students first participate in seminar sessions led by a trained instructor. They learn teaching techniques and human relations skills. From then on, pairs meet on a one-to-one basis, for a half-hour per day, three or four times a week. During the first meetings of the pairs, the seminar trainer is available to provide "at-the-elbow help." The assignments the older students carry out during these meetings range from drills on spelling words, multiplication tables, and Latin vocabulary words, to assistance in sewing, making bookcases, and shooting basketballs. Once a week each older student meets with the receiving teacher to discuss his younger student's progress and to receive instructions for the following week. The older students also continue to have seminar sessions on a once-a-week basis to exchange ideas and experiences.

The plan had just begun at the time of the project team's visit, and no evidence was yet available on its effectiveness. Dr. Lippitt anticipated the following benefits, based on pilot programs in two elementary schools:

A. For the older:
   1. The recognition that he can make a constructive contribution toward someone else's welfare even though he's not fully grown;
   2. The experience of a positive relationship with a younger child;
   3. Cooperative work with teachers;
   4. A pre-professional apprenticeship—a taste of teaching and related helping professions;
   5. An improved attitude toward his own learning as he helps others learn; and
   6. Training in human relations.

B. For the younger:
   1. Either individual help with schoolwork with which he's experiencing difficulty or an opportunity for an enrichment experience which he otherwise would not have;
   2. The experience of a positive relationship with an older child; and
   3. The opportunity to learn in a concrete way how schoolwork done well now will help him do well later.

The assumptions on which the program was built, explained by Dr. Lippitt in a mimeographed statement, suggest related values:

1. Exclusively separate age groups lessen the opportunities for academic or social learning.
2. The process of learning from older peers has greater potential in some areas than learning from adults.

3. Olders have a chance to work out, at a safe psychological distance, some of their unsolved problems of relationship to peers and sibs.

4. The olders have a chance to perfect the skills they teach.

5. Human relations skills and problem solving can be appropriately taught at all age levels and can make a unique contribution to the socialization process.

The olders-youngers plan may promote effective citizenship by fostering more wholesome interpersonal relations among children and a better understanding of how people can live together cooperatively.

The same approach of using students to help other students is applied in a very different manner at DeWitt Clinton High School in New York. A student court squad, composed of above average students with an inclination to serve, counsels students guilty of minor infractions.

Teachers refer to the Student Court those students who have committed infractions so minor that they hesitate to refer them to the deans. Some boys on the squad are designated to screen these complaints and to call students before one of the student justices. The justice then tries to find out what has led to the infraction and makes an effort to help the boy with his problem. The Court follows up on each case, observing the behavior of the boy who has been sent to the Court. If there has been no improvement, he may be referred to the dean for discipline. No other penalty or threat is made when a boy is referred to the Court. Because the offense is not recorded, the boy usually appreciates the chance to come to the Court. Emanuel Lavinsky, sponsor of the Student Court, said that the student justice does not determine guilt:

He tries to help the boy see why he has behaved the way he has, and helps him to see the consequences. He is a kind of big brother, guidance worker, and disciplinarian wrapped in one. The ultimate threat is that he can't do business with us any more. We try to find out what's wrong and what's bothering him. A senior boy can often do more than a guidance worker to improve behavior because other students don't look on him as an enemy.

We also try to protect the teacher. The teacher is always presented in a good light, but a boy can talk his heart out to another boy. The emphasis is on youth moving along on its own ingenuity. If you don't play-act, if you give the teenager real responsibility, he will come through. He learns that he is not going to hide behind anybody else's coat-tail. He grows while he is participating.

Lavinsky feels that one of the strongest features of the program is the benefit it brings to the members of the squad. Although they handle from 300 to 500 cases per term, Student Court members have never received threats of any kind from boys disciplined by the Court.

The Student Court has recently introduced a program designed to help college-bound students prepare for entrance examinations. Members of the Court present a series of eight study sessions in mathematics. An article in the *Clinton News* for October 14 says:

We hope that Clintonites attending our session will achieve higher grades on college entrance exams and preliminary SAT's. The 45 minute lessons to be held on Wednesdays after 8th period will be conducted by a committee of four Court members. Each lesson taught by a team of two committeemen will be checked and approved by Mr. Irving Packer, chairman of the Mathematics Department.

As part of student guidance procedure at DeWitt Clinton, Prefects serve as orientation counselors to younger students. Paul Petluck, faculty advisor for the Prefects, explains that one of the school's problems is its immense size, which makes it very easy for the new student to become lost, both physically and psychologically. He says:

A freshman comes into the school and looks at the big boys and is destroyed. Many times freshmen make bad starts and have difficulty righting themselves and getting back on the right track. Often they do badly and matters go from bad to worse. Some form of guidance is needed, more than could be given by a formal guidance department; so association with another boy is most helpful.

Although the program started as a kind of big-brother program, it became impossible to supply enough boys to maintain a one-to-one relationship, so one Prefect was assigned to each freshman and sophomore homeroom. He was carefully chosen from among student leaders.

At the beginning of the year the function of the Prefect, whom most freshmen admire, is to make announcements and explanations pertinent to the first-year student. He attempts to befriend individual boys and tries to find out what kind of help they need. When the Prefect determines what the boy needs and wants, the boy is referred to the proper person. If the student needs assistance in mathematics, the Prefect sometimes will contact a teacher to encourage the boy to seek after-school help. He may make an appointment with the Guidance Counselor or with some other person in the school who could be of help.

This program started in a minor way in 1964 and enjoyed immediate success. The Prefect attempts to build the boy's confidence and trust. Petluck points out:

The object is to develop a kind of camaraderie between the student and the Prefect. We don't expect to perform miracles, but if every Prefect can change one boy who is on the wrong track in each room it can lift the tone of the whole school. The school will benefit, the boy will benefit, and the community will benefit.

He also points out the effect this program may have on the boys who are members of the Prefect squad. These are students who have already shown their leadership ability, and who are willing to accept responsibility for other students. The Prefect program affords them an opportunity to develop leadership skills. It can also help to recruit teachers. A number of the boys indicated that they would like to go into teaching as a result of their experience as Prefects. Petluck feels that from the experience in 1964, he can say with some assurance that some boys who had been failing were able to pass their courses because of the help given by a Prefect. He believes other students who were doing barely passing work finished the year with much higher averages than they would have without Prefect assistance.

School-Police Cooperation   In Flint, Michigan, a different form of student guidance plan is used with police cooperation. A police detective sergeant is maintained in the school as a regular member of the staff of the Flint community school system. He has an office in the school and permanent full-time assignment to the school district (the high school, several nearby elementary schools, and a parochial school). The police counselor is a member of a counseling team which includes the dean of students, the dean of counselors, the nurse counselor, and the community director. Because the police officer has his office in the school, he knows the school, the community, the youngsters, and the counseling plan. He can be far more effective in an educational and crime-preventive program than as a regular member of the police force. He does not help enforce school rules, but only regular community laws.

Flint had a 52 percent reduction in the number of complaints during 1964, the first year the program was in operation. More students talk with the police sergeant and formerly undetected minor delinquencies came to the surface and were handled. Sgt. Frank Rutherford, police liaison officer at the Bryant Community High School, says, "The mere presence of a police officer helps in the same way that the presence of a traffic officer helps to improve traffic behavior. Apprehension is more certain, regardless of the severity of punishment." He considers the certainty of apprehension one of the strongest deterrents to misdeeds.

The school and police crime-prevention program emphasizes the team approach, the case work approach, and a mental health approach. In addition to a regular weekly conference, the team discusses every immediate problem or tough case. There is constant informal cooperation and referral, and serious cases involve reporting or feed-back to teachers. Sgt. Rutherford and Principal Rodda both feel that continuing feed-back to the teachers might unnecessarily prejudice them against the students, but teacher conferences are sometimes called to inform them as a group of an urgent problem.

During the week of the project team's visit to Flint, the school had handled four cases but had had no complaints from the community, the more remarkable because this week included Halloween and there were no requests from the community for law enforcement to cope with Halloween pranksters.

The principal, when asked if he had any suggestions for persons who might wish to institute such a program in another community, said, "The school should make the overture. There should be a clear understanding that the police officer has no school responsibility. He should not be an enforcing officer for school regulations." The effectiveness of the arrangement depends upon the establishment of a wholesome tone to overcome the image of the policeman as an enemy of freedom and youth and to replace it with a positive image of the officer of the law as one of a number of adult counselors intent upon the improvement of human relations and standards of citizenship.

CONCLUSION

In these quite different ways schools are attempting to meet the needs of the local community by providing the best instructional opportunities for underprivileged students and offering appropriate guidance services for all students. However different these techniques may be, all have promising points and offer possibilities for creating more confident, competent, and effective citizens.

We live in a great century but if
it is to rise to its full opportunity
the scientific achievements of its first
half must be matched by comparable
achievements in human relations
in its second half.

Euston Smith

CHAPTER **10**

School-Community Relations

At one time, schools typically were portrayed as institutions isolated from the practical life of the community. Today, the stereotype evidenced by references to "ivy-covered towers" and "absent-minded professors" persists, but its influence appears to be diminishing. An increasing number of schools are engaging in continuing dialogue with the community and drawing upon it for resources to enrich education. There is constant traffic between the colleges, high schools, elementary schools, business establishments, social agencies, and government offices. The interaction does not mean that schools are any less intent on fostering scholarship; instead, it indicates a commitment to make scholarship meaningful by relating it to today's world.

Recognition that education cannot be compartmentalized within the classroom has been paralleled by a realization in many communities that the school can serve many more community needs than was formerly imagined. The change in school-community relations, in other words, is a two-way street.

This chapter will illustrate some of the ways in which the high school's civic education function has been made a part of the total community life. The initiative for innovations has come sometimes from the community and sometimes from the school.

THE SCOPE OF COOPERATION

Alumni

At DeWitt Clinton High School in New York, the Helping Hand program of the Alumni Association invites its members to sponsor, on a one-to-one basis, present DeWitt Clinton students. Sponsorship involves introducing the boy to the alumnus' line of work. Some sponsors give their boys a part-time job in the office or the factory. Others simply counsel their boys or advise them on the kind of preparation needed to continue in this field of work. In 1964, between 300 and 400 DeWitt Clinton students were paired with alumni. Participating students came from all socio-economic groups; some were in special need of the money they earned while working with their alumni sponsors. A strong bond joins alumni and students of DeWitt Clinton. One teacher told the project team that the opportunity the students have to work with an alumnus is regarded as "sort of a birthright."

Outside Speakers

One example of the utilization of the community is the frequent provision for outside speakers. In the schools of Cleveland, for example, the speakers represent organizations such as Junior Achievement, the Cleveland municipal courts, the State Highway Department, Kiwanis, a number of colleges, the Peace Corps, the Army, the Y.M.C.A., the Zoological Society, the Red Cross, and many private corporations. Students are given the opportunity to hear experts and specialists who know the detailed operation of the many agencies that are part of community life.

Another example of the use of outside speakers is in the schools of Fulton County, Georgia, where an Annual Public Affairs Conference for high school students has been established. The 1965 conference brought together 5,000 students in the Municipal Auditorium to hear an address by Vice President Hubert Humphrey.

The Northampton, Massachusetts, High School extended its staff resources by inviting guest lecturers from Smith College to address large groups of students. The large-group lecture series has included topics such as slavery, the Civil War, 19th-century capitalists, U.S. foreign policy, the literary work of Abraham Lincoln, and a series of demonstration lectures by physicists.

In Ohio, the scientific community is invited to participate in the school program through the Visiting Scientists Program of the Ohio Academy of Science. The Academy has prepared a roster of scientific persons willing to address school audiences and has fostered a program of science lectures in the schools. During the 1964–65 school year the scientists made 470 visits to 366 schools. They spoke to 1,311 classes, 128 assemblies, 60 science clubs, and 29 teachers' groups, reaching an audience of over 88,000. The roster of speakers includes the names of 464 scientists and engineers affiliated with 46 colleges and universities, 20 industrial firms, and seven research institutes.

Volunteer Organizations Innumerable non-profit organizations with programs of civic betterment work systematically with the schools to supplement civic education in their special area of interest. These include groups such as the World Affairs Council, the American Red Cross, the Foreign Policy Association, the League of Women Voters, and the various service clubs.

Specialized organizations such as the Freedom Foundation, the Constitutional Rights Foundation, the American Friends Service Committee, the National Conference on Citizenship, and the education project of the U.S. Department of State are likewise devoted to strengthening civic education and frequently work hand in hand with the schools. Although the organizations mentioned here operate in all parts of the country, the degree of involvement of any of these organizations in a particular school depends on the local leadership and the local school policy respecting cooperation with non-school agencies.

The League of Women Voters was brought to the project team's attention in schools in the San Francisco area, where the League maintains a speakers' bureau which often gives assistance to civics classes. Many San Francisco schools buy for use as a supplementary text the

Pocket Guide to San Francisco City and County Government prepared by the League. The League maintains a group of observers who attend all local board and commission meetings to keep the information up to date.

The best known activity of the League of Women Voters, and perhaps the one most used by the schools, is the regular publication of voter guides containing the pros and cons of all ballot measures and biographical information about all candidates. In addition, students often call or visit the office of the League with questions and requests for information, usually for school papers or research projects. Mrs. Douglas E. Lord, executive secretary of the San Francisco branch, says, "I personally enjoy these visits very much because of the students' lively curiosity and interest in public affairs, and I will spend as much time as possible discussing their projects. We take pride in the fact that we are becoming well known as an information center and will continue to encourage the use of this service."

The American Friends Service Committee operates high school seminars described as workshops in ideas. Week-long seminars in New York and Washington are scheduled in November, April, and May; they are open to students in the last three years of high school. Similar workshops for high school students are conducted throughout the United States by regional offices of the American Friends Service Committee.

News Media Some local newspapers, such as the *Salt Lake City Tribune*, encourage civic education by sponsoring programs. The *Tribune's* "Inquiring Editor" is a weekly televised quiz program based on world, national, regional, and local news. A similar program in the Washington, D.C., area is called "It's Academic"; it is patterned after the "College Bowl" program. In Detroit, a comparable program is called "Quiz-'em."

Many radio and television stations publish and distribute to the schools special bulletins listing scheduled times of broadcasts with unique educational value. Almost all area educational television stations exist primarily for the purpose of cooperative planning with local schools and school systems. For example, the programs of station KQED in

San Francisco during daylight hours are tailored entirely to school needs, and most of its evening programs are also educationally oriented.

**Sponsors Of
Workshops And
In-Service Institutes**
Not the least of the agencies that co-operate with the schools in promoting civic education are the academic groups whose contribution is primarily to the upgrading of teacher competence. Among these is the Robert A. Taft Institute of Government, whose seminars for teachers have already been mentioned. Evaluation of the first 12 programs indicates that those who participate in one of the Institute's political education seminar programs come away with a greater understanding and respect for the two-party system, a sense of the need for political responsibility and, further, a desire to transmit this to their students. Seminars have been held in New York, Michigan, New Jersey, Kentucky, and Minnesota, with each of the 12 institutes enrolling 50 social studies teachers. The attitudes of teachers toward politics and the two party system appear to change significantly after attending the institute, as suggested by the poll of teachers described on pages 226–227 and the remarks by teachers:

Politics became more exciting, politicians more real, governmental processes more definite, clear and understandable, and the virtues as well as the vices of the two-party system were brought to light.

Sessions pointed out how human our politicians are and how interested they become in their work.

Served to remind me as an individual I have a responsibility to participate in political activities.

Previously believed politicians . . . work more for personal gain than service; now feel there is personal sacrifice.

Renewed my personal faith in the integrity of men who aspire to positions of power within the framework of government.

I've decided to become a dues paying member of the party, rather than just giving to campaign funds during an election year.

The seminar has encouraged me to become a candidate for precinct delegate.

. . . a higher opinion of politicians. They have impressed me with . . .
sincerity and desire to be of service.

The Service Center for Teachers of History, an adjunct of the American Historical Association, has for years provided services to strengthen the teaching of history. Among its programs is the preparation of a series of pamphlets on selected historical topics appropriate to the history courses most widely offered in schools. Because many secondary-school teachers have neither the time nor the opportunity to read widely in the monographic literature, these pamphlets are specifically designed to meet their needs. Each pamphlet surveys current interpretations and significant writings in a particular field of historical study. By helping teachers keep up to date in their fields of interest, the pamphlets can materially benefit the teacher and thereby contribute to the enrichment of classroom instruction.

The Service Center also sponsors conferences for history teachers to promote the general objective of maintaining and improving standards of history teaching. These meetings are usually held in conjunction with the department of history at a college or university and are designed for the high school teachers within a convenient radius. The primary purpose is to provide teachers with an opportunity to hear specialists discuss the latest research and writings in their fields and current scholarly historical interpretation on selected topics.

The emphasis in Service Center meetings for teachers is on subject matter rather than methods of teaching. The duration of the meeting depends upon the timing; during the school year conferences range from a half day to a day and a half, but special institutes, as long as a week, are held during the summer. Members of the history department at the host institution collaborate with visiting specialists to lead the program sessions. More than a dozen such conferences are held throughout the nation each year.

City And State Programs   In Webster Groves, Missouri, an outdoor camp is operated as part of the city recreational services. Elementary schools send classes here for special instruction, especially in science and outdoor sports, and the high school

Future Teachers of America take over classes for a day in Cleveland.

provides counselors from among its students. The high school also co-operates closely with the YMCA and Junior Achievement, which now serve 600 students in Webster Groves.

The state of Ohio stages an annual voluntary competitive examination in civic information for high school students. In South Dakota, a State Young Citizens League promotes civic virtues by sponsoring local young citizen leagues in every school. The purpose of the Young Citizens League, as described in its handbook, "is to assist in giving to the children of South Dakota the best possible instruction, training, and guidance in good citizenship. Education is training for living. The child becomes loyal; he realizes his responsibility, duty, and obligaton, and he makes his realization known by his acts of service, protection, and consideration." Each Young Citizens League has, in addition to an executive committee, committees on physical training, patriotism, cleanliness, and courtesy.

Individuals

The nature of the school's involvement is frequently determined by the presence of some local persons or positions. In New Albany, Indiana, school-community cooperation is encouraged by the director of the school radio program, who is also a member of the board of directors of Historic New Albany. This association of business leaders promotes tradition, restores historical relics, and encourages tourism in New Albany. The members of the school radio class have become interested in the community. They wear a crest on their jackets for identification; and they usher at important community affairs, march in the parade that opens the United Fund campaign, and serve as tour guides for community tours arranged by Historic New Albany.

Professional Organizations

In San Angelo, Texas, the annual government day in the high schools is much enhanced by the cooperation of the County Bar Association. This organization submits the names of attorneys agreeable to briefing students in advance of student government day on the duties of the offices of prosecutor, judge, and other positions with legal overtones. The Bar Association also provides sample documents useful in understanding legal functions. Bail bond, affidavit, subpoena, and forms for the use of the jury become more meaningful terms when students can see samples of them.

THREE EXAMPLES OF SCHOOL-COMMUNITY INTERACTION

In a number of schools the interaction of school and community is so significant and affects the civic education to such a marked degree that the program is deserving of detailed description. This chapter presents three examples from these areas—Ithaca, New York; Flint, Michigan; and Washington, D.C.

DeWitt Junior High School, Ithaca, New York

John Bozzone, social studies department chairman at DeWitt Junior High School, is convinced of the importance of utilizing community resources. He describes these resources under the headings of Town and Gown. Industrial, commercial, and governmental resources form the Town part, and academic persons (mostly from Cornell University and Ithaca College) comprise the Gown area. Some notable examples of "Town" and "Gown" activities are given below.

When Cornell students joined a Vietnam protest parade, local newspapers and radio stations were deluged with letters commenting on the demonstration and the news coverage of the event. Someone suggested that radio station WTKO broadcast a discussion by students and teachers focused on "the best way for a community to discuss controversial issues." A regular weekly broadcast series resulted, titled "Youth Speaks Out." One informal student meeting is held to discuss the topic before the taping session for the Saturday broadcast. The program motivates students to give intensive study to current events before participating in the program.

The samples given below give some indication of the range of topics and types of guests used in this interview program:

"How Should a Community Discuss an Issue?"—Round Table Discussion—3 teachers and 3 students from DeWitt Junior High.

"Clergymen Demonstrators"—Interview with Rev. Charles N. Arlin and Rev. John Keene on demonstrations in which they participated at Selma, Alabama.

"The John Birch Society"—Interview with Mr. Thomas Nelson, New York State Coordinator, The John Birch Society.

"The Youth Court"—Interview with Mr. William Shaw, Chief Justice, and Miss Theresa Wehe, Chief Prosecuting Attorney, Tompkins County Youth Court.

Outside speakers are also used for classroom presentations at DeWitt. Topics presented by classroom speakers have included "Persecution of Jews in Nazi Germany (by a former prisoner at Auschwitz);" "Films of a Visit to Nigeria;" and "Recollections of a World War I Veteran."

Other facets of the "Town" resources have included a showing of the film, "How the West Was Won," for the entire 7th and 8th grades, and a color film depicting the nations represented at the New York World's Fair; trips to the DeWitt Historical Museum; and independent research work at the city museum under the guidance of the curator, who meets with students weekly.

The "Gown" side of "Town and Gown" features classroom speakers from the Cornell campus, especially talks by college students from other lands. Among the foreign students who have spoken to classes are some from Thailand, Japan, India, Turkey, the U.S.S.R., Israel, and Nigeria. Faculty speakers from Cornell have addressed student groups on "Education in the U.S.S.R.," "Latin-America," "Travels to the U.S.S.R.," and "Trip to Israel." Other Cornell speakers have given talks on "Hungary under Communism," and "Naziism in Germany," and staged a debate on civil rights. A Peace Corps team spoke to the 9th grade on the work of that organization.

As an in-service offering for the entire faculty of DeWitt Junior High, the social studies department sponsors a Public Affairs Forum, which students and parents are invited to attend. In 1965, the series included meetings on "Communists and the Law in the U.S.," "Which Way Vietnam?," "The Churches and Social Action," "Understanding Reapportionment," "The Ecumenical Movement," "The John Birch Society," and "What Next for the Conservative Movement?"

The junior high school also brings the current world into the classroom through the use of documentary films. Among those that have been used are the following:

"Let My People Go" (Xerox TV Special)
"When I'm Old Enough, Goodbye" (U.S. Employment Service)
"The Hat" (World Law Fund)
"Depressed Area—USA" (CBS News-20th Century)
"The Only War We Seek" (United States Department of State)
"Freedom Ride" (Congress of Racial Equality)
"Battle of Midway" (borrowed from Cornell Film Library)
"Fallout" (Tompkins County Civil Defense Headquarters)

James Campbell, former social studies chairman and present guidance director, feels that the school should be closely integrated with the community life. A school, he says, should reach into the community to discover its needs and then should do what it can to meet those needs. This school is not insulated from the conditions around it. It is educating its students to be thoughtfully aware of their world.

**The Community Schools
And Big Brother Program
of Flint, Michigan**

Flint, Michigan, has approached many of its social problems through the concept of the community school. Each of the 47 schools in the city has a Community School Director who spends almost all his time coordinating and conducting the community activities in the school. Flint recognized that the unavailability of wholesome recreational facilities for youth presented a problem in many areas. Now, all schools operate late afternoon and early evening teen clubs where hundreds of students can dance, play bridge, chess and basketball, and study.

The community school has become the center of systematic programs to improve community recreation, health, and cultural awareness. The programs are concerned with the problems of adults as well as with the problems of youth, and special efforts are made to bring adults and youth together. Family swims, roller skating, music and art programs, and library services are presented as activities for family participation. The community school philosophy stresses:

> . . . that world peace and understanding among men must begin in men's hearts; that neighbor must understand neighbor and that people must learn to live together in neighborhoods and cities before nation can understand nation and a world can live in peace. To this end, people must be provided the opportunity at a grassroots level to learn to understand one another's problems, to work together and to find the means to improve themselves and their cities.

One of the many community problems that has been brought to the attention of schools is how to help the fatherless boy to achieve a wholesome relation with a man who can in some ways take the place of his absent father. From this need, the Big Brother Program has evolved in communities throughout the nation.

Flint, Michigan, is one of 82 communities cooperating in the Big Brother program; it has, in fact, 13 percent of all the nation's Big Brother pairs. In 1965, 857 fatherless boys were paired with male adults in the community who, through the school's cooperation and planning, supervised some of the boys' out-of-school recreation.

Fatherless boys are referred to the program by school counselors. The Big Brothers are recruited mostly from the recommendations of other Big Brothers and in response to television and newspaper publicity. Matching of big and little brother pairs is done after careful analysis of the individuals and some assurance of congeniality in three major areas. Similarity is sought, first, in religion, race, and nationality; secondly, in interests and hobbies; and thirdly, in economic backgrounds and expectations. The director of the program and the eight supervisors who do the matching agree that ideally race, religion, and nationality should not be factors. They point out, however, that there are so many initial tensions, strains, and difficulties that the additional strain of racial, religious, or nationality differences can create a hazard to success.

The Big Brother is required to visit his contact at least once every two weeks for one year. He agrees to do this in a signed pledge. The school, as coordinator of the program, prefers that the visits be weekly for at least two years. One Big Brother in Flint has served during the entire time this program has been in operation and is now working with his third little brother.

At first the Big Brother program was regarded as a measure to prevent juvenile delinquency, but this emphasis has been softened in order to encourage participation by all socio-economic levels. Nevertheless, the program's effect is to reduce juvenile delinquency. The earlier a boy can be recruited into the program, the better. The longer a boy is permitted to be without a father or father substitute, the greater are the chances of frustration, anger, and possible delinquency.

School officials report that boys who acquire a Big Brother subsequently attend school more regularly, behave better, and learn more easily. This program makes it possible for a boy to develop a strong and constructive self-image, and he may later return to the program as a Big Brother to another boy.

Neighbors, Inc., In Washington, D. C.

Another type of school-community cooperation operates in the Paul Junior High School area in Washington, D.C. Here, community leaders organized a campaign to halt migration of white residents from the area. Their strategy was to strengthen the school in every way possible, so that white families would hesitate to move from a community where their children were receiving the best available education.

The neighborhood in which Paul Junior High School is located was predominately white a decade ago. Now, white students constitute fewer than 20 percent of the school population. Neighbors, Inc. was established in the late 1950's, after Washington schools desegregated with the explicit intent, according to Mrs. Ware, executive secretary, to stabilize the community and halt what she called "panic selling." "We had to 'make people stop running.'" One of the first functions of the organization was to recruit white families to return to the area.

After eight years of operation, Neighbors, Inc. makes no claim to having completely stabilized the neighborhood. It does take credit for decreasing the exodus of white families, but Negro families are moving in at a faster rate, and so the racial balance of the neighborhood continues to shift.

As more Negroes have moved into the community, the emphasis in Neighbors, Inc. has changed. Mrs. Ware sees the objective as giving "a sense of community to this neighborhood." She feels that it is developing an *esprit de corps* among residents. The neighborhood has, in her words, a small-town atmosphere, unique in a metropolis such as Washington.

Sometimes the emphasis in Neighbors, Inc. is primarily on community, at other times primarily on the school. As with Flint Community Schools, the answer given by Neighbors, Inc. is that school and community are inseparable.

Perhaps the essence of the community aspect can be seen in the membership appeal in the organization's news bulletin:

Do you value NEIGHBORS, INC. (NI) as an effective civic association that looks after neighborhood housekeeping—such matters as sanitation, public safety, beautification, streets and traffic—and serves as a spokesman of the residents on school appropriation, recreation, zoning, freeways, and the like?

Do you also see the unique qualities of NI as assets to your family and your neighborhood? Do you enjoy the cultural activities promoted by NI, such as the Art and Book Festival, Play Reading Group, a monthly "open house?" Do you take pride in the friendliness and esprit de corps we have developed?

Neighbors, Inc. raises about $7,000 per year in dues, and an additional $1,000 through appeals in the community and fund-raising projects. One of these is the Art and Book Festival, which is a combination fund-raising and cultural activity. The budget in the past for the entire program has been approximately $22,000 a year, including funds from foundation grants.

Much of the organization's work is accomplished through standing committees. The recreation committee works to obtain more playground facilities in the neighborhood and has argued for the use of volunteers to direct D.C. Recreation Department playground activities. The education committee works with Paul Junior High School and with the area's elementary schools. It publicizes activities of schools in the newsletter and works with city newspapers to provide more favorable publicity about area schools.

Another standing committee works with city officials on questions such as street lighting, sanitation, and zoning. This group also promotes beautification projects. A fourth standing committee, on real estate, was created to curb panic selling by white homeowners. Mrs. Ware believes that Neighbors, Inc. played a significant role in obtaining open-occupancy regulations in Washington.

The relationship of Neighbors, Inc. to Paul Junior High School is unique, because the organization's original purpose, to halt white migration from the community, was unrelated to the school. Soon, however, it acquired the goal of making Paul Junior High a "blue-ribbon reputation to overcome fears and prejudices." Finally, it advanced the concept of a comprehensive Democracy in Action program in the school.

A teacher described the advantages of the program:

This Democracy in Action program is outstanding primarily because every student participates. Secondly, it is integrated with the curriculum. This is not just a matter of arranging a few trips for selected students to national shrines in our capital city. It is a closely planned bit of curriculum building to take advantage of the resources for all students.

For example, the 9th-grade European history class always goes to the Washington Cathedral to learn what it can of medieval architecture, music, and the historical associations connected with this great cathedral.

We are having a speaker from the Bureau of Indian Affairs of the Department of the Interior speak to the 8th grade about Indian problems.

We will have a Congressman speak to the 9th grade about citizenship again this year. This year we have Congressman Mink from Hawaii. Of course, we will not have the political rallies we had in 1964, when there was a presidential campaign, so we will substitute more Congressional hearings. I'm hoping to take a group to the Home Rule hearing on Monday. . . . We don't take students to events that are merely ceremonial, but to places where there is solid content, except that we do have a naturalization ceremony for our students to observe. This is an especially meaningful ceremony.

Because Neighbors, Inc. was so directly involved in the controversial issue of integration, it did not want to jeopardize the Democracy in

Action program by causing people to transfer their hostilities to the school. Consequently, the Democracy in Action program of exposing students to governmental and cultural activities has been under the sole supervision of the school since its inception in 1962.

Although Neighbors, Inc. does not participate in the supervision of the school program, it provides powerful community support. One of the links is the Home and School Group, comparable to a PTA, which includes many of the leaders of Neighbors, Inc. among its members. The parents provide transportation, volunteer work, and money. Some parents in this community have also been able to assist in less usual ways, because of their acquaintance with prominent figures in government. When parents who knew Senator Robert Kennedy informed him of the program of school-community cooperation at Paul Junior High School, he became one of its enthusiastic backers.

The school principal, Sidney Zevin, is an enthusiastic and able administrator who shares the concerns of the community. He believes that problems of teenage gangs carry over to the school and should therefore be a matter of concern for school administration. He works with roving youth leaders and is an active member of the area youth council. Zevin has also encouraged an exchange program with Terrell Junior High School, in which the two schools, with similar problems, take part in joint activities. Among the objectives is a reduction of rivalries and tensions between the two schools, and this, like other programs in the Paul Junior High School and its community, is proving to be an imaginative contribution to civic education.

CONCLUSION

In this report the scope and magnitude of cooperation between schools and communities can only be suggested. There is strong indication that the civic education of youth benefits from the use of alumni, outside speakers, volunteer and professional organizations, the news media, foundations and other sponsors of in-service training, and the efforts of interested individuals in the community. In the three cities used as examples—Ithaca, New York; Flint, Michigan; and Washington, D.C.—the role of the school extends beyond the classroom, and the source of initiative for ideas is sometimes difficult to identify. In these cities, as in many others throughout the United States, the school has entered the community and the community has entered the school. The emphasis of each of these agents of civic education is on giving students realistic preparation for problems of adult citizenship.

STUDENT BODY OFFICERS - 1965-1966
STANLEY ATWOOD - PRESIDENT
DAVID SEARLE - VICE PRESIDENT
JOANNE LOPEZ - SECRETARY
DEBBIE SHAFFER - HISTORIAN
KATHY BRADY - GIRL'S ASSOC. PRES.
RANDY PARK - BOY'S ASSOC. PRES.
PEGGY PETTY - HEAD CHEERLEADER
MR. WRIGHT - ADVISOR

Behold, I have set before thee
an open door.

Germantown Friends School motto

CHAPTER **11**

Student Government and School Authority

Some form of student government exists in almost every school. In general, student governments aspire to develop leadership ability, a sense of responsibility, and respect for law and order through the model of relationships among students, teachers, and administrators. The degree to which they are effective, however, depends on whether the school achieves a state of equilibrium between order and freedom, avoiding both the pitfalls of an authoritarian atmosphere and its opposite, anarchy.

In this chapter, several student governments will be examined. No attempt will be made to survey the condition of student governments throughout the nation's schools, nor does the project team offer these descriptions as models to be copied. Each school must find its own balance between order and freedom, just as the schools described in this chapter have done.

KEARNS JUNIOR HIGH SCHOOL IN KEARNS, UTAH

The house of representatives in Kearns Junior High is composed of one representative from each 7th grade and 8th grade homeroom. The senate has one representative from each 9th grade homeroom. The executive includes the three class presidents plus eight officers elected by school-wide election. Pupils who are not academic leaders or athletic stars and who seem to lack some of the traditional leadership qualities nevertheless often appear to succeed as student council officers.

The legislative body meets each day during the last class period. Some meetings are classes in the study of government, and others are used to discuss proposed legislation. The executive can veto a bill, which can then be passed again over the veto by a two-thirds vote of both the house of representatives and the senate. In 1965, for example, two bills were vetoed. In one case the veto held; the other case was reconsidered.

At the time of the project team's visit, four bills had passed both houses and were awaiting executive action. They provided for the establishment of a conduct committee, permission to wear "granny" dresses, mending and cleaning of the auditorium curtains, and permission for house of representatives members to attend home games during the seventh period.

Combined meetings of the house, senate, and executive are scheduled in the auditorium approximately once a month for general discussion and debate or to hear outside speakers. Twice a year, students hear the State of the School address given by the president of the student body.

During the seventh period on the day of the visit, the project team observed a combined meeting, held for the purpose of discussing a proposed resolution: "Be it resolved that military efforts in Vietnam be increased even to the point of risking Chinese intervention, that the major cities of North Vietnam be bombed along with other major military and industrial targets." At the end of the session, 24 members of the student congress voted for the resolution and 20 voted against it.

It was evident that a majority if not all of the members of the Kearns house and senate take great pride in their titles and responsibilities and joy in their role playing in debate. Discussion is a challenge and a game of wits. It involves learning and parliamentary strategy to gain and keep the floor, to outwit an opponent, and to win an argument or a vote.

When the project team asked the president, the president pro tem, and the secretary of the Senate about the significance of the student council to students who are not officers, they replied unanimously, "Everyone likes it; everyone is proud of it, and all the students participate to make Kearns rise above other schools." Although it was difficult for these officers to be specific about the values of student government for the average student, they obviously were enthusiastic.

Student government organizations appear to be alive and useful where there is clear recognition by the school administration of the importance of the student government. At Kearns, as at some other schools, this recognition is accorded by scheduling ample time for meetings and by treating student government deliberations with respect.

STUDENT GOVERNMENT AT McCLUER HIGH SCHOOL, FLORISSANT, MISSOURI

It would be unrealistic to expect a student government to exercise unlimited authority. Like any other governing body, its actions can be reversed, and it is under the jurisdiction of the school administration.

The 3,100 students of McCluer High School, in Florissant, Missouri, appear to have respect for their student government and for the school administration under principal M. A. Ludwig. The student council president told the project team:

I think the students have a feeling that it is their representative representing them in the student council. Even though we do not have a lot of authority, the student council is a form of public government. It gives the students a feeling that they are making some of the decisions, even though these decisions are within limits defined by the administration.

The project team visitor asked this student why he was so enthusiastic about a student government that had no independent authority. The boy explained:

I want to make this very clear. The student council was established as a laboratory for learning and not as a force to take over the school. I don't know if all the students realize this. Some may think we should have independent authority, but that isn't the purpose of the student council. We are given certain things to do by the administration, and the administration always has the final voice.

This articulate boy provided the project team with an opportunity to explore in greater depth a number of his beliefs about the functions and limitations of student government.

"In what areas does the student council have jurisdiction and in what areas does it not?" the project team visitor asked.

The boy said, "Well, we cannot interfere with any classroom by any student council motion, and our action in regard to student parking is definitely limited. We can pass the motion, but our motions are always worded, 'I move that the student council look into the possibility . . .' That is all we can do. Everything has to have the approval of the administration. We are very lucky to have a great administration. Dr. Ludwig wrote his doctoral dissertation on extra-curricular activities, so you know he's all for it. He tries to see our views and looks at them objectively. It must be hard for a principal to look at things the way a student does. In a lot of schools the students see the principal as an enemy, but the students in our school don't feel that way."

The project team visitor then asked this student council president where he had learned his ideas on the function of a student council. "You mean who taught me this?" he asked. "I attended two conventions this summer and this was stressed at these conventions. I think I learned it when I was a representative last year in the student council and we had a learning session. At such sessions it is clearly pointed out to us that student council is a laboratory for democracy. Both our sponsors and a student on the Executive Committee explained that."

The continuing interview with this student leader revealed other significant aspects of his concepts of loyalty to the administration and to his fellow students and his respect for law and order. These are the concepts promoted in the state and national conventions of student government leaders.

VISITOR: *Suppose some students organize a demonstration without your knowledge. Later, with your knowledge but without your approval, they plan a Saturday afternoon march to the principal's house, with plenty of jeering and chanting. They call it a pep session in reverse, to let him know how they feel. As president of the student body, what would you do?*

STUDENT: *I would try to prevent it. Even if I were against the principal's decision, I have certain responsibilities as president of the student body. Once the administration makes a final decision, I have to support it.*

VISITOR: Let's say that you persuade the students to give up their plans for a demonstration. Instead, they circulate a petition requesting some other authority to approach the principal and see what can be done about their complaint. Some of the Executive members of your Student Council support the petition. Would you be willing to take the signed petition to the principal?

STUDENT: If he were strongly opposed, I don't know, but I think I would. I think if the students wanted this badly enough to have a petition, I would take it to him. If he said no, I wouldn't argue with him. I might say, "Sir, consider how many students want it." If he still said no, I would try to quiet the students.

VISITOR: Can you think of any situation in which you would feel completely justified in defying the teacher, the sponsor, or the principal? I mean just quietly going your own way in opposition to what you know they want you to do.

STUDENT: I think the president should be an example as well as an individual. If everybody decided to oppose the teachers or the administration, it would just bring havoc to the entire school. I would have to go along with the administration or the teacher or whoever it would be, because I think I am an example to other students. I would be a poor president if I could not set this example.

VISITOR: Are you saying that if you were not the student council president you would have a little more freedom as a person?

STUDENT: I know I would. It's changed my entire outlook.

VISITOR: Do you feel that other people who do not hold office should be educated, if possible, to assume this same feeling of responsibility to give up some of their freedom of action as individuals?

STUDENT: Every individual isn't made to be a leader, so we can't ask everyone to be responsible.

VISITOR: Let's look at it in a different way. What is your reaction to the current newspaper stories about individuals burning their draft cards?

STUDENT: (Long pause) I think it's phony. An individual has a responsibility to his country, and these people are shirking their responsibility to their country.

VISITOR: But if someone said he felt he also had a responsibility to his conscience and mankind to try to discourage militarism and war, how would you respond?

STUDENT: *I don't think that if you tear up draft cards, you are being responsible to humanity or to mankind. If we didn't try to stop the Communists in Vietnam, the entire world would soon be taken by Communism; I don't think that would be helping mankind. I think these claims about responsibility to God and mankind are just an excuse.*

VISITOR: *An excuse for what?*

STUDENT: *For being afraid to fight for their country.*

VISITOR: *Let's pursue that point. Some people say that it takes courage and conviction to defy the law when a person has much to lose and nothing to gain by doing so. A person who is classified as 4-F and yet burns his draft card, for example, has nothing to gain and may get into serious trouble.*

STUDENT: *That's a tough one. I don't know if draft-card burners weigh the results when they defy the law.*

VISITOR: *You have said that you are interested in American history. How do you feel about the morals of men like Patrick Henry, Sam Adams, John Otis, and Paul Revere who opposed the authority of the government under which they lived for what they as individuals thought was right?*

STUDENT: *Well, that's why I'm a fan of Patrick Henry.*

VISITOR: *How do you justify his defiance of the law? Aren't there some people who would say that he metaphorically tore up his British draft card?*

STUDENT: *I guess he didn't think the British were right. I think this is a way new and stronger ideas about freedom develop.*

VISITOR: *Do you think there is any justification for these people to have strong ideas about opposing the war?*

STUDENT: *It's possible, but I don't think so. Maybe people that tear up their draft cards and defy the law cause others to think, but I don't know if it's the right type of thinking. Maybe it's true that when fellows like Patrick Henry did what they did, people didn't think it was the right kind of thinking. Later it proved to be so. It's hard to tell. Maybe in 10 years you can tell whether this defiance of law is necessary.*

VISITOR: *I've been asking you about this to discover the circumstances in which you feel that resisting authority is justified. To return to*

your school, it appears that you don't feel that there is a conflict be-
tween your individual conscience and loyalty to the principal. Is it fair
to say that you can support your principal and your principles at the
same time?
STUDENT: *That's right, because we have a great principal.*

Although the statements by the president of the student council at
McCluer High School are uniquely his own, the tone is relatively representative of many student leaders the project team interviewed throughout the nation. Students who hold the positions of leadership in student councils are likely to emphasize loyalty, respect for law and order,
and awareness of the need for dedicated leadership to insure stability.
There can be little doubt that experience in student government has contributed to their views on civic responsibility.

At the McCluer High School, it must be emphasized, the student
council exists primarily as a learning situation. Because Principal Ludwig
considers this a fundamental way of teaching civic participation, he
treats it as a significant part of the school program by allotting ample
time, facilities, and staff to make it important. Two teachers are re-
lieved of one class each to act as sponsors of the student council. About
120 students hold student council office and an additional 500 are active
in committee work.

Miss Regina Jerzewiak and Miss Eileen Smith discussed the theory
and practice of student councils with the project team, emphasizing
that at McCluer the student council is considered a laboratory for
democracy. These two sponsors wrote a chapter for the *Handbook* published by the National Association of Student Councils, describing the
student council class as a year-long program. They believed the year-
long learning program must center around two main ideas: (1) that the
course be a continuous program of learning about the democratic processes; and (2) that it must be accompanied by activities compatible
with the learning program.

Miss Jerzewiak and Miss Smith believe student council members
must learn very early that one of the important objectives of the public
school is to help students acquire and apply the kinds of knowledge that
will enable them to become good citizens. The student council must

acquire the "know-how" for citizenship and apply this knowledge in practice.

At McCluer High School, time is available for a planned, progressive orientation which allows for absorption, application, and evaluation of ideas. There are daily student council sessions within the school hours. The officers and committee chairmen meet every day, and representatives meet three times a week.

Teaching aids are important to the student council class. A room library with pertinent literature is available for representatives and officers. Magazine racks and bookcases are filled with copies of *Student Life*, *School Activities*, *The Student Council in the Secondary School*, *Student Council Yearbooks*, parliamentary procedure pamphlets, and other resource materials. Other valuable material was obtained from the National Student Council office at minimal cost. Miss Jerzewiak and Miss Smith called attention to the importance of the student council librarian, who helps students make good use of the varied materials. They also pointed out the work tables, typewriters, duplicating machines, tape recorders, film strips, file cabinets, portable blackboards, easels, bulletin boards, mailboxes, stationery, and art supplies in McCluer's student council library room. All student council members participate in McCluer's learning sessions, but some, through natural leadership or by virtue of their positions, are better equipped to serve as teachers. In setting up the learning program, the student council uses foreign exchange students, students outside the council with special experiences, faculty members, and individuals from the community.

In any learning program some areas will take priority over others. McCluer High School places strong emphasis on the student council movement. The aims and objectives of the student council, its relation to students, and the relation of the student council to the state and national organizations are incorporated into the lesson sessions.

Another teaching area is parliamentary procedure. Three sessions are used for this subject. The parliamentarian, who receives preparation during the spring term preceding the school year in which he serves, has charge of the program. In his presentation, he makes use of three film-strips, diagrams prepared by himself or previous parliamentarians, pamphlets obtained from the League of Women Voters, *Robert's Rules of Order*, and slide guides. Parliamentary procedure pamphlets are distributed to all members of the student council. After the direct teaching sessions have been completed, one period is used for a mock meeting.

A third learning session is devoted to "How To Give A Report." Again, an executive member is in charge of the program. Sometimes mock minutes are read, and student council members are asked to report extemporaneously; a check list is used by executive committee members or representatives to aid in the evaluation of these reports. The tape recorder and public address system are also used.

The McCluer High School student council has 12 standing committees, and special committees are created when needed. The 12 standing committees have their year-long program outlined in the by-laws, and additional projects may be assigned to them or initiated by them from time to time. The standing committees deal with areas such as assemblies, elections, safety, and school spirit. Chairmen of the 12 committees are appointed by the student council president with the consent of the council in the spring preceding their term of office. This practice makes an orientation program possible before the retiring chairmen leave school. It gives the new chairmen an opportunity to study annual reports and become acquainted with the files before starting committee work.

Committee meetings are held after school. The chairman meets with his sponsor to prepare the agenda, and he then gives copies of the agenda to all committee members.

Although committee meetings are less formal than the student council business meetings, they are conducted in a business-like fashion. Every committee has a secretary who types duplicate copies of the minutes. One copy is given to the president of the student council for his weekly report to the principal. The second copy is placed in the committee chairman's file. The secretary may also assist the chairman with his weekly and semester reports.

Not all committee work is carried on in business meetings. In committees such as "Bulletin Board" and "Sign and Poster," for example, the business meeting may be relatively short, and most of the time is likely to be spent in work sessions.

In the "Foreign Relations" committee, activities center around projects such as the UN Day collection, the sale of stock in the Students Abroad Corporation, receptions and other programs involving the exchange students, and a training program for students who apply for a year of study in a foreign country.

Because faculty sponsor time is arranged and because school time is provided for meetings, it is possible to perform the careful detailed planning so necessary for a successful organization. The faculty sponsors are selected with equal care. The McCluer Student Council meetings are planned as precisely as if they were regular academic classes.

Committee chairmen use a special checklist to assure that they have forgotten nothing which will contribute to a smooth meeting:

1. *Have you notified your sponsor about the meeting?*
2. *Have you put your announcement in the bulletin? Signed by the sponsor?*
3. *Do you have the materials ready for the meeting?*
4. *Have you checked the minutes of past meetings for deferred business?*
5. *Are committees ready to report?*
6. *Do any projects of the next few weeks require the appointment of subcommittees now?*
7. *Is there any correspondence to be read?*
8. *Are there any announcements?*
9. *Do you want publicity on any of your projects?*
10. *Will you need to notify any other committees of your plans?*
11. *Do you feel you need to discuss a project with the Executive Committee?*
12. *Do you have a printed agenda ready for the next meeting?*
13. *Have you allotted adequate time to dispose of the business on the agenda?*

It is worth noting that at McCluer the student council representatives are chosen by their constituencies in the homerooms, which meet daily. Here, time is available for continuous involvement of all students in discussion of student government projects. In some schools where social studies courses are required of all students every year, the social studies class is the basic unit for student government; other schools place all student government on a before-or-after-school basis. These are advantages and disadvantages to all these alternatives; McCluer has selected the homeroom as the best for its purposes.

STUDENT COUNCIL ROLES, FUNCTIONS, AND ACTIVITIES

It is fashionable in some circles to demean the student council as simply a juvenile bureaucracy charged with deciding on the themes for school dances, devising an acceptable method of raising money for a worthy school or community cause, and making recommendations for improving traffic control in the corridors or relieving congestion in the cafeterias, although student councils are called upon to deal with a wider variety of problems.

These functions are not insignificant. A student government body that performs only these functions will provide the student with valuable experience in working with adults and in handling money other than their own personal funds.

A Cafeteria Boycott In Kansas City, Missouri

An experience at Central High School, in Kansas City, Missouri, illustrates the responsible leadership student government officers can exercise. The event was a cafeteria boycott.

A few years ago a number of Central High School students decided to boycott the cafeteria to show their dissatisfaction with its food and service. The school administration disapproved, but it did not act hastily. Instead, it tried to convince students that the complaint should first be taken to the proper authorities. One student told the project team that the student council and its president, who wrote a very strong editorial which was sent to all the homerooms, were instrumental in breaking the boycott. The editorial, in the form of a letter, said:

I would like to call your attention to the "Thought for Today" that appeared in the Kansas City Times on Monday. It read, "A man who has committed a mistake and doesn't correct it is committing another mistake."—Confucius, philosopher of ancient China.

That is the position in which the students of Central High School find themselves today. Because of the dastardly actions of a few Centralites, who refuse even to come forth in defense of their actions, we are faced with the problem of either correcting our mistake or leaving it to show forever as a black mark against our school.

Someone spread the rumor that the student council supported yesterday's boycott of the cafeteria. I assure you that the student council did not support this action in any way, shape, or form. What the student council does support, however, is an orderly deliverance of grievances to the proper authorities. There will be a council cabinet meeting today in room 405. Any student wishing to present a grievance at this meeting is welcome to do so. As a matter of fact, I challenge any supporters of "the strike" to appear before the council with a list of grievances.

Throughout history, strikes have served one purpose—to call attention to a disagreement so that it could be mediated. The time has now come for us to work for a solution to our differences. The student council is ready and willing to work for a solution, but the actions of these persons who have supported the boycott indicate that neither their identities nor their objectives are to be known. Those who are sincerely interested in seeking a solution will welcome this opportunity to be heard. Or was it the plan of the organizer of this protest to be heard?

Following this letter, the boycott soon collapsed. The majority of students agreed, upon reflection, that the grievances should have been presented in an orderly manner.

Codes of Conduct

In many schools the student council is the focal point for extended student discussions of proper behavior which eventually find expression in formal codes of conduct or dress codes. Teachers and administrators readily concur that when these codes are developed from student meetings and enforced largely by student officers, they are more effective than when they are formulated and carried out by the administration. Allowing students to draw up codes of conduct provides the dual benefit of giving students experience in self-government at the same time that it relieves the faculty of "policing functions."

The comprehensive code of conduct at the Edison Junior High in Wheaton, Illinois, is revised each year by the student council. It contains sections on honesty, appearance, scholarship, citizenship, and punctuality. Following is the recent code for citizenship:

Learn how to participate in our form of government.

Be helpful in maintaining good order.

Practice good sportsmanship by being a good winner or loser; respecting the abilities of our opponents; following the rules of play; and yet never lose willingly.

Be a good representative of our home, church, school, and community.

Have respect for authority in all its forms; including school, parents, law, and student leaders.

Respect the rights and property of others.

Dress codes vary considerably with the current fads in the neighborhood. Items causing greatest concern in 1965 were long hair and hanging shirt tails for boys and mini skirts and granny dresses for girls. Some codes have specifically banned the long granny dresses and skirts that are shorter than one inch above the knee. Following is a dress code for girls at Lincoln High School in Cleveland, Ohio:

1. *Girls must wear simple dress, jumper and blouse, or skirt and loose sweater or blouse. Sheer blouses may not be worn.*

2. *Skirts should fit properly and should reach to the mid kneecap.*

3. *Slacks may be worn to and from school in severe weather, but must be changed immediately upon entering the building.*

4. *Hair style must be presentable with no exotic styles or colors. No pin curls or rollers may be worn to the class.*

5. *Make-up, if any, must be appropriate for daytime wear. Make-up is no substitute for soap and water.*

6. *Face and hands should be clean.*

7. *Full slips must be worn with overblouses and sweaters.*

Some student councils concern themselves with formulating honor codes. Unquestionably the concern of student government groups to formulate and apply effective honor codes helps some students achieve an awareness of the responsibility of the individual citizen for his own

behavior. Following is the code signed by students at Webster Groves, Missouri:

I pledge that I shall conduct myself according to the standards and ideals of the Honor Code. I shall act in such a manner as to reflect honor on the reputation of this student body. I shall treat all classmates with fairness and respect. I have the greatest responsibility to myself; I shall use good judgment in maintaining my self-respect and integrity. I shall give my full support to the student honor system at Webster Groves High School.

Acting in any manner inconsistent with the Honor Code, or any violation of school rules shall be considered as basis for being reported to the Guidance Council.

At Ladue High School, also in Missouri, the honor code is limited to specific test situations. If the individual class votes to accept the honor system, written examinations include the statement on the examination paper, "On my honor as a Ladue High School student, I am aware of no cheating related to this examination." Students are asked to sign this statement at the beginning of the examination. If they subsequently become aware of cheating, they are expected to cross out their signatures.

Tutoring And Awards

Tutoring as a means by which students can serve others and awards—which reinforce commendable conduct—are handled through the student council in many schools. The student council at New Albany, Indiana, for example, has a student tutoring service for failing students which works with the Honor Society to secure volunteers and with the faculty to screen these volunteers for fitness. With faculty help, it schedules 60 accepted tutors to meet with as many of the 250 failing students as are interested. At Lincoln High School in Cleveland a similar system operates. Here the Student Council secures from teachers the names of students needing help and sends these names to the Future Teachers Club, which holds tutorial sessions for an hour before school. Average attendance is 25 students, helped by seven future teachers.

At Webster Groves the student council helps to plan the competition for a sportsmanship award granted each year to the school in the St. Louis area judged outstanding in the spirit shown by players, coaches, cheerleaders, and spectators at football games. This award is reported to have helped greatly in creating good feeling among schools and reducing the tension that sometimes arises from excessive competition.

A complex award system at the George Washington High School in Philadelphia keeps the student council involved in assigning point values to student activities. A pin is awarded to 7th-grade students who earn 10 points; a gold grade key requires 125 points of seniors. Point values are assigned for every kind of office or service; one point is given for every 100 hours of community service, for example, and 18 points are given for serving as president of the student association.

A Citizenship Committee

At Pine Bluff, Arkansas, the high school Citizenship Committee, now a self-perpetuating group, supplements the regular student council. The Citizenship Committee, after several years of operation, remains an experiment to obtain greater student involvement than was provided by the usual formal programs. It began with 40 student members, appointed by the principal. The committee started with no patterns for procedure and no specified objectives other than the intangible goal of improving citizenship.

Beginning in September 1961, these 40 students, with their counselor sponsor, met regularly one period each day in open discussion sessions. One of the members later described these sessions as being "frustrating but enthusiastic," and, he added, "At first, the whole attempt was so intangible that we met each morning with no specified work—just to talk. No one really knew what we were doing or how or where we were going. Then, things began to take shape."

The first two or three weeks were spent in defining for themselves the traits of good citizenship and desirable values and attitudes. Every student was encouraged to express ideas and thoughts, and discussions were candid and often controversial. Next, they identified "problem" areas and selected the five they considered most important. It was interesting to note that these were closely related to, in fact almost identical with, the ones identified by the school staff. The 40 students then formed subcommittees, each working on one of the five problem areas and reporting to the entire group once a week. A general chairman was elected to coordinate the work of the subcommittees and to conduct the full group discussions.

Each subcommittee initiated projects which it thought would help to improve the area on which the students were working. In doing so, they learned much about human relations and gained an understanding of problems from the points of view of administrators, teachers, and other students. One of the projects the students thought was most successful, for example, was an attempt to promote school spirit and sportsmanship. They felt that behavior at ball games was poor, and after consideration, they worked out a plan of procedure to improve it. They had observed that much of the undesirable behavior was coming from elementary and junior high school students and from adults as well. They made tags which said, "I'm a booster—Not a Boo-er," and pinned them on everyone coming through the gate. They also contacted the coaches, football players, cheerleaders, and grade school principals and arranged for the "hero" image football players and cheerleaders to visit the assemblies and talk about citizenship and sportsmanship. The difference in attitudes, as demonstrated at the next ball game, was very noticeable. A similarly effective concern for school spirit was evident in New York City's Dodge Vocational School, as well as in many other high schools visited by the project team.

Sampling Student Opinions Some schools, including Horace Watkins at Ladue, Missouri, maintain an informal cabinet in addition to the formal council, to provide opportunity for expression to more students and to give the principal an opportunity to sample student opinion. The function and value of the cabinet may be judged from an item in the student newspaper:

To create better understanding between students and administration the Principal's Cabinet will be meeting again this year.

Composed of four students from each grade, the Cabinet acts as a sounding board for ideas proposed by the administration. Although it has no tangible power, students are given the opportunity to sound off without a feeling of pressure because they represent no one but themselves, explained Mr. Richard Stauffer, principal.

Past discussion topics have included the amount of homework teachers should assign, the necessity of grades to motivate students, new classes to be offered, and dancing standards. Mr. Stauffer refers the opinions expressed to the appropriate people, so that the students help formulate school policy and decision.

Anyone interested in serving on the Cabinet must be able to be at school by 7:45 every Thursday morning. Names are chosen at random from three class boxes located in the office, in which interested students have placed their names. Students may sign up anytime during the year. Each group meets only four times, so many and varied viewpoints may be discussed.

CONCLUSION

The thrust of student government influence varies with the school. In some it is procedural, with heavy emphasis on parliamentary law. In others it leans towards the promotion of school spirit. In still others the dominant spirit is concerned with community service.

It is obvious that student councils frequently do more than tally the votes in a school election, raise money for charity drives, and assign themselves to clean up the cafeteria; and even when the council confines itself to this sort of routine operation it can still be a force for civic betterment through the confidence it gives students in their ability to carry through to completion extended and sometimes complex operations. Among the many other values are the experiences student government provides for young people to work with adults, as well as with their peers, on meaningful jobs, and the responsibility of handling other people's money.

For many students election to the student government provides an important experience in responsibility and prudence. A faculty sponsor at Ladue, Missouri, told the project team about a recent situation in which the Council favored a fund-raising plan which would have required a considerable investment of funds and some risk of financial losses. The sponsor strongly advised the students against this proposal and discouraged them from attempting it—an example of a way in which student council experience is likely to be directed toward conservative, or at least prudent, action. The principal of this school realizes that perhaps the reason why he has never had to veto a major proposal of the student council is that the students realize he exercises the ultimate authority and choose not to test it. They have something they want to keep. They know that the administration, while permitting no defiance of its authority, considers suggestions made in an orderly manner.

One of the key elements of civic education is the creation of a wholesome relationship between the citizen and governmental authority. Unquestionably the tone of the student-faculty relationship in high school has some bearing on the student's later attitudes toward authority, and in high school the student government organization plays a role in crystallizing the attitudes of individual students. As the project team observed this role, it appeared to give students an opportunity for participation in matters of direct concern within a framework of orderly procedures and respect for law and order.

The ideal in democracy is for each adult citizen to contribute effectively to society through his own inner sense of right. Transfer of authority from the outer symbols of law, the parent, teacher, and uniformed officer to a personal basis in knowledge, wisdom, and conscience is at the essence of civic education. Consequently, the responsibility of the school is to provide the essential authority and discipline, but to bend every effort to educate students away from dependence on it.

The project team saw a number of high schools which maintain a good balance between freedom and authority. While retaining the ultimate authority for student behavior in faculty and administration hands, many administrators are attempting to establish appropriate situations in student governments and elsewhere in the school where students can discuss, analyze, and propose standards for student conduct, and take initiative to encourage the willing adoption of these standards by the entire student body. This kind of effort, the project team believes, is a most hopeful sign of civic education.

*Our purpose is to cultivate
in the largest possible number of
our future citizens an appreciation of
both the responsibilities and the benefits
which come to them because they are
Americans and are free.*

James B. Conant

CHAPTER **12**

How Civic Education
Can Be Strengthened

In this final chapter, the project team will present its conclusions and recommendations, based on its experiences in visiting 83 schools in 27 states and on the collective professional judgment of the four team members.

These conclusions can be summarized in five basic statements.

1. The project team did find promising practices in civic education in both private and public junior and senior high schools. It believes that many of these practices could be extended to other schools, with whatever adaptation local conditions demand.

2. These effective practices were found in a variety of classroom and extra-curricular experiences—in English classes, vocational training programs, science projects, school clubs, volunteer work, and other activities—as well as in social studies departments.

3. In an age of increasing automation, the interaction between an individual teacher and his students remains one of the key ingredients in effective civic education.

4. Dedicated school administrators, especially at the building level, can establish a favorable climate for effective civic education.

Ultimately, civic education is a focus and point of view for the school.

5. The school has a dual responsibility, to foster civic education and academic excellence. Neither can be neglected without detrimental effects on the quality of the preparation the student receives.

These five conclusions are implicit in the following discussion of the ideal qualities of civic education.

IDEAL CIVIC EDUCATION

Successful civic education is distingushed by four features. It is realistic; it is comprehensive; it is conducted by competent teachers; and it is encouraged by dedicated administrators. Although programs lacking some of these qualities can and often do contribute to civic education, the most commendable civic education is likely to be characterized by all four qualities.

Realistic Civic Education
The word "realism" can mean many things; in this context three levels of meaning are attached to the word. Effective civic education is realistic in its treatment of conditions in the world today, in the expectations it has for students, and in its contact with the particular environment in which the student lives.

Often, the traditional civics class has avoided the realities of the world in which we live and has taught about the formal structure of government at the expense of the basic theory and function of government. By equating practical aspects of power politics with coarseness and corruption, and by tainting the very word "politician" with overtones of questionable morality, a school may also fail to prepare students for the realities of politics. Teachers who close their eyes to the realities of public affairs may be uninformed, or they may have the romanticized view that students should be protected from knowledge of the less agreeable aspects of political life.

Today, increasing numbers of teachers are aware of the inappropriateness of a dichotomy of purity and evil. Many of them are adopting a more tough-minded approach, recognizing that political power is an inescapable reality that can be used for good as well as for evil. They realize that power is not always left for the use of the selfish and corrupt, for they see some of the most successful wielders of political power using it for unselfish causes. Teachers have learned, also, that it is impossible to protect youngsters from the harsh and the indecorous when television daily brings dramatic reports of reality.

When teachers retain a realistic approach to problems of public life, or any other kind of problem, they gain the confidence of a sophisticated younger generation that asks for unvarnished facts. When students are exposed to public realities outside the school, they feel that they are being treated like children if their teachers present less than the whole truth. Marshall McLuhan, the communications authority, asserts that a major cause of dropouts is the fact that the outside world has more interesting data than the inside of a classroom.

A school that presents a realistic civic education provides opportunities for students to come to terms with social reality. Its students are encouraged to examine critically the social, political, economic, and moral issues facing contemporary society. Their confrontations with real issues are unhampered by fearful teachers or the existence of unstated but recognized "closed areas."

To offer a realistic program requires courage and determination, for the obstacles are formidable. Community pressures can easily dissuade the timid teacher from pursuing an issue he deems pertinent. The desire to cooperate in a smoothly functioning administrative operation can prevent him from attempting an innovation that may require an adjustment of the class schedule and the possible annoyance of an administrator. The absence of key leadership in the faculty or in the community may make the enthusiastic teacher feel alone and out of step and may discourage his efforts to deal with controversial issues.

Some efforts at civic education flounder through failure to use the available community resources, either because of ignorance or timidity. A "don't rock the boat" attitude is so dominant in some school communities that teachers are either afraid or embarrassed to use materials or speakers sponsored by recognized voices of the political right or left. In these schools, a National Association of Manufacturers pamphlet or an AFL-CIO film might be equally suspect, a Socialist speaker or a John Birch Society speaker equally unacceptable. In few schools is the civic education concept so well developed that schools utilize the community, not merely as a setting for field trips, but as a laboratory for experiments, case studies, and surveys.

The lack of realism in much of what is called civic education may be ascribed partly to the dilution of reality in some textbooks, which are excessively cautious and theoretical. This weakness, however, is being overcome by publication of new and factual texts, and by the use of multiple materials, including a wide variety of periodicals and other fugitive materials.

These conditions too often prevail: reliance on a single text, often weakened by the necessity to cover too much material; reluctance to handle controversial issues honestly or imaginatively; unqualified and unimaginative teachers or administrators; and willingness to restrict learning to the classroom. These limiting factors often conspire to screen out or dilute material that describes the world as it is, leaving materials which describe what it once was, or what one would like it to be. Too many schools develop what Jerome Bruner calls a "middle language" which describes not reality, but notions—often erroneous—about reality.

Another obstacle to realistic civic education results from the expectations the school has for its students. Although teachers must work to create an interest and commitment to civic affairs, they cannot realistically expect that every student will react positively to every suggestion of civic participation. Not all students respond with enthusiasm to cars or football or dancing, and it is unreasonable to expect all to become enthusiastic about an opportunity to write to their congressman, work for a political party, or contribute to a worthy charity. To label as irresponsible the prospective citizen who confesses his lack of interest in local politics is likely only to deepen his alienation.

When a teacher says, "Every good citizen does this or knows that," branding all others as bad citizens, he engages in the kind of careless thinking that justifiably leads students to consider him hypocritical. Probably all good citizens should vote, pay taxes, and obey laws, but even these fundamentals may have exceptions.

It is equally unrealistic to believe that high school students should feel guilty if they remain ignorant of some "basic fact." No one can retain all the information that another person considers essential, but many of today's students are relatively well informed. In the 1965 National Citizenship Test, St. Louis honor students had average scores of 83, the same as political workers in Philadelphia, 11 points higher than the League of Women Voters in New York, and only two points below congressmen and their wives. This is not to say that students should not be encouraged to improve their performance by reaching higher than their grasp; rather, it is to suggest that civic education is better attained when the demands made on a student are realistic.

Louis Untermeyer, the poet and former consultant in poetry at the Library of Congress, testified to the unfortunate effect that an unrealistic curriculum has on students. Untermeyer, a dropout from high school, was awarded his diploma 63 years later at the age of 80. While he was reminiscing about his failure to complete the high school program, he said, "It was not defiance, merely defeat. My formal education was over." Just before he received his diploma at the special ceremony, he told a reporter that he would not advise anyone to drop out of school, but added that if he had to take that same geometry course again, he would again leave school!

To maintain constant contact with the realities of the student's environment and to help him to expand his world and fit it congenially into the effective adult world requires knowledgeable and understanding teachers. These teachers must be capable of comprehending the world by standards different from those of their own family and neighborhood. It requires flexible persons who are able to earn the confidence of the bright student and the slow, the non-white and the white, the rich and the poor, the eager learner and the reluctant.

Comprehensive Civic Education

Ideally, a realistic approach to civic education will also be comprehensive, in terms of meeting the needs of all students, involving all departments of the school, and using a variety of techniques to reach the student. In this sense, civic education at its best is not a unit, a course, or even an entire program within a school; it is a focus of concern that pervades every aspect of the school. Within a comprehensive concern for civic education, the social studies department is likely to provide the "heartbeat," but each part of the school will have a vital role.

Meeting the needs of the entire student body is by no means an easy task, especially in schools containing students from varied and/or culturally deprived backgrounds. The historian Arnold Toynbee was aware of the problems when he wrote:

The importance of the home's contribution comes to light when an educational institution that has been the preserve of some privileged minority is thrown open to a wider public. One of the most effective privileges hitherto has been the privilege of being heir to a richer cultural heritage than is accessible to the underprivileged minority, and this richer heritage is transmitted through the family as well as through schools and colleges. This becomes apparent when children with a poorer cultural heritage are admitted to the minority's schools. They find it difficult to obtain as much benefit as their privileged school fellows obtain from the same course of formal education, because they bring less with them. To him that hath shall be given. This is not just, but it is one of the facts of life.[1]

In order to bring all students to a reasonable level of civic awareness and participation, the school can use multiple paths, including volunteer clubs and service activities, differentiated assignments, individualized reading stimulated by the popularity of paperback books, and a variety of other procedures and programs reported throughout this volume.

The need for flexibility in the school, with opportunity and encouragement for students to learn what concerns them as individuals, is reflected in many reports and in the pleas of students themselves. The 1965 National High School Student Conference on Education, sponsored by the Charles F. Kettering Foundation, offered 101 high school seniors a chance to express themselves on the problems of education. Writer James Cass summarized their views in the *Saturday Review* as follows:

They would eliminate the lock-step inflexibility that wastes students' time while placing tradition or administrative convenience first. ("Why allot the same time to every subject? Some don't require as many hours as others.") They would substitute a far more free-wheeling learning environment for the tidy, ship-shape school that runs on a split-second schedule. ("Administrators are more concerned with their school's image

---

[1] Edward D. Myers, *Education in the Perspective of History.* Harper and Row, 1960, p. 270.

than they are with their students.") They would do away with poor teachers who are inadequately prepared for the subjects they teach. ("Even worse than a poorly trained teacher is one who isn't interested in his subject.") They would eliminate dull textbooks or use them only for reference. ("I'd rather read twice as much in a good paperback on the same subject.") They would assign homework much more selectively. Admitting its necessary role in the education process, they felt that too much of it was repetitive busy work. ("I always do my homework just to have something done, but it doesn't mean anything. Research papers stimulate you to get involved in a subject.") Some of the pressure for high grades and academic achievement would be reduced ("All high school did for me was to get me into college."), and a more relaxed environment would be substituted. ("Learning can be fun, if you only have a chance to find it out.")

One recurrent theme that appeared in many of the discussions was the need for mutual respect among the diversity of teachers, students, and administrators that make up a school. We may not be adults yet, they said in effect, but neither are we children any more. We, too, are interested in education; we, too, have given thought to its problems.[2]

Schools that have a strong commitment to civic education use a wide variety of activities and techniques. Instruction is not limited to a single course or a single textbook. A variety of offerings to accommodate the diversity of backgrounds and talents of the students is clearly in evidence. The multiplicity of instructional materials is striking. A great number of student clubs and activities are available. Attention to civic education is not limited to the social studies department; the program is all-embracing.

Teacher Competence   Like Jesse Stuart in *The Thread That Runs So True*, the project team "visited schools . . . looked for virtues . . . hunted for faults . . . wanted to know the answers . . . wanted to heap the information before it like cords of wood and throw out the

---

[2] *The Saturday Review*, March 19, 1966, p. 75.

bad sticks and accept the sound and durable."[3] The characteristics of a great teacher, however, cannot be gathered "like cords of wood." As Margaret Mead has written:

Teaching is an art that has no appeal when it is described only in words. *Books on education are usually as poor a substitute for living models as books on lovemaking are for a lover's gentle hands or as cookbooks are for the sight of a chef actually mixing a sauce. Talk about education is dull. But teaching, practiced as an art by a teacher in love with her subject matter, is a creative delight.*[4]

Knowledge of subject matter, intelligence, interest in students, the ability to convey ideas, imagination and creativity, conscientiousness, integrity, compassion—the list of characteristics of effective teachers is endless. What are the specific characteristics most needed for effective teaching today?

Contrary to a popular view, functions of the teacher have not remained unchanged through the ages. In the ancient world, for example, few manuscripts were available to the student and perhaps the chief characteristic of the great teacher was his possession of information. His principal function was to transmit knowledge. After the invention of the printing press, the "informative function" of the teacher became less important. The personality of the teacher, however, remains important in making knowledge meaningful as part of the learner's life.

It is clearly beyond the scope of this report to attempt to cover the entire range of factors that constitute successful teaching today. Instead, teacher traits that appear to belong within this range will be cited.

It is probably impossible to overemphasize the importance of knowledge and planning. In almost every effective class, club, or student council meeting, both students and teacher had prepared carefully. Background study is one part of preparation; practical planning and management is another. Even meetings that appear to be spontaneous

---

[3] Jesse Stuart, *The Thread That Runs So True.* Charles Scribner's Sons, 1950, p. 258.

[4] Margaret Mead, "Where Education Fits In," *Think*, November–December 1962, p. 20.

discussions more often have a direction and control when there has been preplanning.

The ever-present dilemma of freedom versus order in the classroom, one of the bases of the long-continuing dispute between so-called traditionalists and progressives, must be solved by each teacher personally in keeping with his personality and the way he sees his role. Presiding in classes that appear to the project team as vital and creative were strong, confident teachers who exercised authority without being authoritarian. These teachers maintained standards and exacted high student performance while allowing a degree of sharing in both the formulation and the administration of class activities. In every case the teacher fully accepted his classroom responsibilities.

Effective teaching involves control and restraint as well as imagination and creativity. It means helping students to resolve for themselves the ever-recurring dilemma of order and freedom.

The creative classroom is often characterized as one that affords an opportunity for the most students to apply their own personalities and styles to the problems at hand rather than be forced to adopt a precise style and attitude prescribed by the teacher. It permits the student to retain the personal dignity of his convictions, expression, and style, while the teacher remains in charge of the general content and procedure planning.

Arthur Combs offers a helpful list of factors in an educational atmosphere which encourages the students creativity:

1. *The encouragement of fantasy and fun;*
2. *The provision of wide choices;*
3. *Trust in students so that they, in turn, can trust themselves;*
4. *Encouraging cooperation and discouraging competition;*
5. *Encouraging cooperative interaction;*
6. *Creating feelings of belonging;*
7. *Encouraging difference, uniqueness, and integrity;*
8. *Encouraging communication;*
9. *Encouraging problem-solving approaches;*
10. *Valuing openness and flexibility;*
11. *Valuing individuality;*

12. Eliminating censorship;
13. Encouraging experimenting and trying.[5]

In addition to arranging knowledgeable and well-planned presentation of material and maintaining a flexible equilibrium of freedom and control in the classroom, the best teachers use imagination and creativity. The creative teacher may sometimes be a thorn in the side of the administrator. He may be a unique, outspoken, individualist who does not fit comfortably into the mold of a tranquil world for the administrator. He may want to do something new and different, which will require adjustments in the schedule or unusual meeting times or materials. He may say or do things that parents will not understand, and they may complain to the superintendent. This clearly places a responsibility on the administration to support and encourage the strong teacher who, although effective with his students, may alienate insecure elements in the community who hold other notions of the role of the school.

Outstanding teachers are likely to have the knowledge and temperament to be patient with students' mistakes without ignoring or condoning them. Some teachers try so relentlessly to provide the perfect environment for students to learn the right responses that they create an unconscious despotism that negates the democracy they advocate. In one school where explanations of the citizenship program by teachers appeared almost too good to be true the project team asked a group of students after school, "Are you free to make a mistake in this school?" The chorus of "no" belied the democratic spirit described earlier.

A relaxed and accepting attitude on the part of the teacher can do much to help students learn a difficult subject. Classic philosophy and ancient history are not necessarily beyond the understanding of the student with a limited cultural background or below-average ability. With these students in particular, however, the tone, vocabulary, and standards of acceptance of the teacher are crucial. As one student said, "Some teachers are so devoted to their subject that they are impatient with slow-learning or culturally deprived students."

The teacher who lacks flexibility frequently needs the assurance he

---

[5] A. S. Combs, "Creating Effective Teachers," *The Professional Education of Teachers.* Allyn and Bacon, Inc., 1965, p. 36.

can derive from teaching about things that he believes are past, settled, unchanging and unchallenged. Teaching about current problems can be unsettling because the teacher may feel insecure when he knows his information is not up to date, or when there is no one right answer.

Another characteristic of outstanding teachers is objectivity. Teachers qualified to bring civic competence to all our youth must be able to separate their personal convictions on specific issues from the basic attitudes they are justified in encouraging in their students. They must be able to accord equal dignity to students who resist change, those who accept it, and those who create it. If such a teacher recommends books by Arthur Schlesinger, Jr., Hubert Humphrey, or William O. Douglas, for example, he should at an appropriate time offer balance with readings from J. Edgar Hoover, William Buckley, or Barry Goldwater. It is not enough for the teacher to assign only "liberal" or only "conservative" readings and keep a few titles representative of the other view on the library shelves "to show we are impartial." To be impartial, the opposing view must be given consideration.

In conclusion, the five qualities described here—knowledgeable organization of material, flexibility in the balance between classroom order and freedom, creativity, patience, and objectivity—are attributes of the ideal teacher. These qualities are likely to be found in the outstanding teachers of today.

Dedicated Administrators

In schools where civic education is flourishing, principals and superintendents do more than affirm in words the importance of civic education; they support programs that produce civic competence by allocating the time and resources needed to make them succeed. When a school ad-

ministration considers any school activity significant enough to be given the constant consideration due to an important activity, that effort has a good chance of succeeding. At the McCluer High School in Missouri, the administration believes the student council is important to civic education. Consequently two teachers are given a reduced teaching load in order to serve as co-sponsors; half a dozen other teachers are enlisted to assist by sponsoring committees; and schooltime is allocated to student council activities every day. In Detroit, where community programs and special projects are deemed important, special divisions of the central administrative staff are established to administer these projects and throughout the city hundreds of persons devote the bulk of their time to making the programs creative. In towns and cities where school administrators consider it important to expose students to the crucial controversial issues of our day, they work to create a community climate receptive to honest discussion of pertinent issues. These principals and superintendents defend their teachers' right to deal with controversial material, not only because it is good practice to support one's teaching staff, but also because they believe that forthright treatment of critical issues is an essential part of training for citizenship.

The central administrative staff and the principal's office can contribute to civic education in many ways. They can select teachers committed to the behavioral goals of civic education and allocate adequate time in the school schedule for appropriate activities. They can encourage the treatment of controversial issues. They can support in-service programs for teachers and provide salaried teacher time for curriculum revision. They can facilitate the acquisition of the kinds of instructional materials their teachers need. As mediators, they are in a position to create a school environment conductive to the free exchange of ideas; to promote cooperation with community agencies and with other schools; and to ease the way for student and faculty participation in state and regional conferences. Above all, administrators can contribute to civic education by being honest, courageous, and dedicated individuals, ready to do whatever must be done to assist teachers to enrich the lives of their students. As one assistant superintendent put it, "I weigh every decision in the light of what difference it will make in the lives of students."

School administrations frequently encourage teacher growth by paying travel expenses to conventions, compensating teachers for attendance at summer workshops, publicizing the achievements of individuals and committees, and especially by being receptive to ideas offered by teachers. Although these are not new practices, they are not as widely used as they might be.

Summary

The ideal of a realistic and comprehensive program in the hands of competent teachers and dedicated administrators is approached in some schools. Many schools are aware of the ideal and are making strides to improve their contributions to civic education. Some districts are encouraged by Federal programs such as Upward Bound, Operation Head Start, and the Teacher Corps, which have similar objectives. The project team hopes that the successes of some schools in activities reported here will encourage other schools to redouble their efforts to provide all students with the fullest opportunity to gain the knowledge, analytical ability, and commitment for effective participation as citizens.

SOME RECOMMENDATIONS FOR THE STRENGTHENING OF CIVIC EDUCATION

While the project team was primarily concerned with observing and reporting promising practices, it could not fail to be aware of areas that were weak or deficient in some schools. In this section attention is directed to observed conditions that appeared to possess potential for great improvement in some of the schools visited.

In-Service Institutes

Instruction is antiquated where teachers teach only what they were taught 10, 20, or 30 years earlier. When society is changing as fast as it is today, the continued growth of the teacher is crucial. It is not enough for the social studies teacher to be an alert reader of the newspaper; the student can read newspapers for himself. The teacher needs thoughtful, systematic, depth understanding of the forces at work creating the changes in our world. Consequently, one of the most valuable devices for teachers is the in-service institute. Whether it is a weekly lecture or television presentation or a six-week summer institute, some form of continuing training is essential. Provision should be made for this training to be a regular and normal part of every teacher's program. Several summer institutes for teachers of civics, sponsored by the U.S. Office of Education for the summer of 1966, and the several dozen for the summer of 1967, as well as the parallel institutes for teachers of history, geography, and economics, contribute to the unending job of keeping teaching contemporary. Equally valuable are the local in-service programs operated in some schools, which can be tailored to fit precisely the goals and facilities of the local district. In-service courses and institutes help upgrade the teacher's information and skills and stimulate his thinking by reviewing contact with authorities in his field.

Continuous learning is essential to keep teachers abreast of a rapidly changing world and to maintain their receptivity to new ideas. In schools where many teachers participate in conferences and institutes, a constant flow of fresh ideas permeates the atmosphere. In schools where few teachers attend conferences and institutes, the tone is more likely to become passive, lethargic, and perhaps stagnant.

Many schools have splendid student government plans which are losing their value because they are becoming institutionalized and taken for granted. They no longer have the impact they once had. The sponsors are worn out, and an infusion of new ideas or new spirit is needed. Alert and sensitive faculties become aware of such needs. Effective in-service programs point the way to solutions.

A faculty committed to the ideal of keeping itself intellectually active finds constant regeneration of interest in its school institutions. Schools which keep their teachers intellectually invigorated tend to keep the curriculum updated.

Curriculum Development

Faculties that are exposed to appropriate continuing education tend to be engaged in curriculum revision and course development. To date, too little of this curriculum planning has centered around the kind of unified schoolwide approach to citizenship goals recommended earlier in this chapter. Little attention has been paid to devising courses of study that will do for citizenship objectives what the new mathematics and new science curricula are beginning to do for those subjects. It is highly desirable for teachers and curriculum-makers to concern themselves with the construction of sequences of content and activities leading to the mastery of citizenship skills.

From time to time social studies leaders have randomly emphasized skills, from map-making to distinguishing between fact and opinion, but few courses of study have given adequate attention to these skills. Such courses—whether they be history, geography, or an integrated social studies curriculum—might include attention to research skills and techniques for using the library; basic principles of logic; rules of evidence; and mastery of fundamental concepts and knowledge in the social sciences. The important point is that courses of study can be designed with primary emphasis on valid citizenship goals, drawing upon the assistance of the social sciences. Unfortunately, the reverse is more often true; the competencies necessary for citizenship are brought into programs only as they appear to contribute to mastery of the academic subject.

Where in the school can suitable experiences be introduced to help students learn to accept social dilemmas as natural phenomena? The preoccupation of many Americans with security, both personal and national, has made many people susceptible to excessive anxiety in the face of uncertainty or dilemma. Uncertainty is inseparable from change, and our coming generation will be forced to live with it. Currently much of the school experience in decision-making seems artificial to the point of removing the key element of dilemma. In a world of shifting values, conflicts of loyalty are inevitable, and young people must learn to cope with conflict. There is too little evidence that schools are helping them to identify and resolve these conflicts.

Progress towards an improved civic education program may include attention to integrated social studies, with no immovable barriers between anthropology, sociology, history, government, psychology, economics, and political science. In an integrated social studies program, the student seeks answers to human problems without regard for narrow subject boundaries. It is true that some social studies teachers link the several social sciences, but usually in a hesitant and limited manner. They use maps in a history course, for example, or study the history of the banking system or the tariff acts in an economics course, or combine study of the Constitution with a study of the historical events surrounding its writing. These instances of the overlapping of two or more social science disciplines are frequent and they are commendable, but they can be carried much further.

The writing of the U.S. Constitution, for example, is more than a topic of history and political science. It is equally an event influenced by economics, geography, sociology, and psychology. The Constitutional Convention itself was the outgrowth of a series of conferences designed to facilitate economic cooperation among the states; the geographical problems, including distances and barriers to trade, were vital; the concepts of social class and ability to govern, as well as the individual ambitions and idiosyncrasies of the delegates, were as significant then as they are in comparable situations today. Human problems are seldom understandable by reference to a single academic discipline. Civic education needs to be concerned with broad human problems, and the contributions of the several disciplines must be brought to bear on these problems.

Although the project team is aware of the unhurried pace of curriculum change, it is reassured that changes are taking place, at least in some schools. At the high school level, some classes are indistinguishable from the classes of a generation ago, but others are marked by wider reading assignments, more visual aids, greater variety of class activities, more reliance on exchange of ideas through group discussion, and much greater use of community resources.

Making Use Of The Past

Because, from one view, schools exist primarily to transmit the accumulated heritage of the culture, it is to be expected that the curriculum should be heavily weighted with history. Schools do transmit much of the record of man's past achievements, in courses in national political history, world history, cultural and other non-political history, in other subjects, and in extra-curricular activities. This emphasis is obviously essential to human progress.

One discouraging observation made by the project team, however, was that although history courses still constitute roughly 50 percent of the offerings of social studies departments, the lessons of the historical approach are repeatedly ignored. Very often student clubs operate from a short-sighted basis of attacking each problem as if it were a brand new topic that had never been considered before. Each year, the student council may raise the question of improving the food service in the cafeteria, having a senior dance at a downtown hotel rather than the school gymnasium, improving the supervision of the halls, controlling smoking, or regulating student parking. Seldom is any reference made to the arguments that have been presented on these same topics in previous years. Why can not faculty sponsors of student councils encourage students to train themselves in the basic procedure of consulting the records? Consulting the student council or club minutes of the preceding year or two, to see what arguments were presented and what action was taken, can provide continuity for the organization. It can also teach a lesson in group action and expedite a solution to the problem at hand. The study of history is enlightening in itself, but history can also be used as a tool for attacking current problems.

Similarly, current problems of national and international significance are frequently discussed, in history classes and elsewhere, with little or no reference to their historical backgrounds. Sometimes the very teachers who justify the study of history on grounds that it provides help in understanding current problems fail to refer to historical origins when they turn to the study of current events. Too frequently, history remains an isolated formalized record of the past, with no methodological influence on the handling of current problems. The social studies concept is not yet firmly enough established in the thinking of some high school teachers or students for them freely to relate history to geography, economics, political science, psychology, and anthropology or any of these to today's absorbing headline news.

Libraries Although libraries are evolving into instructional materials centers, books remain the staple medium for recorded communication. Books are the heart of the academic process, the success of which is vitally affected by the number and quality of books that are available for student use.

The variation in size and quality of school libraries is truly astounding. Some adequate school libraries have been mentioned earlier. In contrast to these is a high school where the librarian spends only one period a day in the library; during the rest of the day, she teaches social studies classes. This high school library includes no works by Faulkner, Salinger, Marx, Plato, Toynbee, Barzun, Golding, Montaigne, Darwin, Eisenhower, Goldwater. One title by Hemingway is in this library, and one by Tolstoy. Here is a library lacking some of the most important books ever written. Students are deprived of contact with many of the great men and great minds of history. Some might excuse these deficiencies on the basis that this is a small town that cannot easily afford many books. However, the inadequacies of school libraries are not limited to those in small schools. Amazingly, some large city schools, and not only in deprived areas, are culpably deficient in their library holdings.

One city high school with a library of over 15,000 volumes has no works by William Faulkner, J. D. Salinger, Karl Marx, Bertrand Russell, or Martin Luther King. This metropolitan school made available to its 2,000 students only two of Hemingway's novels and only one play by Tennessee Williams. Here the library reflects a situation where controversy is avoided, new ideas are suspect, and democracy is a word for the dictionary.

A widespread deficiency in most high school libraries visited is their failure to offer even a gesture of recognition that literature exists in languages other than English. If the school is to help to produce citizens of the world by making students aware of the contributions of other cultures through formal language courses, these efforts might be supplemented and encouraged by having some foreign language publications available. Today few high school libraries have on their shelves any books written in a language other than English, and only a few subscribe to foreign language periodicals.

Other Features   The recapitulation of strengths and weaknesses could continue indefinitely. Every aspect of the school program in some manner affects civic education, and therefore, every aspect of school operation could be considered within the scope of this report. The most conspicuous features have been summarized. Some others are listed below.

1. Student councils are vital forces for citizenship in some schools but

mere ceremonial groups with no responsibility in other schools.

2. Variations in teaching effectiveness are startling. The quality of performance can never be uniform, but it may properly be expected to rise consistently above the low level that still prevails in some classrooms.

3. The quality of democracy expressed in the granting of dignity and human acceptance to members of minority groups also ranges from inspiring to appalling. In some schools students and teachers alike work in a free atmosphere where every individual knows that his worth as an individual will be recognized and strives to make a worthy contribution to the group. In other schools so-called "outsiders" are merely tolerated. These students from minority groups, and usually from less fortunate economic circumstances, are made to feel inferior because of language difficulties and cultural differences. Schools with minority groups in their student bodies can make a substantial contribution to civic education through citizenship programs designed to help all students learn and practice techniques for overcoming barriers and by approaching in practice the equality of personal acceptance and opportunity that is the goal of democratic citizenship.

Many practices observed by the project team deserve to be reported much more thoroughly than was possible within the limits of this study. The contributions to civic education of practices such as simulation games, flexible scheduling, the infusion of anthropology and sociology into the curriculum, deeper involvement of students in community affairs, and many others deserve further study. As experiences with these and other innovations are reported, it is to be hoped that some observers will pay particular attention to their value for developing informed and analytical citizens who are dedicated to helping bring about a better nation and a better world.

THE NEED FOR WIDESPREAD COMMITMENT TO CIVIC EDUCATION

Although this report is couched in positive terms, no reader should be misled into believing that the project team admired every class situation it observed or that it did not encounter some deplorable teaching practices. Even in schools recommended for their excellence, indefensible practices occur. Even in schools where promising practices flourish, some teachers talk too much and with insufficient planning. Some test only for memory of isolated facts, become intemperate or biased in discussion of public affairs, ignore viewpoints that do not accord with their own convictions, offer no encouragement to student thinking, and in other ways violate the basic tenets of teaching.

There are schools where the air is infected by totalitarianism, although all the outward forms are democratic. These are schools dominated by highly autocratic personalities, and the relationship with students is an armed truce. Other schools reflect total commitment to materialism and egocentrism. Specific weaknesses already mentioned include woefully inadequate libraries, student councils that do little beyond managing fund-raising campaigns, classes where inquiry and controversy are discouraged, and schools where commitment to civic education is not evident anywhere.

Favorable situations far outnumbered the unfavorable, however, and inspiring successes are being achieved in many schools. Nevertheless, much more must be done before anyone dare be satisfied with the civic education offered in our secondary schools. As effective as many present programs are, they are not enough. Too often the promising practices are isolated examples of someone's ingenuity or of one teacher's skill. Seldom found is a consistent schoolwide concern for creating better citizens.

The liberating effect of education is multiplied when specialized academic competence is given significance by being related to the larger goal of creating informed and analytic citizens, committed to the betterment of society. In absence of this commitment there is danger that superior teachers in each subject will implant in their students a distorted picture of citizenship based upon a limited area of competence. The schoolwide commitment to civic education can provide the cohesive element that can make of the separate academic, vocational, and social excellences a genuinely informed, analytic, and committed civic spirit.

Commendably, many schools have come alive with intensified concern for academic standards, rigorous intellectual effort, and excellence of performance. Such aspirations for intellectual achievement must be encouraged and rewarded in every reasonable way. One way to encourage intellectual excellence is by relating learning to a worthy and appropriate goal. Admission of a large number of a school's graduates to the colleges of their choice, commendable as it is, should not be the primary goal of an American high school. At the same time, graduation of young men and women prepared for and committed to civic participation, and also qualified for admission to an excellent college, is completely laudable. The ideals of civic competence need not be submerged by the goals of personal reward typified by high grades, college admission, scholarships, and other success symbols.

Goals for Americans need not be uniform, but they must be larger than self. Democracy demands diversity and a pluralism of ideals, and not a mere collection of ambitions for personal material success. If, as *Webster's New International Dictionary* says, patriotism is devotion to the welfare of one's country, then it becomes the patriotic duty of the schools to promote goals that transcend intellectual excellence without reducing that excellence. Commitment to civic excellence can enhance commitment to academic excellence by giving it purpose beyond personal benefits.

In a 1966 article in *Harper's*, Allan R. Talbot says of the programs of financial aid from the Federal government, "What is, however, sadly lacking [in the schools] is the kind of vigorous leadership that could convert ideas and money into solid, functioning programs. This cannot be done by professional edicts emanating from a lonely voice in the superintendent's office. It can only be done with men and women who can function as public entrepreneurs—leaders with the ingenuity, verve, and energy so much more evident in other areas of national life than in public education."[6]

Ingenuity, verve, and energy spring from commitment. A commitment to the ideal of the improving society can inspire teachers in every department to dedicate their teaching to the creation of adults who will personify the 11 goals of citizenship described in Chapter 2. By doing this, teachers can produce as many or even more scholarship winners and specialized champions and at the same time contribute to the growth of bolder, far-seeing individuals who will constitute collectively a stronger society.

---

[6] "Needed, A New Breed of School Superintendent," by Allan R. Talbot. *Harper's*, February 1966, p. 81.

The project team does not advocate indoctrination, except demonstration by example in the highest standards and values of our society, but it does not on that account reject the school's obligation to offer direction and inspiration for goals beyond self advancement. Without such goals, our society loses its cohesiveness. With these goals, education becomes meaningful; it becomes civic education. As a recent social studies publication expressed it, "We, the teachers, have an obligation. Our society has established free education for all as one of its values. It is expected that in attending school a child will be exposed to and prepared to meet the problems of a citizen in our democratic society. Therefore, creating good citizens has become a publicly accepted goal of the public schools. In short, the public may clamor against 'indoctrination' and 'value determination,' but at the same time, under another label, it demands a value-oriented program."[7]

A bold civic education program affords opportunity for the study of all pertinent issues; a wide variety of student experiences and community action programs; participation in decision-making by both faculty and students; and a school climate characterized by mutual confidence among administration, faculty, and students. In such schools, the administration and faculty are alert to better ways of teaching, but they do not adopt an innovation just because it is new.

To urge that schools engage in wholehearted concern for civic education seems more than appropriate. The clearly recognized political apathy, massive alienation, and high rates of crime and delinquency in this country suggest that it is imperative. These flaws in our democratic society may be interpreted as evidence that our schools have not yet succeeded in igniting commitment to an improving society through the virtues of knowledge, analysis, and dedicated action. Further, many schools have not yet succeeded because they have not yet attempted this basic task. Some have been totally committed to the narrower academic goal which Arnold Toynbee and others have recognized as being originally a kind of vocational education. Toynbee says:

One lesson is that we must try to keep the several essential subjects of education in balance with each other. Undoubtedly the most important

---

[7] Roy Price, Warren Hickman, and Gerald Smith, *Major Concepts for Social Studies*, Social Studies Curriculum Center at Syracuse U., November 1965, p. 21.

subject of all is man. The human race could not survive if, in each generation, we did not learn from our predecessors at least a modicum of the art of managing our relations with our fellow human beings with ourselves. This is the essence of a humane education, but it cannot be learned just from a study of "the humanities" in book form. In the present day world, it is true, a considerable amount of book learning has come to be a necessary part of everyone's education. At the same time, the essence of a humane education has still to be acquired mainly through the informal apprenticeship that is the heart of education in all societies and all social classes at all levels. This is what makes and keeps us human. Book learning in the humanities can be a valuable supplement to it, but can never be a substitute for it. And it must be remembered that while an apprenticeship in the art of living with one's fellows is an indispensable part of the education of every human being born into the world, the bookish supplement to it originally came into existence as a vocational education for administrative officials in government service and for ministers of the higher religions. [8]

Academic and intellectual goals can be strengthened by placing them in perspective and making them part of the larger goal of civic competence. The details of the larger purpose are suggested throughout this volume. A totally committed school might well employ a dozen or more of the practices cited in this report, or it might engage in parallel practices.

There is no pattern, no formula, and no checklist for civic education. Every school, aware of its resources and its goals and mindful of the limitations on what it can accomplish but undismayed by these limitations, will devise its own combination of promising practices for the transformaton of its youth into knowledgeable and analytical citizens committed to active participation in the making of a better society.

---

[8] Edward D. Myers, *Education in the Perspective of History*, Harper and Row, 1960, pp. 281–82.

APPENDIX

Schools Visited	Principal
R. B. Hudson High School	
Selma, Alabama	William J. Yelder
(Phoenix) West High School	
Phoenix, Arizona	Donald F. Stone
Verde Valley School	
Sedona, Arizona	Zdenek Salzmann
Fresno High School	
Fresno, California	Arthur L. Miller
Rim of the World Junior Senior	
High School	
Lake Arrowhead, California	Lester DeMent
Hollenbeck Junior High School	
Los Angeles, California	Paul L. Currin
Mark Twain Junior High School	
Los Angeles, California	Arthur Ramey
Oakland Technical High School	
Oakland, California	Donald W. Lucas
Portola Junior Senior High School	
Portola, California	Glynn B. Lee
San Carlos High School	
San Carlos, California	Philip Maslin
Woodside High School	
Woodside, California	Willard Bradley
Abraham Lincoln High School	
Denver, Colorado	David S. Brainerd
East High School	
Denver, Colorado	Robert P. Colwell
Lake Junior High School	
Denver, Colorado	William R. Schumacher
Darien High School	
Darien, Connecticut	Stewart B. Atkinson
Mather Junior High School	
Darien, Connecticut	Jack A. Forte
Middlesex Junior High School	
Darien, Connecticut	Albert Benson
Glastonbury High School	
Glastonbury, Connecticut	Theodore Bartolotta
Brien McMahon High School	
South Norwalk, Connecticut	Luther A. Howard
Paul Junior High School	
Washington, District of Columbia	Sidney H. Zevin

Schools Visited	Principal
Miami Beach Senior High School Miami Beach, Florida	Steve Moore
Ferry Pass Junior High School Pensacola, Florida	Julian Wilson
Sylvan Hills High School Atlanta, Georgia	Gerald W. Culberson
Trinity High School Bloomington, Illinois	Sister Marie Bertrand
St. Scholastica High School Chicago, Illinois	Sister M. Catherine Lynch
University of Chicago Laboratory School Chicago, Illinois	Willard J. Congreve
Lakeview High School Decatur, Illinois	William W. Fromm
West Leyden High School Northlake, Illinois	George R. Cox
Maine Township High School (East) Park Ridge, Illinois	Milo Johnson
Maine Township High School (South) Park Ridge, Illinois	Clyde K. Watson
Maine Township High School (West) Park Ridge, Illinois	Herman Rider
Edison Junior High School Wheaton, Illinois	Donald J. Burr
New Albany High School New Albany, Indiana	Delbert A. Brown
Labette County Community High School Altamont, Kansas	Curtis D. Sides
De La Salle High School New Orleans, Louisiana	Brother A. Amedy Walsh
High Point High School Beltsville, Maryland	Allan L. Chotiner
Fairmont Heights Senior High School Fairmont Heights, Maryland	G. James Gholson
Mount Hermon School Mount Hermon, Massachusetts	Arthur H. Kiendl
Central High School Detroit, Michigan	James R. Irwin
Denby High School Detroit, Michigan	Miss Julia Wilde

Schools Visited	Principal
Durfee Junior High School Detroit, Michigan	Miss Edith Edwards
Frank Murphy Junior High School Detroit, Michigan	John D. Zinnikas
Pershing Senior High School Detroit, Michigan	Alfred Meyers
Phillip Murray Senior High School Detroit, Michigan	Thomas Quinlan
Redford Senior High School Detroit, Michigan	Robert R. Baumgartner
Skills Center Detroit, Michigan	George D. McWatt
Spain Junior High School Detroit, Michigan	Theodore Meyer
Bryant Junior High School Flint, Michigan	Robert W. Rodda
Northwestern High School Flint, Michigan	Jack A. Mobley
Meridian High School Meridian, Mississippi	Charles Armstrong
McCluer High School Florissant, Missouri	Merlin Ludwig
Central High School Kansas City, Missouri	James F. Boyd
East High School Kansas City, Missouri	L. Clayton Dickson
Lincoln Junior High School Kansas City, Missouri	A. Leedy Campbell
Horton Watkins High School Ladue, Missouri	Richard F. Stauffer
Webster Groves High School Webster Groves, Missouri	Howard A. Latta
Henniker High School Henniker, New Hampshire	Theodore E. Gladu
Passaic Valley High School Little Falls, New Jersey	Michael F. Gatti
Monmouth Regional High School New Shrewsbury, New Jersey	Thomas J. Bradshaw
DeWitt Junior High School Ithaca, New York	Curtis L. Rohm
DeWitt Clinton High School New York, New York	Walter J. Degnan

Schools Visited	Principal
Erasmus Hall High School New York, New York	Saul Israel
Grace Hoadley Dodge Vocational High School New York, New York	Stuart C. Lucey
Oneida Junior High School Schenectady, New York	Harvey Handel
East High School Cleveland, Ohio	Jay Robert Klein
Lincoln High School Cleveland, Ohio	Guy F. Varner
Wilbur Wright Junior High School Cleveland, Ohio	Robert A. Lazzaro
Euclid High School Euclid, Ohio	William A. Hunter
Mayfield High School Mayfield, Ohio	Theron S. Gurney
Sunset High School Beaverton, Oregon	William Logan
Lebanon Union High School Lebanon, Oregon	Lawrence F. Page
Marshall High School Portland, Oregon	Gaynor Petrequin
Washington High School Portland, Oregon	Harold A. York
George Washington High School Philadelphia, Pennsylvania	Morris S. Miller
Germantown Friends School Philadelphia, Pennsylvania	Henry Scattergood
Dubose Junior High School Alice, Texas	L. O. Endsley
Kearns Junior High School Kearns, Utah	Lee Burton
Yorktown High School Arlington, Virginia	Ralph Kier
John Marshall High School Richmond, Virginia	Fred Dixon
Mountlake Terrace High School Mountlake, Washington	Albert Christensen
Ingraham High School Seattle, Washington	John Maxey

Index

All references to schools are cited here under names of schools. Use the *List of Schools Visited* (pages 251–54) to identify school locations.

356 / INDEX

semblies, 67; scientific inquiry, 68; team teaching, 251–52
Ladue H.S., 318–19
Lakeview H.S., Instructional Materials Center, 244–45
Lanford, Oscar E., 19
Language in Action, 102–03
Lavinsky, Emanuel, 282–83
League of Women Voters, 289–90
Lebanon Union H.S., 77–78; analogies in thinking, 108–10; international relations club, 172–73
Lerner, Max, 26
liberal education, 9–10
liberty, belief in, 25–26, 152–65
libraries, 243–45, 343–44
Lin Yutang, 22
Lincoln H.S. (Cleveland), 39, 192, 233; Americanization program, 275; dress code, 317; tutoring, 319
Lincoln H.S. (Kansas City), United Fund drive, 193
Lindsay, James W., 130–32, 138
Lippitt, Peggy, 280
Los Angeles public schools, 7
Ludwig, M. A., 231, 307

M

McCluer H.S., 231; research skills, 58; student government, 307–15; team teaching, 250–51
McLain, Lt. Col. William E., 196
McLaughlin, Mr., 253
McLeod, Alan, 125
McLuhan, Marshall, 247, 327
Mahan, Margaret, 126
Maine Township East H.S., 256–57
Maine Township South H.S., art course, 186–87; foreign affairs course, 180–81
Maine Township West H.S., economics, 78; games, 257
Manning, Robert, 186
Manpower Regional Development Act, 8
Marburger, Carl, 221
Maritain, Jacques, 31
Mark Community School, in-service education, 223–24
Mark Twain Jr. H.S., 97–102
Marshall H.S., team teaching, 252
Mather Jr. H.S., 192
Mayer, Frederick, 30–31
Mead, Margaret, 332
Meridian, Miss., 7
Miami Beach H.S., 166–67; Bill of Rights study, 163; communism study, 63–64; English course, 242; SHARE program, 190–91
Michigan, Employment Security Commis-

sion, 273; see also Detroit, Flint, and individual schools
Mickina, Gil, 256–57
Middlesex Jr. H.S., 178–79, 192
Mississippi Youth Congress, 259
Missouri—see Kansas City, Ladue, and individual schools
mock elections, 144–47
model congress, 149–50
model UN, 181
Monmouth Regional H.S., 29, science course, 68–70; administrative cabinet, 233; English course, 242; independent study, 252–53
Moore, Donald, 74–77
Morley, Frank, 218, 228
Mount Hermon School, 40; economics course, 72; foreign policy, 167–68; American history, 101; independent study, 252; liberal studies program, 241–42; religion, 113–14
Mountlake Terrace, Wash., government workshop, 122–25
Murphy, Alvin, 247
music, 182–84

N

National Association of Student Councils, *Handbook*, 311
National Citizenship Test, 328
National Council for the Social Studies, Advisory Committee to project, x
National High School Student Conference on Education, 330
national pride, 26–28, 165–81
Negro history, 152–54
Neighbors, Inc., 299–302
Neuman, Mr., 77
New Albany H.S., 232–33; economics, 74–77; social studies, 238; television, 246; tutoring, 319
Newman, Jonathan U., 161–62
New Jersey—see individual schools
New York state—see Ithaca, New York City, and individual schools
New York City, school administration, 219–20; in-service education, 225; textbooks, 154–55
news media, educational programs, 290–91
Nicholas, Ivan, 218, 227
Northampton H.S., speakers, 289
Norwalk, Conn., Action Project, 141; independent study, 252

O

Oakland Technical H.S., Americanization, 274–75; drama, 184–85; sex education, 116–18

SELECTED PUBLICATIONS
OF THE NATIONAL COUNCIL FOR THE SOCIAL STUDIES
1201 Sixteenth St., N.W., Washington, D.C. 20036

Yearbooks

Thirty-Sixth Yearbook (1966), *Political Science in the Social Studies,* Donald H. Riddle and Robert E. Cleary, editors. $4.00; clothbound $5.00.

Thirty-Fifth Yearbook (1965), *Evaluation in Social Studies,* Harry D. Berg, editor. $4.00; clothbound $5.00.

Thirty-Fourth Yearbook (1964), *New Perspectives in World History,* Shirley H. Engle, editor. $5.00; clothbound $6.00.

Thirty-Third Yearbook (1963), *Skill Development in Social Studies,* Helen McCracken Carpenter, editor. $4.00; clothbound $5.00.

Thirty-Second Yearbook (1962), *Social Studies in Elementary Schools,* John U. Michaelis, editor. $4.00; clothbound $5.00.

Thirty-First Yearbook (1961), *Interpreting and Teaching American History,* William H. Cartwright and Richard L. Watson, Jr., co-editors. $4.00; clothbound $5.00.

Thirtieth Yearbook (1960), *Citizenship and a Free Society: Education for the Future,* Franklin Patterson, editor. $4.00; clothbound $5.00.

Twenty-Ninth Yearbook (1959), *New Viewpoints in Geography,* Preston E. James, editor. $4.00; clothbound $5.00.

Twenty-Eighth Yearbook (1958), *New Viewpoints in the Social Sciences,* Roy A. Price, editor. $4.00; clothbound $5.00.

Twenty-Seventh Yearbook (1956–57), *Science and the Social Studies,* Howard H. Cummings, editor. $4.00; clothbound $5.00.

Twenty-Sixth Yearbook (1955), *Improving the Social Studies Curriculum,* Ruth Ellsworth and Ole Sand, co-editors. $3.50; clothbound $4.00.

Bulletins

Bulletin No. 39 (1967), *Productivity and Automation*, J. J. Jehring, editor. $2.50.

Bulletin No. 38 (1966), *Reading Guide in Politics and Government*, by Robert H. Connery, Richard H. Leach, and Joseph Zikmund II. $1.50.

Bulletin No. 37 (1965), *The Study of Totalitarianism: An Inductive Approach* (A Guide for Teachers), by Howard D. Mehlinger. $2.00.

Bulletin No. 35 (1964), *Improving the Teaching of World Affairs: The Glens Falls Story*, by Harold M. Long and Robert N. King. $2.00.

Bulletin No. 34 (1963), *Guiding the Social Studies Reading of High School Students*, by Ralph C. Preston, J. Wesley Schneyer, and Franc J. Thyng. $1.50.

Bulletin No. 31 (rev. ed. 1962), *World History Book List for High Schools: A Selection for Supplementary Reading*, prepared by The World History Bibliography Committee of NCSS, Alice W. Spieseke, Chairman. $1.50.

Bulletin 15 (rev. ed. 1964), *Selected Items for the Testing of Study Skills and Critical Thinking*, by Horace T. Morse and George H. McCune. $1.50.

Bulletin 9 (rev. ed. 1960), *Selected Test Items in World History*, by Howard R. Anderson and E. F. Lindquist. Revised by David K. Heenan. $1.50.

Bulletin 6 (rev. ed. 1964), *Selected Test Items in American History*, by Howard R. Anderson and E. F. Lindquist. Revised by Harriet Stull. $1.50.

Curriculum Series

Number Twelve (1965), *Social Studies in Transition: Guidelines for Change*, Dorothy McClure Fraser and Samuel P. McCutchen, editors. $2.25.

Number Ten (1958), *The Social Education of the Academically Talented*, Ruth Wood Gavian, editor. $2.00.

Number Eight (1953), *Social Studies in the College: Programs for the First Two Years*, William G. Tyrrell, editor. $2.00.

Number Seven (rev. ed. 1965), *Social Studies in the Senior High School: Programs for Grades Ten, Eleven, and Twelve*, Willis D. Moreland, editor. $2.25.

Number Six (new ed. 1967), *Social Studies for Young Adolescents*, Eugene Cottle, editor. $2.25.

Number Five (new ed., 1960), *Social Studies for the Middle Grades: Answering Teachers' Questions*, C. W. Hunnicutt, editor. $2.25.

Number Four (rev. ed.), *Social Education of Young Children: Kindergarten-Primary Grades*, Mary Willcockson, editor. $2.00.

Orders which amount to $2.00 or less must be accompanied by cash.

Shipping charges will be prepaid on cash orders, but orders not accompanied by cash will be billed with shipping charges included.

A complete publications list sent free on request.

DATE DUE

DEMCO 38-297